Thank you Peter for your support!

S. Paulson

Meal after meal, day after day, Mother tried
to get Jimmy to eat. "It's delicious today, Jimmy.
I promise. Now open wide."
    Then Taro tried. Jimmy refused Taro too.

Jimmy didn't understand why his family couldn't be together at home near the Pacific Ocean, at home where they could eat in their own kitchen. Why couldn't his mother cook the good rice and noodles, fresh vegetables and fish that he was used to?

Soon Jimmy stopped asking about the Pacific fish
and could no longer remember how the ocean looked
and smelled. He stopped running with the other children.
Mother and Taro feared that Jimmy was becoming ill.

Taro could not sleep, as his mind filled with troubling thoughts. He worried about Jimmy. He worried about their father and remembered the night in December when the men took him away.

"You must help your mother and take care of Jimmy until I return," his father had said.

Quiet as a breeze, Taro wrapped the shears he had secretly borrowed from the camp garden in his mother's scarf and slid them into his pocket. He slipped out the front door.

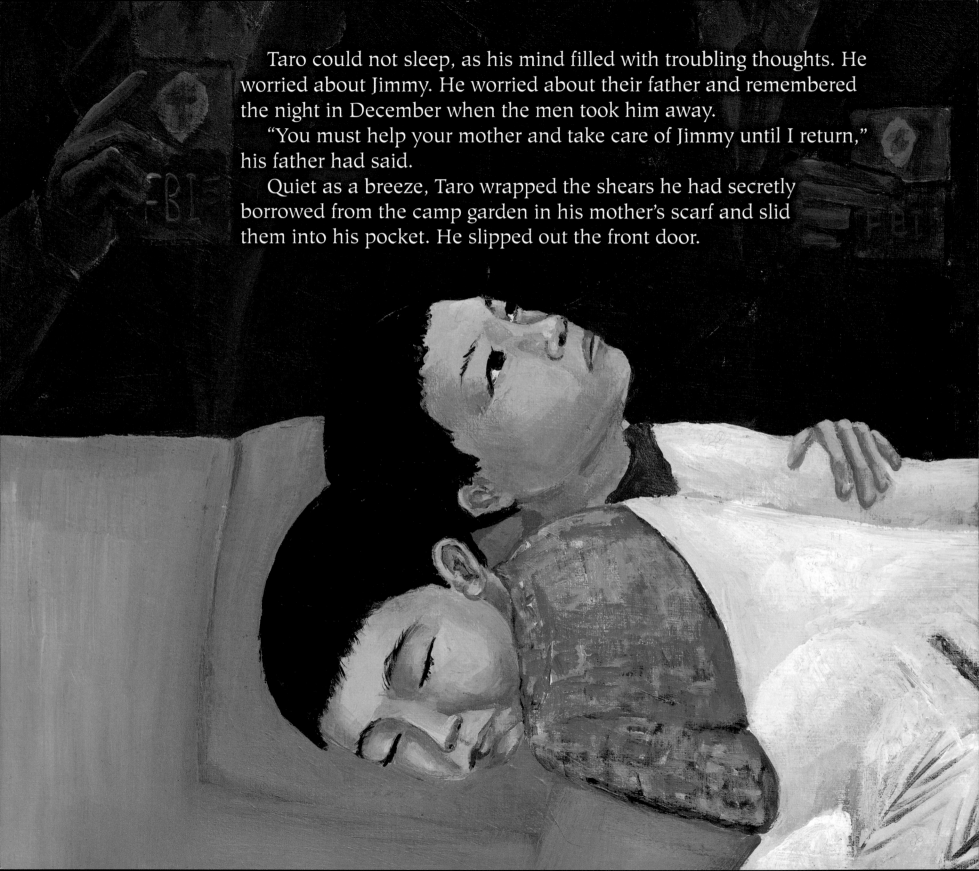

Taro crept from shadow to shadow until he arrived at the fence. He glanced at the guards in the distance. Impossible as it was, he feared they could hear his heart pounding in his chest.

He clipped the fence and slipped into the darkness.

Taro ran fast and far until, breathing heavily,
he arrived at a mountain. A trickle of water
led to a quiet pool, where still, black water
reflected the night sky.

Standing in the pool, Taro felt fish bump against his legs. He slowly lowered his hands into the water and let his fingers sway like reeds. He silently asked the river fish to help his brother.

A fish swam to the swaying fingers, and Taro caught it. He caught another and another until he had seven fish for Jimmy.

With the fish wrapped in his mother's scarf, Taro retraced
his steps. He felt the fresh air of freedom. The cool mountain
air was so different from what he breathed in the barracks.
   Back at camp, he slipped through the hole in the fence
and once again crept from shadow to shadow back to
his prison home.

In the morning there was fish for Jimmy.
As Mother cooked the fish in their barrack,
Taro's belly rumbled. He realized how much
he too had missed the fresh food of home.

"Are these Pacific fish?" Jimmy asked.
"Did they come from far away like us?"
    Mother laughed as Jimmy ate at last.
Taro had forgotten the sound of his mother's
laugh, and it was beautiful.

With bellies full, Taro and Jimmy went outside to draw pictures in the dusty earth. And when other children came by, Jimmy went off to play with them.

Many months later
Father was released from
prison and was permitted
to join the rest of the family
at the camp. Taro showed
Father how, each week, he
would creep beyond the
fence to the free air of the
mountains to find fish
for Jimmy.

Dear Reader,

This story is based on a true story from my own family's history in the Japanese internment camps. In the real story, my grandfather's cousin snuck out of the camp to find fish for his very young son. In the book, what happened to Taro and Jimmy's father is based on what happened to my great-grandfather Anko Hirashiki.

On December 7, 1941, the Japanese bombed Pearl Harbor, in Hawaii. Many American soldiers were killed, and the next day the United States declared war on Japan. The years that followed were extremely hard times for people of Japanese descent. More than 110,000 American citizens of Japanese descent and Japanese resident aliens, including my great-grandparents, aunts, and uncles, lost their homes and were sent to live in internment camps in desolate parts of the country. They were sent there because the government feared people of Japanese descent couldn't be trusted. Many innocent Japanese men, such as my great-grandfather, were also arrested and sent to prison the night of Pearl Harbor for fear they were spies for Japan.

The camps were closed in 1945, and in 1988 the United States government admitted it had made a mistake and offered a formal apology to the victims of the internment.

KATIE YAMASAKI's
great-grandmother Toshi Hirashiki,
great-aunt Akiko Hirashiki, and
great-grandfather Anko Hirashiki
interned at the Granada Relocation
Center in Amache, Colorado

Granada Relocation Center, Amache, Colorado

1987 TEEN CHALLENGE GRADUATES

Rick & Donna Fernandez

South Florida Women's Home Directors
Davie, Florida

"For I know the plans I have for you,"

declares the LORD, "plans to prosper you and not to harm you,

plans to give you hope and a future."

JEREMIAH 29:11 NIV®

TEEN CHALLENGE

50 YEARS OF MIRACLES

DAVID BATTY | ETHAN CAMPBELL

Teen Challenge: *50 Years of Miracles*
By David Batty & Ethan Campbell

Design: Don Jones, www.brotherjones.com

Teen Challenge USA
PO Box 1015
Springfield, MO 65801
Phone: 417-862-6969

Teen Challenge Brooklyn
444 Clinton Ave.
Brooklyn, NY 11238
Phone: 718-789-1414

Global Teen Challenge
PO Box 511
Columbus, GA 31901
Phone: 706-576-6555

ISBN: 978-0-9817280-0-1

TEEN CHALLENGE offers special discounts for bulk purchases
of *Teen Challenge: 50 Years of Miracles*.
Contact the Teen Challenge USA office for more details.

Printed in the United States of America by Color House Graphics, Grand Rapids, Michigan.

First edition: June 2008

CONTENTS

"This whole strange adventure got its start late one night when I was sitting in my study reading *Life* magazine, and turned a page."

David Wilkerson
The Cross and the Switchblade[1]

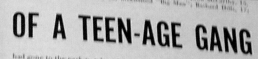

TEEN-AGE DEFENDANTS, created from six months confinement and police as drawn in court by Lou Glassman, are: Leroy Birch, 18, called "The Magician" "Jello" and an immigrant from the Dominican Republic; John McCarthy, 15, George Melendez, 16; Louis Alvarez, 16, named as president of boys' gang. All are and named as boy who led the way to the park; Leoncio DeLeon, 16, nicknamed an epileptic; Charles Horton, 16, nicknamed "Big Man"; Richard Hills, 17; pleading "not guilty" as required by state law in first degree murder cases.

MASS MURDER TRIAL

OF A TEEN-AGE GANG

In a New York criminal court seven stony-faced boys, aged 15 to 18 and dressed in their Sunday best, went on trial for their lives. On a hot night last summer in an uptown Manhattan park, a 15-year-old polio victim named Michael Farmer had been beaten and stabbed to death by one of the teen-age gangs which have terrorized sections of the city. Charged with the murder are the boys above. Eleven others then under 15 years old, who were legally too young to be prosecuted, are in reform school.

The trial, which promises to be lengthy, is remarkable both for the age and number of defendants involved and for the number of defense attorneys—27 in all. Each boy has several lawyers, all of whom, including such eminent criminal lawyers as James D. C. Murray and Harold O. N. Frankel, were appointed by the court. They jam the small courtroom so tightly there seems barely room to try the case.

The prosecutor, Assistant District Attorney Robert Reynolds, began with testimony from 16-year-old Roger McShane (left). He and Farmer

had gone to the park to take a furtive swim in the pool, which was closed for the night. There they were set upon by a gang armed with knives, metal pipes, dog chains and a machete. McShane, stabbed twice in the back, ran to safety. But Farmer, unable to run on his polio-weakened leg, was left dying in the grass.

The frightening, senseless reason for the attack was told by the second prosecution witness, Ralph Lago (right), member of a gang that called itself the Egyptian Dragons. Though one of the youngest (14) of the gang, Lago was their "war lord," responsible for planning intergang battles. Bitter enemies of his gang were the Jesters who fought with the Egyptian Dragons over the public park pool, which each claimed as their territory. Then, on that summer night, 18 vengeful Dragons, some fortified with wine, lay in ambush for the Jesters near a place in the pool fence where after-hours swimmers had pried open a hole for easier entrance. The first boys to come were McShane and crippled Michael Farmer.

IN COURTHOUSE 15 OF THE 27 DEFENSE LAWYERS GATHER BEFORE TRIAL

SESSION BEGINS. EACH OF THEM, AS A COURT APPOINTEE, WILL BE PAID $500

PANION and a key witness, Roger McShane walks home detective assigned to him after he received threatening letter.

GANG "WAR LORD," Ralph Lago leaves court after testifying. rifle introduced as evidence though allegedly not used because bull

^ **LIFE MAGAZINE,** February 24, 1958

8

Dear Reader,

In the summer of 1988, I was a 36-year-old failure, a hopeless heroin addict who had brought his wife and three kids to utter despair. What was such a sorry excuse for a man to do with himself?

Fortunately, a young pastor from rural Pennsylvania had responded to God's call on his life 30 years earlier. In 1958, David Wilkerson travelled to New York City to start a ministry to teenagers involved in gangs. Over the course of the next 50 years, the organization he founded would transform thousands of men and women like me, breaking our cycles of drug addiction, alcoholism, gang life, and other life-controlling problems.

That ministry, Teen Challenge, would eventually expand to include more than 1,000 ministries in 82 countries around the world. The graduates of its recovery programs, once prisoners of addiction and the streets, would go on to start Teen Challenge centers, take up leadership roles in their churches and in their careers, and establish other ministries that would reach out to thousands more.

Teen Challenge sponsors after school programs, musical groups, soup kitchens, coffee houses, and community development projects, and publishes classroom materials used by Christian teachers across the globe. The book *The Cross and the Switchblade*, which tells the story of its founding, has sold more than 15 million copies in 30 languages, and inspired a feature film that would play in sold-out theaters.

Through both government and privately funded research projects, Teen Challenge would also become recognized as one of the most successful addiction recovery programs in the world, with a 70–86% success rate. It would earn endorsements from prominent leaders like Billy Graham and Chuck Colson, three U.S. Presidents, and dozens of world leaders.

Who knew in 1958 that any of this would happen? David Wilkerson certainly didn't. He simply followed God's lead into a riotous neighborhood. What happened next can only be described as a 50-year miracle.

This book is a celebration of Teen Challenge's first five remarkable decades. Along the way, you will hear dozens of stories of lives that were changed—from people who were helped by Teen Challenge, those who did the helping, and those like me, who have been given the honor and privilege of both. These stories represent only a tiny fraction of literally thousands of miracles that the ministry has witnessed since its earliest days.

I had no idea, all those years ago, that God would transform me from the failure I used to be into the Executive Director of the very organization He used to bring me liberty. The story of Teen Challenge is full of people just like me—and the same miracles are still occurring *daily*. The last 50 years truly have been an amazing adventure, and I know the next 50 years will be, too!

Changing Lives Together,

Samuel Sierra, *Executive Director*
TEEN CHALLENGE — BROOKLYN, NEW YORK

THE CALL

In the summer of 1957, eighteen members of a gang called the Egyptian Dragons beat and stabbed two teens named Michael Farmer and Roger McShane in Highbridge Park, in Manhattan. Farmer was a former polio victim, partially crippled, and he died from the gang attack. Seven of his assailants were put on trial for murder. The other eleven were too young to be tried as adults, and they faced charges in children's court. Edward R. Murrow, the popular broadcaster from CBS News, covered the explosive case in a documentary, playing up the fact that Farmer had been an innocent non-gang member, and handicapped. Instantly, the trial became a national sensation.

At the time, David Wilkerson was 26 years old, the pastor of an Assemblies of God church in Philipsburg, Pennsylvania. Philipsburg was a quiet mountain town, but Dave had found success there in his ministry—the church had steadily grown to more than 250 members over the course of four years. He and his wife Gwen had two baby girls, Bonnie and Debbie, and were expecting their third child. What they didn't expect was how dramatically their quiet lives were about to be upended.

Dave usually spent the hours from midnight to 2 a.m. watching late-night talk shows, but one night in early February, 1958, he sensed God telling him to sell his TV and set aside those hours for prayer. Two weeks later, praying alone in his office on a Tuesday night, he felt drawn to a copy of *Life* magazine on his desk. After a few unsuccessful attempts to refocus on his prayer, he finally picked up the magazine and opened it to a story about the Michael Farmer trial in New York City. The article covered only two pages, but it featured a large ink drawing of the seven defendants in court. In Dave's own words, from his book *The Cross and the Switchblade:*

I started to flip the page over. But as I did, my attention was caught by the eyes of one of the figures in the drawing. A boy. One of seven boys on trial for murder. The artist had caught such a look of bewilderment and hatred and despair in his features that I opened the magazine wide again to get a closer look. And as I did, I started to cry. . . .

I was dumbfounded by a thought that sprang suddenly into my head—full-blown, as though it had come into me from somewhere else. *Go to New York City and help those boys.*[2]

THE JURY IS STILL OUT

by *IRWIN D. DAVIDSON*

Judge, Court of General Sessions, New York Cour[t]

and *RICHARD GEHMAN*

The inside narrative of one of history's most dramatic trials as revealed for the first time by the presiding judge: the facts behind a brutal murder, the personalities of the adolescent killers, and the sobering lesson it holds for all of us today.

The Michael Farmer Murder in Highbridge Park, Manhattan

The Crime

The following information is taken from the *New York Times* on August 1, 1957:

"Four youths were arrested last night in the aftermath of a teenage gang fight in Washington Heights in which one youngster was fatally stabbed and another wounded seriously.

According to the police, each of the rival gangs had white and Negro members. They said racial tensions had not been involved. The two gangs had been feuding for the last five weeks.

The trouble started when 40 members of the Egyptian Kings attacked five Jesters near George Washington Bridge. Last Saturday, a Jester was stabbed by a member of the Dragons, a gang friendly to the Egyptian Kings.

The victims in the fight Tuesday night were members of the Jesters. The dead boy was Michael Farmer, fifteen years old, of 575 West 175th Street. He had polio when he was ten years old, and he walked with a limp in his left leg. The second boy is Roger McShane, sixteen, of West 170th Street. He was in serious condition last night at Mother Cabrini Hospital.

They were stabbed, near the swimming pool at Highbridge Park, West 173 D Street and Amstam Avenue."

The Crime Scene

To the right is Highbridge Park in Washington Heights, Manhattan. It runs along Amsterdam Avenue between 155th and Dyckman streets, and was the site of a municipal swimming pool. This is where the Egyptian Dragons (read the note below "The Defendants" about the two gangs merging into one) fell upon Michael Farmer and his friend Roger McShane.

Apparently Michael Farmer was mistaken for a member of the Jesters (there were rumours that he was part of the Jesters, and other stories denying this) who were in a long running battle with the Egyptian Dragons over the pool.

∧ **DAVE WILKERSON** tried to contact all seven defendants from the Michael Farmer murder trial, but they were either sent to jail or rushed out of the city by their families. [Source: David J. Van Pelt].

< **IRWIN DAVIDSON,** the judge who threw Dave Wilkerson out of his courtroom during the Egyptian Dragons murder trial, wrote about the incident in his 1959 memoir: "A lean, youngish man with light brown hair and a determined, almost fanatical look in his eye rose suddenly from his seat in the fifth or sixth row and strode down the aisle toward the rope that separated the spectators from the court well. He was brandishing a Bible. 'Judge Dav idson, Your Honor!' he cried. 'Would you respect me as a minister of the gospel and let me have a moment, please?' ... To one reporter he said, 'I have sixty-five teen-agers praying and fasting for two days that God give me the opportunity to speak to these boys about their salvation.'"

CHAPTER 1 - *The Brooklyn Story*

◄ A photo of Dave Wilkerson holding a Bible outside the courtroom at the Egyptian Dragons trial appeared in the *New York Daily News*. Later, when Dave talked to teens on the streets of New York City, they recognized him from this picture.

EARLY FAILURE

With the prayers and financial support of his church members, Dave followed God's call and drove to New York two days later with his youth pastor, Miles Hoover. They did not meet with success right away. In fact, their attempts to reach the teen gang members on trial ended in utter failure. Dave was thrown out of the courtroom after an attempt to speak with the judge, and an embarrassing photo of him holding up a Bible was splashed across the *New York Daily News*. He and Miles were denied access to the young men in jail, despite obtaining permission forms from their parents with the help of another Egyptian Dragon named Angelo Morales. They could only watch the news helplessly as four of the gang members were sentenced from twenty years to life, and the other three were rushed out of the city.

But their efforts were not entirely in vain. During his second visit to the city, Dave discovered one result of the courtroom incident and newspaper photo he did not expect. Several Egyptian Dragons had been in the courtroom the day he had been thrown out, and gang members throughout the city were closely following news reports of the trial. Without realizing it, Dave had suddenly become a celebrity among local teen gangs. As he explained, "Their logic was simple. The cops didn't like me; the cops didn't like them. We were in the same boat, and I was one of them."[3]

Dave took advantage of his newfound popularity to preach the gospel, both in street meetings and in the crowded rooms of gang hideouts and heroin "shooting galleries." He spent much of his time in the run-down Fort Greene and Bedford-Stuyvesant neighborhoods of Brooklyn, in part because a gang member had told him they were "New York at its worst."

Conversions to the Christian faith for teens caught up in the gang culture of drugs, fighting, and casual sex, even prostitution, did not come quickly or easily, but after a few months, Dave and the workers with him began to see signs of encouragement. Several members of the Bishops gang (who were African American), the Mau Maus (who were Puerto Rican), and others came to accept Christ at the street meetings. With the help of 65 Assemblies of God churches from Spanish Harlem, Dave began to imagine a city-wide Christian rally in St. Nicholas Arena, a boxing ring in Manhattan.

^ Dave Wilkerson and Rev. Bedzyk review story of courtroom eviction.

> Dave Wilkerson's journal entry from July 8th, 1958, the opening day of meetings at St. Nicholas Arena where Nicky Cruz came to Christ.

TURNING POINT

The rallies took place July 8–12, 1958, but the last night stood out from the rest, a night that would mark a turning point for the ministry. The Mau Maus, Bishops, and members of several other gangs were in attendance, but not to hear the preaching—in fact, they planned to use St. Nicholas as an arena for an all-out gang fight. A rowdy crowd greeted Dave as he stood up to deliver his message.

One young man in the crowd that night was 18-year-old Nicky Cruz, a violent brawler who planned gang attacks as "war lord" for the Mau Maus. Dave had met Nicky several times over the past few weeks, during street meetings in front of Public School #67 in the Fort Greene Projects. Nicky had spit in Dave's face, loudly mocked, and even threatened to kill him. He had, Dave recalled, "the hardest face I have ever seen."

When Dave saw Nicky's hard face in the audience at St. Nicholas on July 12, he was struck with a sudden inspiration—he would take up an offering, and allow Nicky and his gang to collect it. Everyone in the room expected the Mau Maus to run once they had the money in hand, but remarkably, they didn't. Even more miraculously, Dave made it through his sermon without a fight breaking out, and afterward, dozens of gang members came forward to accept Christ as Savior.

The conversion hardest for me to believe was Nicky's.

There he stood, a great grin on his face, saying in his strained, stammering way, "I am giving my heart to God, Davie." I couldn't believe him. The change was too sudden. He was puffing his perpetual cigarette, the little jets of smoke streaming out the side of his mouth, telling me that something new had happened in his heart. What about the narcotics addiction? What about the stealing and the mugging, the heavy drinking, the stabbings and the sadism? Nicky must have read my thoughts, because he defended himself by the only technique he knew, cursing:

"Damn it, Davie, I've given my heart to God."[4]

Volunteers at the event handed out free Bibles to everyone who came forward. In one of the strangest but most memorable scenes in *The Cross and the Switchblade*, a group of boys who had been saved at the rally went to the police station the next day to ask officers to sign their Bibles. Their conversions were not short-lived flashes in the pan, either. Both Nicky Cruz and Angelo Morales attended the Latin American Bible Institute in La Puente, California, and embarked on careers in Christian ministry. Israel Narvaez, President of the Mau Maus, was sent to prison six months later, as an accomplice to the murder of a rival gang member, but eventually he returned to the faith and started a ministry of his own in Seattle.

Nicky Cruz (left), Israel Narvaez (right), and other gang members exchange their weapons for Bibles after the St. Nicholas Arena rally with Dave Wilkerson.

Teen Challenge's Place in New York History

Alcohol and drug addiction are not new problems in New York City — in fact, they have been a part of the city's life from the beginning. In their Pulitzer Prize-winning history *Gotham*, Edwin Burrows and Mike Wallace describe how early Dutch settlers viewed drinking as the cause of many other social ills:

> In 1685 the Assembly increased the fines for public drunkenness, describing that "Louthsome and Odious sin " as " the root and foundation of many other Enormous Sinnes as bloodshed, stabbing, murder, swearing, fornication, adultry, and such like."

One Methodist minister observed in 1888 that "where there was but one Protestant church for every 4,464 inhabitants, the saloon-to-inhabitant ratio was one to 150." In response, many Christian charities built shelters, predecessors of recovery programs like Teen Challenge. These included the Jerry McCauley Mission and the Bowery Mission, both of which are still in operation.

Street gangs have also long been a part of New York City's underworld. In the book *Teenage*, Jon Savage describes how teen gangs in the 1890s "created an alternate map of Manhattan," each marking out its own turf. After World War II, the Mafia flooded the streets with heroin, and by the late 1950s, teen addicts and criminals had made it impossible to walk safely through many neighborhoods.

In that chaotic setting, God raised up Teen Challenge to bring hope and healing to those caught up in gangs and addiction. Teen gangs still exist today, but their scope is far more limited.

[Sources: Edwin Burrows and Mike Wallace, *Gotham: A History of New York City to 1898* (New York: Oxford UP, 1999), p. 35, 111, 776, 1162.

Jon Savage, *Teenage: The Creation of Youth Culture* (New York: Viking Penguin, 2007), p. 38.]

TEEN AGE EVANGELISM

As dramatic as the scene at St. Nicholas Arena had been, however, the hard work had just begun. The street meetings and rallies continued, but Dave's vision expanded into other types of outreach as well. He had already written several evangelistic tracts, which he passed out to kids on the street, but he needed money for more. On October 5, 1959, Assemblies of God pastor Reg Yake pulled together a group of fellow clergy to consider supporting him. According to Frank Reynolds, a Staten Island pastor who attended the first meeting:

> Pastor Yake invited 200 ministers to a meeting at Glad Tidings Tabernacle in Manhattan, to discuss how we could help this young man. Only 20 of the 200 invitees showed up, but it is amazing how God has always been able to get along on 10 percent![5]

> The group decided to support Dave with $100 a week, and Frank agreed to serve on a steering committee for the growing ministry.

^ **DAVE WILKERSON** preaches at a rally in 1963.

^ These men, some still in their teens, are volunteers and staff who helped begin the ministry to gangs in New York City. Pictured above in 1960 (left to right): David Demola, Jimmy Picasso, Thurman Faison (one of the first full-time staff members to work with Dave Wilkerson), Rev. Arce, Nicky Cruz, and Nicky Bruno.

Run Baby Run

Nicky Cruz

The story of Nicky Cruz's conversion, from a gang warlord on the streets of Brooklyn to a respected Christian leader, plays a central role in David Wilkerson's book *The Cross and the Switchblade*. But Nicky also wrote his own autobiography, *Run Baby Run,* which tells his side of that miraculous story. In the excerpt below, Nicky describes his first encounter with Dave.

Israel punched me and nodded his head in the direction of the two men. "Come on, Nicky, let's go." I could see that he was serious and I pulled back. There was something sinister about this whole thing ... something dangerous and deceptive. It smacked of something I was deathly afraid of.

The crowd began to hoot and shout. "Hey, look at our leader. He's afraid of the skinny preacher."

Israel pulled at my jacket. "Come on, Nicky, let's go." I had no choice but to go forward and stand in front of the two men.

Israel shook hands with the two men. I was still afraid, hanging back. The skinny man walked over to me and stuck out his hand. "Nicky, my name is David Wilkerson. I'm a preacher from Pennsylvania."

I just stared at him and said, "Go to hell, preacher."

"You don't like me, Nicky," he said, "but I feel different about you. I love you. And not only that, I've come to tell you about Jesus who loves you, too."

I felt like a trapped animal about to be caged. Behind me was the crowd. In front of me was the smiling face of this skinny man talking about love. No one loved me. As I stood there my mind raced back to that time so many years ago when I had heard my mother say, "I don't love you, Nicky." I thought, "If your own mother doesn't love you then no one loves you—or ever will."

The preacher just stood there, smiling, with his hand stuck out. I always prided myself on not being afraid. "You come near me, Preacher, and I'll kill you," I said. I was afraid, and didn't know how to deal with it.

If he had come at me with a knife, I would have fought him. If he had come begging and pleading, I would have laughed at him and kicked him in the teeth. But he came saying, "I love you." And I had never come up against this kind of approach before. ❧

∧ In addition to printing more than 2 million copies of *Run Baby Run,* Nicky has inspired countless audiences of teenagers around the world with his story of Christian hope in the midst of despair. He serves as the founder and director of a youth outreach ministry called TRUCE, To Reach Urban Communities Everywhere.

The President
Israel Narvaez

Israel Narvaez started the Puerto Rican gang the Mau Maus in 1954, when he was 13 years old. Israel decided to let only the toughest street fighters into his new gang. To prove his worthiness, a new recruit had to let a gang member throw a knife at him or take a beating. Israel thought there wasn't anyone tougher than himself, until he met Nicky Cruz.

Israel and Nicky both met Dave Wilkerson on the street in the summer of 1958, but they laughed off the clueless country preacher. They decided to attend his rally at St. Nicholas Arena only because other gangs would be there, and they were itching to fight.

The Israel Narvaez Story

Second Chance

by DARLA MILNE

He made it back into society. Could he find his way back to God? Don't miss this unforgettable follow-up to **RUN BABY RUN**

But God had other plans. In his autobiography, *Second Chance*, Israel wrote that as Dave spoke of Jesus hanging on the cross, "The proud Empire State Building of my heart came crashing down." When Dave invited those who wanted to know Jesus to come forward, Israel rushed to the platform. He received a new Bible, and marvelled at seeing his name inside. "With my name mentioned so many times in the Bible," he wrote, "I knew for sure that God must have something special planned for my life."

The next morning, Israel, Nicky, and several other Mau Maus turned in their weapons to the police. Two months later, Dave invited them to Philipsburg, Pennsylvania, to meet church members who had been praying for them. Israel got his directions mixed up, however, and waited on a street corner for a ride that never came. Disillusioned, he returned to the Mau Maus. Six months later, he was serving a five-year prison sentence as an accomplice to a gang murder.

Dave tried to contact Israel in prison, but only letters from his immediate family could reach him. Israel didn't meet his old friends again until 1966, three years after his release, when Nicky showed up on his doorstep. Nicky told him about *The Cross and the Switchblade*, which had sold a million copies, and asked for help with his own book, *Run Baby Run*.

As Israel and his new wife Rosa sat in a hotel room with Nicky and the writer Jamie Buckingham, he told stories of the old days in the gang, and of his decision years ago at the St. Nicholas Arena rally. He started to cry, and decided there to recommit his life to Christ.

Israel and Rosa joined Nicky and his wife Gloria in their new ministry, Youth Outreach, in Fresno, California. Eventually they started a ministry of their own, the Association for Youth Evangelism, in Seattle. ◆

Ripples of Influence
A.R. Bernard

Rev. A.R. Bernard, founder of the largest church in New York City, came to Christ through the ministry of Nicky Cruz.

He grew up in the Bedford-Stuyvesant neighborhood of Brooklyn in the 1960s, when racial tensions were at their peak. As a young black man, he struggled to find his social and religious identity. At the age of 17, he joined the Nation of Islam.

In 1974, while working as a banker, Bernard hired a Christian woman as his secretary. They often talked and debated about religion, and she invited him to a service at the Baptist Temple in Brooklyn. The guest speaker that night was Nicky Cruz.

"Nicky's English was not that great," Pastor Bernard recalls. "But the power of God was so on his life that as I sat there hearing him, I was faced with a decision." He knew instinctively that God was speaking to him, and he walked to the front. Nicky asked, "Do you want to receive Jesus in your heart?" When Bernard said yes, "I felt like someone put a blowtorch to my chest. It had me weeping like a baby."

So began his journey into a completely new kind of life. As he grew in faith, he realized God was calling him to ministry. He and his wife Karen started a Bible study group in a friend's kitchen, then opened a tiny storefront church.

From the beginning, the Christian Cultural Center attracted men and women who had graduated from Teen Challenge, and others who were looking for help. Pastor Bernard says, "I became part of the Teen Challenge family because so many graduates were coming to my church." The CCC keeps a close relationship with Teen Challenge through referrals of those seeking help with their addictions.

The ministry that got its start in a storefront now sits on an 11-acre campus in Brooklyn, and more than 28,000 people call it their church home. Both *New York Magazine* and the *New York Daily News* recently named Pastor Bernard one of the city's most influential people. ◆

Dave gave his new organization the name Teen Age Evangelism. On February 1, 1960, he moved into an office at 1865 Victory Boulevard in Staten Island. A year later his younger brother Don and mother Ann joined him in the office.

In those early months, Dave was supported mainly by churches that believed in his mission. A group of Spanish Harlem Assemblies of God churches donated $1,000, which Dave spent on Operation Saturation, an outreach program to teenagers through printed literature. Harald Bredesen, who pastored a Dutch Reformed Church in Mount Vernon, New York, introduced Dave to magazine editor Chase Walker, of *Guideposts*, who in turn introduced him to a man who would play an enormous role in getting Teen Challenge off the ground—W. Clement Stone, founder of the Combined Insurance Company of America. Stone's first donation of $10,000 allowed Dave to make *Vulture on My Veins*, one of a series of informative anti-drug films.

W. Clement Stone

Clement Stone began his business career at age 6, when he sold newspapers to support his widowed mother. At age 16, he opened an insurance company with her, and in the 1920s, built the Combined Insurance Company of America, which exceeded $1 billion in assets by 1979.

Stone was famous for his striking appearance— thin mustache, bright suspenders, and polka-dot bow ties—and his habit of shouting "Bingo!" He gave away $275 million to Christian organizations, including his own Religious Heritage of America, which helped add the phrase "under God" to the Pledge of Allegiance.

Stone donated half a million dollars to Teen Challenge in its early years, including a crucial $10,000 answer to prayer described in *The Cross and the Switchblade*. He passed away in 2002, shortly after his 100th birthday. ✵

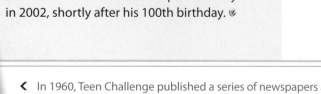

❮ In 1960, Teen Challenge published a series of newspapers about the ministry's early outreach efforts to gangs. Staff and volunteers also spread the word about Teen Challenge through films such as *Teen Age Drug Addiction, Vulture on My Veins, Youth in a Fix,* and *Teen Revolt.*

Generous donations also allowed Dave to host a weekly 15-minute television program in 1960. The "Teen Challenge" show, which aired Sunday afternoons on Channel 9, WOR-TV, featured a choir of 80 church youth group teens, along with former gang members and drug addicts, who sang gospel songs and gave testimonies of their new lives in Christ. The show was taken off the air in response to complaints from one of WOR's advertisers, a tobacco company, fearful that stories of teens dropping their cigarette habits would hurt its business.

Several other Teen Challenge choirs produced albums after the show's cancellation. Dino Kartsonakis, better known years later as the Christian recording artist Dino, played piano for the "Teen Challengers" on an album in 1962, and in 1966, a college student named Andrae Crouch wrote songs and performed with the Teen Challenge Addicts' Choir of Los Angeles. It was the very first long-play album recording for the young man who would later write and sing such gospel hits as "Soon and Very Soon" and "My Tribute."

With new sources of income, Dave wrote several new tracts and found ever more innovative ways to get them in the hands of teens in the city. One of his most successful was entitled *Chicken*—the workers handing it out dared teens to read it and not be "chicken." Dave also developed a flip-top box, which looked like a cigarette box and could carry several tracts in an eye-catching display case, and the plastic "truth capsule," which enclosed a small rolled-up tract. He organized "literature rumbles" (a reference to the physical "rumbles" between warring gangs), mass distributions of tracts and pamphlets to targeted neighborhoods or groups.

As successful as the TV, film, music, and literature campaigns were, however, over time Dave felt they lacked the personal connection that God was calling him to have with youth in the city. He began to dream of establishing a home where troubled teens could stay and be welcomed. And he knew exactly where such a home should be: right in the middle of Brooklyn, in the neighborhood of Bedford-Stuyvesant.

Teen Challenge used what looked like cigarette flip-top boxes to distribute Christian tracts to teens in New York City in the early years of the ministry.

A PERMANENT HOME

On December 15, 1960, Dave's call from God became even more specific:

> At two o'clock in the morning while I was deep in prayer, I received the sudden clear impression that there was a particular street in Brooklyn we were supposed to investigate. We knew that our home should be close to the heart of the troubled Bedford-Stuyvesant area. So we had been making our first tentative inquiries along Fulton Street. But now came the name Clinton Avenue.

> Quickly I got out a map and located the street. There it was, just a black line on a piece of paper, but I drew a line around it as if it were already settled that this was to be the future address of the Teen Challenge Center.[6]

The next day, he set out with Harald Bredesen to find a house for sale. The only one that seemed even close to affordable was a run-down, colonial-style house made of red brick — 416 Clinton Avenue. It looked grand from the outside, but what waited inside was a disaster:

> An old recluse lived in the place now, illegally. He was one of these old men who finds his security in accumulated junk, and he had filled every room in the house with newspapers, broken bottles, skeleton umbrellas, baby carriages and rags. Most of the water pipes were broken, plaster fell from the ceilings and walls, banisters lolled on their side and doors were ripped from their hinges.

> We walked through the sad debris, silent until all of a sudden in a loud and clear voice, almost as if he were preaching, Harald said: "This is the place. This is the place God wants for us."[7]

Dick Simmons, a Presbyterian minister and friend of Bredesen's, bargained with the owners to buy the house for $42,000, a one-third reduction in price. Dave couldn't afford even that much, but the Sunday before Christmas, after speaking at Glad Tidings Tabernacle, he raised $4,400, the exact amount needed for the 10% down payment and the lawyers' fees. Over the next few months, volunteers from local churches hauled out eight truckloads of garbage, repaired and painted the house, and installed a new sprinkler system.

What had started mainly as an effort among Assemblies of God churches suddenly took on an ecumenical flavor. "I realized how much God wanted all sorts of people to be a part of our work," Dave wrote.[8] His first Board of Advisors for the house project included Episcopalian, Presbyterian, Baptist, and Dutch Reformed members. Dave also made numerous contacts through speaking engagements at colleges across the country.

Teen Challenge purchased its first building at 416 Clinton Avenue in Brooklyn in December 1960. Twenty Bible college students stayed at the house and ministered to teens and addicts on the streets of Brooklyn in the summer of 1961. Later it housed Teen Challenge's first residential discipleship program. The Teen Challenge men's program is still located in this facility.

> There was a large fireplace against one wall. A richly carved mantle stuck out into the room, and as I talked to Gwen I leaned up against this mantle. I reminded her of the evening, just a year and a half earlier, when I stood in the moonlit churchyard in Philipsburg, watching the wheat wave in the breeze. Now the Lord had brought us to the harvest field.

> "Darling," said Gwen, "look." I stood forward and tried to make out what she was pointing to on the mantelpiece. And then I saw, too. There, beautifully carved into the fireplace, in our chapel, was the bas-relief of a sheaf of wheat, brought in, tied and harvested.

— David Wilkerson, *The Cross and the Switchblade*

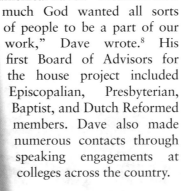

In the summer of 1961, twenty students from Central Bible College in Springfield, Missouri and Lee College in Knoxville, Tennessee came to Brooklyn to minister to teens and addicts at Teen Challenge.

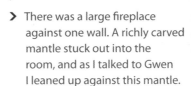

I n June of 1962, Dave shared this vision with a congregation in Lebanon, Pennsylvania, and a Mennonite farmer named Arthur Graybill offered to sell him a farmhouse and sixteen acres of farmland outside of rural Rehrersburg. Teen Challenge purchased the property and made plans to develop the very first Teen Challenge Training Center for men. Someone at an early prayer meeting called it "God's Mountain," and the name stuck. The new center's first challenge was to find the right person to pioneer its program and develop the property. After Frank had spent months of searching and holding prayer meetings into the night, God answered his earnest prayers in much the same way He had answered Dave's. Frank remembered later:

One night, after such a meeting, I was in prayer regarding the matter, and something within me said, "Could you be the one? You were raised on the farm. God blessed you with four boys. You grew up with brothers. You already carry a great vision for this work and you know how to use a hammer and saw."[15]

After further prayer and wrestling with God, Frank took the job of Executive Director himself. On the very same day that Frank and his wife Gladys left Staten Island for Rehrersburg, Dave asked if they could also take a recent convert named Harvey Kuflik. Frank agreed with Dave that the young man couldn't survive much longer in the city, so Harvey moved into the farmhouse with them and their four young boys. Eventually, a total of seven ex-addicts would come to live in the Reynolds house— which gave Frank all the more incentive to finish building the new dormitory.

With the Rehrersburg Center, also known as "the Farm," Frank's vision of a long-term Christian discipleship program was finally realized. By the late 1960s, he had established a model of addiction

▷ Harvey Kuflik was the first graduate of the Teen Challenge Training Center in Rehrersburg, Pennsylvania. He also helped Frank Reynolds with the construction of the first Teen Challenge building on the property.

▼ Frank Reynolds milks a cow on the Farm in 1965. Frank served as the first director of the Farm's programs, and later as the first President of Teen Challenge USA. His pioneering method of discipleship training served as a model for Teen Challenge centers nationwide.

From Dragon to Lieutenant Colonel

Johnny Melendez joined the Dragons gang of Spanish Harlem as a teenager in the 1950s. The gang gave him a strong sense of identity, as the son of Puerto Rican immigrants, and offered him protection. But his friends from the Dragons also introduced him to drugs, and he was forced to put his life on hold.

In John's own words, "For seven years, I was lost in the streets."

He finally came to his senses in 1964, after a second overdose left him alone and near death. A friend gave him a card from Teen Challenge. Though he didn't want to use it himself, the friend told John, "This is where you should go if you want to kick your drug habit."

When John called the phone number on the card, Nicky Cruz answered. "I really need some help," he said, and Nicky agreed to let him enter the program that very night.

As soon as he got to the house at 416 Clinton Avenue, Nicky pulled him into an empty office.

"Kneel down, Johnny," Nicky ordered. "We are going to pray for you." John had no idea how to pray, so he just listened as Nicky spoke the words aloud to God. Slowly, he began to feel something inside himself begin to open up.

Early the next morning, Nicky approached John again and said, "The Lord healed you last night. You know that, right?"

John didn't exactly know what Nicky meant by the word "healed," but he answered, "I guess so." What Nicky meant was that at that moment, God had begun the work of removing John's addiction and restoring his life. And He would carry that work to completion.

A year later, after many more prayers from Nicky and other staff, John graduated from the Farm in Pennsylvania. He continued to serve Teen Challenge for several years as a counselor, teacher, and dean, both at the Brooklyn center and in Rhinebeck, New York. In 1976, he completed a Masters of Divinity from Fuller Theological Seminary and joined the U.S. Army as a Chaplain.

John often felt shocked by the ways that God used him in the Army. He travelled to combat zones all over the world, including Iraq, where he ministered to soldiers preparing to fight in Desert Storm. He preached to servicemen at every rank of the military, from Generals to Privates, and saw many of them come to the Lord.

When he retired in 2002, after 26 years of service, John Melendez, the former Dragon from Spanish Harlem, had earned the rank of Lieutenant Colonel. ◙

"We don't know how to be Christians"

the response of the first drug addicts who accepted Christ, which led to the opening of the first residential recovery program in Brooklyn, New York in 1961.

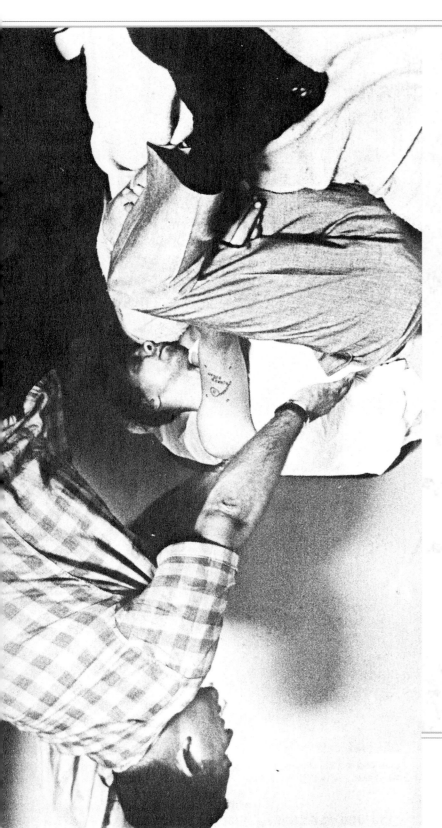

often preach to people they can barely see. Sometimes we go into the shadows after them.[10]

Don Wilkerson, writing in 1969, observed that New York street gangs had crumbled in the wake of this new threat: "Gangs, once so powerful that the law could not even come close to breaking them up, were wiped out by drugs."[11]

In spite of these new challenges, the ministry in the 1960s thrived and moved in directions that Dave had never dreamed. The workers who focused daily on helping drug addicts quickly learned many valuable lessons. The first, and most important, was that a young person's decision to follow Christ was often not enough, in itself, to ensure a long-term change in lifestyle or attitude, especially among those addicted to drugs. In the book *The Jesus Factor*, Don Wilkerson admitted to the writer David Manuel that they had been naive about the powerful hold drugs held over the addicts they were witnessing to.

He and his brother had been brought up to believe that all a person needed was to be saved and filled with the Holy Spirit, and so they were having the addicts kneel with them on the street and give their lives to the Lord right there. And they would even take the addict out with them the very next day to help with the evangelism.[12]

God could perform incredible miracles in the lives of people shackled by drug addiction and other life-controlling problems—but most of the time, He did it through the long, often painful process of Christian discipleship. After a few years of trial and error and false starts, Teen Challenge staff members sensed the need for a structured program that could saturate young men and women in a healthy environment with Christian teaching over an entire year.

An outspoken advocate for this new type of ministry was Frank Reynolds, the Cornell-educated Assemblies of God pastor on Teen Age Evangelism's first steering committee. In his autobiography, *Is There a God?*, Frank wrote that he initially dismissed Dave as an ignorant country preacher, after his disruption at the Michael Farmer trial in 1958. But after meeting him personally and witnessing Teen Challenge's early success, he came to see Dave as "a warrior who had been given a vision from God."[13] Like many others, Frank marvelled at the continual reports of miracles coming from the Brooklyn center. At the same time, he recognized that addicts who had been delivered from bondage to drugs faced an enormous challenge when they tried to return to their old neighborhoods and attend churches. Temptations from their old lifestyle remained strong, churches often proved unsupportive or ill-equipped to deal with their problems, and many Teen Challenge converts fell back into old habits. "We certainly did not claim to be experts," Frank wrote, but the committee knew they had to try something different.

Many were being delivered from their addictions right on the streets and in the Brooklyn Center. But within just days or weeks they would begin shooting up again. We would ask, "Why are you doing this? God did a miracle for you!" The answer was always the same. "Hey, man, we don't know how to be Christians in real life!" If we could just get them away from this scene and [teach them] how to live the Christian lifestyle, we knew they would be able to make it.[14]

NEW NAME, NEW DIRECTION

Supporters of this early work were diverse not only in denomination and in age, but also in their career backgrounds. Several successful businessmen made notable contributions in those early years, including Clement Stone and his wife Jessie; Walter Hoving, the head of Tiffany & Company; and Grant Simmons, Jr. of the Simmons Mattress Company, who donated beds and mattresses for the house. These early partners did much more than donate money and supplies—they also helped to make key decisions that shaped the direction of the ministry.

For example, Walter Hoving, who served as the first President of Teen Age Evangelism's Board of Advisors, sold thousands of silver Tiffany's pins engraved with the words "Try God," in order to provide seed money for a new women's program in Garrison, New York, now known as the Walter Hoving Home. He was also the first to suggest the name "Teen Challenge"—first for the TV show, then for the organization as a whole.

The new name was the first step in a gradual, necessary shift in strategy over the next few years. Narcotics use increased sharply across the city, and with it came a corresponding decline in teen gang activity. More and more of the people who came through the doors of 416 Clinton Avenue were struggling with life-controlling addictions, and many were older than the college students volunteering to help them. Soon it became clear that the needs of the community had changed. Evangelism, street meetings, and outreach to teens remained essential, but Teen Challenge's mission grew broader, to encompass addiction treatment, counseling, and training in practical life skills. The ministry focused not only on Christian conversion, but also on Christian

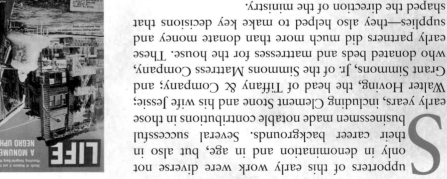

An article in *Life* magazine from March 5, 1965 described this shift: "The Reverend David Wilkerson started Teen Challenge to retrieve young toughs from New York street gangs," it said. "With the spread of addiction, the emphasis shifted to drugs, and many of the patients are beyond the teens."[9] Dave described it himself in a 1966 book entitled *The Little People*:

Our street evangelism had changed since I first preached on a corner in a Brooklyn slum. Then I got plenty of competition from the brutal energy of the street gangs, always so ready to erupt. My background noises came from screeching tires, police sirens, moans, curses, and screams. My audience was loud, and their language was foul. Our audience isn't the same any more. They don't say much, and our street workers

A Sign of Quality

As president of the jewelry company Tiffany's from 1955 to 1980, **Walter Hoving** had a few simple rules: no diamond rings for men, no cellophane tape on gift-wrapped boxes, and absolutely no silver plating.

He made only one exception to the silver plating rule, in 1967, when Tiffany's sold pins engraved with the words "Try God." Proceeds went to build a new Teen Challenge facility for women in Garrison, New York. In response to this generous gift, founders John and Elsie Benton named it the Walter Hoving Home.

In addition to being an enormously successful businessman, Hoving held exacting standards of honor and etiquette. He sealed a deal with Donald Trump, allowing him to build the Trump Tower next door to Tiffany's, with a handshake, and he wrote a best-selling book on table manners for teens. He insisted on making a set of gift calendars for President John F. Kennedy with silver rather than plastic, and he allowed Hollywood producers to film *Breakfast at Tiffany's* in his store only after learning that the elegant Audrey Hepburn would play the lead.

Hoving co-founded the Salvation Army Association of New York and supported many Christian charities. He met David Wilkerson in 1959 and immediately took an interest in the young preacher's emerging ministry. He served on Teen Age Evangelism's first Board of Advisors, and later suggested changing the organization's name. Like Tiffany's "blue box," another of his innovations, the name Teen Challenge is respected today as a sign of the highest quality.

Why the Name "Teen Challenge"?

When Dave Wilkerson started writing Christian tracts and making anti-drug films in 1958, he knew that having a specific audience would keep the message focused. Since the first converts at his street meetings were teen gang members, he decided to target the young generation, and called the effort Teen Age Evangelism. But from the start, workers in the new ministry offered help to anyone who needed it.

In 1960, as Dave prepared to launch a weekly TV show, Walter Hoving and the board of directors suggested calling it Teen Challenge. Hoving believed the title would appeal to non-Christians, and better reflect the broad range of activities the ministry was engaged in. A year later, the whole organization had adopted the new name.

After *The Cross and the Switchblade* sold a million copies in the mid-1960s, Teen Challenge became a household name for many Christians. At the same time the ministry was shifting its focus to residential programs for addicts who were teens and adults. Today, Teen Challenge programs nationwide serve every age group, including after school programs for children and feeding programs for the homeless.

"It doesn't matter what you call it," says George Callen, a 43-year-old drug addict who came to Teen Challenge for help. "This is a place where God works on everybody."

The Teen Challenge Couple

Mike Zello and Kay Ware came to Brooklyn in 1961, as part of a missionary team from Central Bible College in Springfield, Missouri. Dave Wilkerson had recruited the college students to start the outreach ministry of Teen Challenge, and for an entire summer, they held street rallies, passed out tracts, and shared the gospel with anyone on the street who would listen. A year later, Mike and Kay married, and helped pioneer Teen Challenge in Chicago. Together they have served God through the Teen Challenge ministry for over 45 years.

Mike, a native New Yorker, began working with David Wilkerson in 1958 as a volunteer at age 17. He has witnessed Teen Age Evangelism transition from a teen gang ministry to Global Teen Challenge. During the height of the drug saturated hippie movement, in 1964, he was appointed Evangelism Director for the new Teen Challenge center in San Francisco. He led outreaches to the Hell's Angels motorcycle gang in the Bay area, handing out gospel tracts and witnessing to young drug users.

In 1968 Mike and Kay moved to Washington, D.C. and pioneered a new Teen Challenge center, where they served for 25 years. Later, Mike spent five

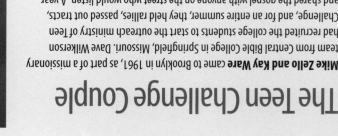

years as Executive Director of the ministry he helped start as a college student, Teen Challenge in Brooklyn. In 1996 Mike and Kay joined Global Teen Challenge, helped train hundreds of leaders from around the world, and assisted in establishing new programs in more than 30 countries.

Mike presently serves as the Global Teen Challenge Regional Representative for Africa. He and Kay have four children in full-time ministry and eleven and eleven grandchildren. ✐

In the late spring of 1961, an infusion of twenty new full-time workers arrived in New York City: sixteen students from Central Bible College in Springfield, Missouri, and four from Lee College in Tennessee. Throughout the summer, they conducted street rallies, shared the gospel with anyone who would listen, and offered shelter at the house to young people in need. Nicky Cruz and his new wife Gloria came directly after their college graduation to join the team, in February of 1962. The pay for these young workers was minimal, and the rough streets of Bedford-Stuyvesant often led them into

▶ From the very beginning, Teen Challenge worked not only with teens, but with adults and young children as well. Here, Dave Wilkerson looks on as a Teen Challenge volunteer plays with a group of Brooklyn kids.

danger, but the ministry flourished, and the rewards of their efforts were incalculable. The house at 416 Clinton was filled at all hours with the sounds of praying, singing, praising God, and general ruckus, as young people once trapped by gangs and drugs and hopelessness explored their new lives in Christ.

Several years later, in order to tap into the energy and idealism of college students like these workers, eager to serve the kingdom of God, Dave founded the Collegiate Urban Renewal Effort, or CURE Corps, in 1967. The name was expressly designed to appeal to students who considered joining secular programs like the Peace Corps, or the VISTA teaching program, but who wanted to do similar work in the service of Christ.

Living Her Faith

Faith Brown moved to the South Bronx in 1968, to join a new Teen Challenge ministry called CURE Corps—College Urban Renewal Effort. Nearly half of her new neighbors on Fox Street lived in poverty, and drug addiction was epidemic.

Faith and her teammates reached out to local kids through Bible clubs. Nothing went smoothly at first, and the children were unruly. But soon the group had opened three storefront clubhouses and started a preschool.

Faith's one-year commitment stretched to decades. In 1970, Don Wilkerson appointed her to oversee Seekers fellowship groups at NYU and Bronx Community College. Faith continued to provide leadership for the ministry after it became independent of Teen Challenge.

Now called Urban Youth Alliance, this ministry runs a highly successful job placement service, jail ministry, and youth mentoring program in the Bronx, and the Seekers have chapters at 35 colleges and high schools in New York City. ✐

▶ Teen Challenge students, staff, and volunteers in the backyard of 416 Clinton Avenue in the summer of 1962.

‹ Arthur Graybill sold his dairy farm outside Rehrersburg, Pennsylvania to Teen Challenge in 1962. The property would come to house the Teen Challenge Training Center, also known as "God's Mountain," with a capacity of 300 men.

recovery that would become the signature of Teen Challenge programs nationwide. The Farm took in men recruited by the Brooklyn center, after they had demonstrated an interest in getting help, and gave them eight to ten months of a structured Christian environment. The structure of the program developed largely through trial and error. According to Don Wilkerson, the rules, discipline, and schedule of the programs at Brooklyn and the Farm "just kind of evolved."[16] So did the policy for how long men would stay at the Brooklyn center—at first, it depended solely on the space available at Rehrersburg. In the early days of the Farm, inductees would stay in Brooklyn for two weeks, but as the Farm's beds were filled and the program grew backlogged, the average stay stretched to several months. Frank had no strategic plan, but he quickly learned that men who had been in the induction center for 3-4 months were the best prepared.

The Pioneer

Romans 1:16 describes salvation as "first for the Jew." **Harvey Kuflik** liked that verse, not only because he was Jewish and loved the Bible— he made it a goal to memorize a chapter daily —but also because it reminded him of an important milestone. In 1963, he became the first graduate of the Teen Challenge Training Center in Pennsylvania.

Growing up Jewish, Harvey heard plenty of teaching about morality, but he rarely listened. His family lived above a synagogue—and Harvey

stole from it to support his drug habit. When his former partner in crime, Sonny Arguinzoni, visited him in jail and described the freedom he'd found in Jesus Christ, Harvey said, "I'm a Jew. We don't look to Jesus for help."

But Harvey did listen to his friend eventually. He entered Teen Challenge Brooklyn after his jail stint and committed his life to Christ soon after. That fall, he had to appear before a judge for writing hot checks and forging drug prescriptions. The judge was Jewish, and Harvey was nervous about telling him of his new life as a Christian. To his surprise, the judge was impressed, and he suspended Harvey's 3-5-year sentence. A year later, Harvey made history as the first of thousands of young men to graduate from the Farm, free from addiction.

After attending Bible college, Harvey worked as a drug counselor for a veterans' hospital in California for more than 30 years. He went to be with the Lord in 2002. ❧

After Relapse, Singing a New Song

Calvin Hunt's early career as a musician took him to many nightclubs where the liquor and the cocaine were free. At least, they were free at first—until he got hooked. Eventually, he was spending thousands of dollars to keep drinking alcohol, sniffing cocaine, and smoking crack.

Calvin learned about Teen Challenge through a different sort of musical venue: an outdoor praise-and-worship meeting on Scholes Street in Brooklyn. He liked what he heard there about the chance to know Christ and change his way of life.

But Teen Challenge was just the beginning of Calvin's journey out of addiction. After a few months in the program, he fell back into using cocaine, and sank even lower than he had before. With no further to fall, he entered another Christian program called Youth Challenge. He finally came home to his wife and children in 1988, and on New Year's Eve, he sang the song "I'm Clean" in front of his church.

Since that time, Calvin has sung for The Brooklyn Tabernacle and Christ Tabernacle Choirs, recorded three CDs as a solo artist, and produced a video. He frequently tours the country, singing praises to God, telling his story, and sharing the good news of God's healing grace. ❧

 "Nothing is impossible with God." Luke 1:37 NIV

A favorite verse of many Teen Challenge students

> **AUTO MECHANIC SHOP**
Students at Teen Challenge have the opportunity
to learn life skills that will be valuable beyond their
12 months in the program.

Today, residents at the Farm complete 3-6 months of training before arriving. They number more than 250 total and come from Teen Challenge centers and similar ministries throughout the Northeast. They hold jobs either at the Farm itself, including positions in the printshop and mailroom, or at an auto mechanic shop in town. At the same time, they take classes in Bible, spiritual discipline, GED preparation, and job-related skills.

The Farm's program of structured Christian discipleship was so successful, it soon became a model for other Teen Challenge programs taking root in other cities in the early 1960s (for more on the history of these programs, see the next chapter). The Brooklyn center adapted its own program to flow more continuously into the Farm's. This discipleship model first birthed at Rehrersburg is still in place at Teen Challenge centers across the country and around the world, the legacy of Frank Reynolds' inspired vision. Frank himself became the first national director of Teen Challenge USA in 1973.

Growth in Stages at the Farm

Reg Yake, an Assemblies of God pastor from New Jersey who directed the Teen Challenge Training Center in Rehrersburg from 1973 to 1987, described how a sense of humility and larger perspective would settle over the men during the course of their stay.

You can almost predict where they're at by what month they're in. Sometimes, when the choir is away, I'll have two guys from each class get up and testify. The first-month guys will say, "Oh, glory to God, am I so glad that the Lord brought me to Teen Challenge! And oh, is it great to be on the mountain here!" In the third to fifth months, you'll hear the guys say, "Boy, am I being tribulated! I almost wanted to split last week, but I'm hanging in there!" The seven-month guys are more subdued. They say, "I almost split during my third month, but the Lord wouldn't let me go. And now I'm beginning to see why." And the guys in their termination month say things like, "What a privilege it is to go through this program! I'm ready to graduate, but I know now that God has only just begun His work in me. I've got so much more to learn."

[Source: David Manuel, *The Jesus Factor* (Plainfield, NJ: Logos, 1977), p. 134-36.]

∧ **JOB RELATED SKILLS** Students hold various
positions in the printshop, mailroom, and kitchen.

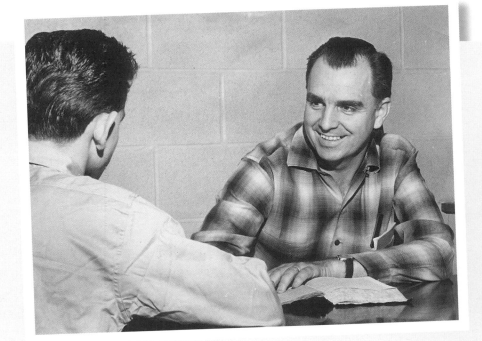

> "We prayed a lot—not because we were overly spiritual — we prayed to survive! And we saw God do miraculous things."
>
> Don Argue
> Director of Evangelism 1962

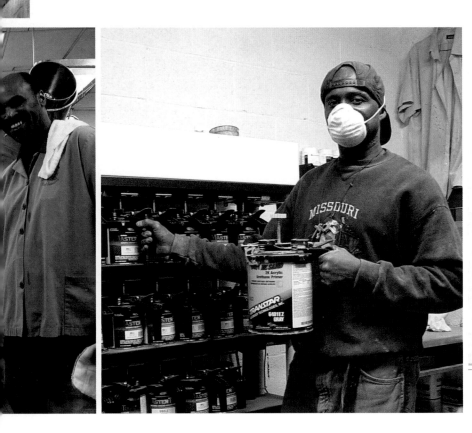

If There Is a God ...

In the middle of the Great Depression, George Reynolds walked out on his wife and eight children. A short time later, his teenage son Frank contracted polio, which left his arm crippled. Feeling abandoned and alone, young **Frank Reynolds** cried out, "If there is such a thing as a God, where is He?"

But Frank was determined to succeed in life. He enrolled at Cornell University, and by the time he graduated in 1944, he was a cynical, skeptical atheist.

That all changed when Frank met Gladys, a nurses' aide at the Reconstruction Home, where he had once been treated for polio. He asked her on a date, and she invited him to church instead. There, Frank witnessed something his atheistic beliefs hadn't prepared him for—a woman was miraculously healed of a cancerous sore on her leg, through prayer. He kept going to church with Gladys, and spent hours researching Christianity at the Cornell Library. He accepted Jesus a few months later, in January 1946.

After they married, Frank and Gladys pioneered an Assemblies of God church in Canandaigua, New York, then another in Medford, New Jersey. Frank accepted a position as the District Home Missions Secretary for the denomination, and oversaw the planting of 35 new churches in five years. Frank became pastor of El Bethel Church in Staten Island, New York, two weeks before David Wilkerson came to New York City and ended up on the front page of the newspaper in early 1958.

Given his experience with forging new ministries, it was fitting that he would join David Wilkerson in his fledgling outreach to teens in gangs. At first, Frank thought the country preacher was naive about his chances of success. But the first time they met, "When I grasped his hand in mine, I somehow knew that this meeting was ordained of God and that my life would be intertwined with his."

Frank's premonition came true in an astounding way. In 1962, he became the first director of the Teen Challenge Training Center in Rehrersburg, Pennsylvania. Frank literally built the Farm from the ground up, and developed the men's discipleship program that would become the model for Teen Challenge centers worldwide.

But Frank's greatest joy in life was seeing members of his own family come to Christ. His brother Carl became a Christian on his deathbed, and Frank even reunited with his father. The man who had prompted Frank's earliest doubts about God came and worked at "God's Mountain" in Rehrersburg during the early years of the ministry. 🌿

[Source: Frank Reynolds with Joan Kruger, *Is There a God?* (Lenexa, KS: 3CrossPublishing, 2006), p. 14, 60.]

> **THE EARLY DAYS OF THE FARM**
Both work time and free time provide the setting for students to learn how to apply the teachings of the Bible in their lives.

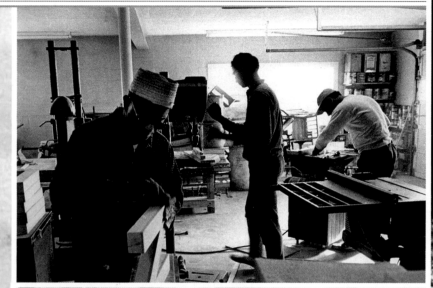

 "A sense of humility and larger perspective would settle over the men during the course of their stay."

Reg Yake, Executive Director of Teen Challenge Training Center 1973-1987

A PROGRAM FOR WOMEN

> The current Teen Challenge women's program in Brooklyn started in 1986, and is now located at 380 Clinton Avenue.

From the earliest days of Teen Challenge's outreach efforts, women were coming to Christ and wanted to see change in their lives. For a short time, the facility at 416 Clinton Avenue housed a number of young women, on a separate floor from the men. But as the ministry shifted its emphasis to drug addiction, Teen Challenge made an important discovery. Men and women tended to recover from addiction in very different ways, and they both adapted to their new lifestyle most effectively when kept separate from members of the opposite sex.

The problem of keeping men and women separate at the Brooklyn center was solved in 1965, when Teen Challenge purchased a building across the street, at 405 Clinton, and started a program exclusively for women. The program also owned a house in Rhinebeck, New York, a mansion formerly owned by John Jacob Astor. With no examples of all-women's discipleship programs to follow, Teen Challenge tested several different strategies. For example, the program initially started with a short induction phase at the Brooklyn facility and used the Rhinebeck house as a training center, similar to the Farm in Rehrersburg. But what worked well for the men created problems for the women, who were much less excited about a major move. The entire program eventually moved to Rhinebeck, and later to Garrison, where it is now the Walter Hoving Home.

The women's program that operates today at the Brooklyn center started in 1986, with the purchase of 380 Clinton

^ THE WALTER HOVING HOME
This old mansion is a beautiful setting where women can experience God's transformation in their lives.

Avenue, an ornate mansion built in 1907 by the brewer of Rheingold beer. Unlike the men, the women spend all 12-16 months of their program in Brooklyn, where they receive both spiritual and practical instruction. In their last few months, the women take part-time employment, either with the Teen Challenge center or an outside employer. Most Teen Challenge centers nationwide employ a similar model of keeping centers for men and women separate with only a few co-ed activities, such as chapel services.

The Walter Hoving Home

John and Elsie Benton began their ministry on the streets of New York City, reaching out to prostitutes and young women addicted to drugs. When they saw the success Dave Wilkerson had in bringing young men to Christ through the residential center in Brooklyn, they dreamed of opening a similar program just for women.

The dream became a reality in 1967, through a donation from Tiffany's president and longtime Teen Challenge supporter Walter Hoving. Today, the Walter Hoving Home in Garrison, New York, has a capacity of 30 women. In 1985, the Bentons opened a second women's center in Pasadena, California, and another in Las Vegas in 2006. ❧

∧ Ann Wilkerson, Dave and Don's mother, started the Lost Coin and the Living Room coffeehouses in the early1960s as an outreach to teens and college students in Greenwich Village, Manhattan

Wisdom from Mom Wilkerson

Ann Wilkerson joined her sons Dave and Don in New York City in 1960. With the help of Fay Mianulli, a native of Little Italy, she established two Christian coffeehouses in Greenwich Village, called the Lost Coin and the Living Room. In a 1969 issue of the Teen Challenge magazine, Ann offered advice to those who wished to start similar coffeehouses.

Rent a room near the kids' hangouts. Fix it up suitably in rather a mod fashion with bright colors, low lights, mismatching tables and chairs, intriguing pictures. Records playing softly in the background will keep the voices down, but you must have only good Christian music. Don't try to entertain. These young people know where to find entertainment that is better than you can provide.

We serve coffee, tea or cocoa and cookies free at the Lost Coin. No smoking or necking is permitted, nor holding hands. This is a new atmosphere for many, but they seem to enjoy it and confess they like the peacefulness of the place. We permit the hippies and others to talk on any subject—sex, civil rights, Viet Nam or politics—but they can only go so far. They are always brought back to the Bible.

You will find that people with various backgrounds, drug addicts, alcoholics and the very lowest of creatures are all on a search for the true meaning of life. Have patience. And don't count numbers! Christ asks you only to sow the seed; the rest is His responsibility. ✑
[Source: Ann Wilkerson, "Starting a Coffee House?" *New York Challenge* July 1969, p. 2-3.]

NEW PROGRAMS

New programs sprouted up quickly as new needs revealed themselves. In 1967 John Fester, a radio engineer, built a recording studio at Teen Challenge. Don Wilkerson helped him put together a taped program and mailed it to radio stations across the country. The first to accept was station WCPK in Martinsville, Indiana. Within four months, Teen Challenge's weekly half-hour programs were being carried by 15 stations across the country. The program *Youth in a Fix* was directed toward Christians, while *Youth Beat* challenged non-Christians about issues of faith.

The Teen Challenge Institute of Missions in Rhinebeck, New York opened in 1966, providing Bible training for Teen Challenge graduates. Some of the men and women who completed this training went on to higher education, and many others returned to Teen Challenge as staff members. In the years that followed, other Teen Challenge staff training schools were established, including the Teen Challenge International Ministry Institutes in Los Angeles and Jacksonville, Florida.

In 1960, Dave and Don's mother Ann Wilkerson moved to New York City and established two coffeehouses in Greenwich Village called the Lost Coin and the Living Room. With the help of Fay Mianulli, "Mom" Wilkerson made each cafe a place where local teenagers, college students, homeless people, and others could relax, eat free food, listen to live music, and talk to Christian volunteers about the gospel. During their time of operation, they made dozens of referrals to the Teen Challenge program and saw many young people come to Christ.

Chicken Soup Chaplain

Mario Haas left his home in Switzerland at age 14, after his parents divorced. He drifted through Europe as a merchant marine until, ten years later, he ended up in New York City, lonely and addicted to alcohol.

Mario's sister sent him a copy of *The Cross and the Switchblade* in German, and he read it cover to cover, desperate to hear his native language again. He thought the story was fake, until one day he stumbled across the Lost Coin coffeehouse and met "Mom" Wilkerson. She convinced him to enter Teen Challenge.

Mario is now married with five children and serves in a prison ministry. Inmates know him as the "Chicken Soup Chaplain," for his readings from *Chicken Soup for the Soul.* ✑

NEW LEADERSHIP

In 1971, Don Wilkerson took over as Executive Director of Teen Challenge in Brooklyn, a position he held for 16 years. Under Don's leadership, the Brooklyn center instituted a new induction strategy called LIGHT groups, an acronym for Living In Group Harmony through Truth. The men were divided into groups of eight to ten new inductees, which were assigned a single staff member and lived together as a unit. Each LIGHT group went through all of the program's activities together—working, eating, studying, worshipping, and going on trips. These tight-knit communities gave extra encouragement to men who wanted to leave the program, and helped all of them learn to work out their problems together.

Don led the men's program and CURE Corps to summer retreats at a scenic location in the Pocono mountains known as Camp Champion. Over time, his vision for the camp grew, and in 1977, the men's program relocated there. Teen Challenge opened a full-time ministry for families with life-controlling problems on the same site. Both programs met with much success in their mountain locale, but financial concerns eventually led Teen Challenge to sell the property and refocus its efforts on New York City. The family program closed in 1986, the same year that the ministry expanded to include a new women's program in Brooklyn.

∧ Camp Champion, in upstate New York, was the setting for summer ministry to children and teens from inner-city neighborhoods in New York City. In 1977, Teen Challenge relocated its men's residential recovery program to this camp and also operated a residential program for families there until 1986.

Younger Brother, Big Influence

Don Wilkerson was a college sophomore when his older brother Dave travelled to New York City to start Teen Challenge. On a trip home in the summer of 1958, his sister Ruth told him that Dave was holding a rally for teens in Brooklyn, and Don decided to attend. At that rally in St. Nicholas Arena, several gang members, including Nicky Cruz and Israel Narvaez, accepted Christ. Don, too, felt the call of God, and after graduation he moved to New York to work with his brother.

For the next few years, Don visited churches along the East Coast, spreading the word about the new ministry and screening Dave's anti-drug films, such as *Teen-Age Drug Addiction* and *Vulture on My Veins*. He continued his advocacy work even while working as a pastor in Barre, Vermont, but in 1962, he moved to Rehrersburg, Pennsylvania, to help the fledgling ministry at the Teen Challenge Farm full-time.

During the summer of 1963, Don ran a camp for 25 Farm residents, at the Glad Tidings Tabernacle's campsite in Kingston, New York. This early test run of a residential addiction treatment program worked so well, Don returned to Brooklyn to help Dave implement it at the recently purchased 416 Clinton Avenue. The Teen Challenge center in Brooklyn soon became an "induction center" for the Farm, taking in drug addicts and preparing them with 3-4 months of Bible training, counseling, and disciplined living. In 1971, Don took over as Executive Director, a position he held for 16 years.

Don and his wife Cindy were also pioneers in the establishment of Global Teen Challenge, a story you can read more about in Chapter 3. ❧

< Don and David Wilkerson with their mother, Mrs. Ann Wilkerson, cut a cake bearing the inscription "We've Come This Far By Faith," at the 1970 Teen Challenge Homecoming in Brooklyn, New York.

With the publication of the book *The Cross and the Switchblade* in 1963, Teen Challenge found itself suddenly in the national spotlight, deluged both with offers of support and pleas for help from Christians across the country and around the world. Well before that important moment, however, Dave's ministry had already attracted attention from a variety of media outlets.

It started when Dave himself wrote several articles for *The Pentecostal Evangel*, the Assemblies of God denomination's official magazine, starting in 1959. His first article was a warning against the excesses of rock music, and there he mentioned his work with teen gang members. Future articles covered topics such as drug addiction, gang lifestyles, and the Holy Spirit, and drew directly from his experiences on the New York City streets.

In March of 1961, Harald Bredesen wrote an article entitled "Gang Preacher" for *Christian Life*, a mainstream Christian magazine with a much larger circulation. It described Dave's earliest attempts to reach the Egyptian Dragons at the Michael Farmer murder trial, and his success with the St. Nicholas Arena outreach events—stories that would later become well-known to millions of readers. The article also featured a sidebar by John Sherrill, a staff writer for *Guideposts* magazine.

John had met Dave earlier that year, and he was inspired by the Teen Challenge ministry. Shortly after the *Christian Life* article was published, John and his wife Elizabeth wrote "Too Strange to Be Coincidence," a two-part article published in November and December of 1961 for *Guideposts*. It covered the entire story of Dave's ministry, from his first calling to New York, to his failure at reaching the gang members on trial, to his street meetings and theater rallies and hundreds of conversions. Since *Guideposts* was an interfaith magazine, a few aspects of the article made the editorial board members nervous—in particular, descriptions of miracles and other elements of the story that were deemed too "Pentecostal." In the end, though, the editors decided to run the articles, and reader response was overwhelmingly positive. The Sherrills became convinced that mainstream American readers were ready to hear the story of Dave's remarkable journey. The next logical step was a book.

▼ Several Christian publications, such as *The Pentecostal Evangel*, *Christian Life*, and *Guideposts*, showed early interest in Teen Challenge's ministry in New York City.

A Force Greater than Hell

Jimmy Jack was the youngest of nine children, and the wildest. By age 15, he had been arrested for multiple robberies. Once, the police hauled him off in handcuffs during basketball practice, as his coaches and teammates stood watching.

Jimmy prayed for the first time when his friend Billy overdosed on heroin. "Oh God," he said, "save Billy and I will commit my life to you." Billy revived, but Jimmy didn't give up his lifestyle right away.

He tried Teen Challenge for one night, then left the next morning to get drugs. In his own words, "A force greater than hell pulled me back into that program."

Jimmy's girlfriend Miriam also entered the program, and four months later they married. They graduated from the Teen Challenge Family Ministry at Camp Champion in 1985. After college, Jimmy and Miriam pioneered the Long Island Teen Challenge and Freedom Chapel Assembly of God church. ◼

Family Plan

Dianne Lloyd knew she needed help for her heroin addiction, but something was missing at most rehab programs. When she asked a counselor how to deal with the empty feeling inside, he said, "You'll just have to live with it." That same week a friend invited her to church, where she accepted Christ into her life and found the fulfillment she had been searching for.

She became a passionate advocate, determined to reach her family, most who were also addicted to drugs. Her husband Bobby, a heroin addict for 12 years, was the first to change. He went to Teen Challenge in Brooklyn in 1984, and discovered new life with Jesus.

Next Dianne set her focus on her brother Jimmy Jack, who entered Teen Challenge a few months later with his girlfriend Miriam. Eventually, 38 members of Dianne's family would complete the Teen Challenge program.

Today Bobby and Dianne direct a ministry called Long Island Citizens for Community Values, working to reduce sexual violence against women, children, and families. ◼

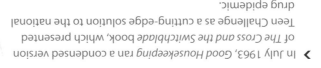

❯ In July 1963, *Good Housekeeping* ran a condensed version of *The Cross and the Switchblade* book, which presented Teen Challenge as a cutting-edge solution to the national drug epidemic.

A t first, Dave was uncertain about the book project, and he asked God for signs that they should proceed. The first to come was that Bernard Geis Associates, the Sherrills' first choice for publisher, accepted their proposal immediately and offered a $5,000 advance. The second was that Bernard Geis himself, who was not a Christian believer, offered the three writers their most important piece of editorial advice.

Dave was blown away by John and Elizabeth's first manuscript draft, and found himself spontaneously praying over each page as he read—which he learned later the Sherrills had done as well. The manuscript was the result of 14 months of taped interviews, and Dave could see his own portrait and hear his own voice in every chapter. The only part that bothered him was the ending—a description of the Holy Spirit's work and teens speaking in tongues at the Brooklyn center. At the time, the issue of tongues was an intense and divisive controversy among Christian churches, but it was largely unknown or dismissed in the secular world of drug addiction treatment. "I had spent years trying to get the social agencies in New York to accept us as a proper house of therapy," Dave recalled in his follow-up memoir, *Beyond the Cross and the Switchblade*. "And now I was afraid we would become the laughingstock."[17] He wondered aloud if they should cut the last chapter.

To his surprise, Bernard Geis's reaction was just the opposite. In his editorial notes to the Sherrills, he wondered why they didn't speak more about the source of their program's power, and he recommended expanding the conclusion into two chapters.

In the end, the book went through six rewrites. The final version included a powerful, personal testimony of the Holy Spirit's work in the lives of former gang members, with vivid descriptions of young men and women speaking in tongues. Dave later attributed much of the book's success to those last two chapters, but more importantly, he had learned a lesson about God's mysterious ways:

I saw now why the Lord had chosen Bernard Geis, who is Jewish, to publish a Christ-centered book. The reason was very simple. If we had taken the story to almost any Christian publisher in those days, their reaction to that last chapter would have been the opposite of Bernard Geis's. "Tongues are too controversial," they would have said. "You'd better tone that down." Geis's motive, perhaps, was good journalism. The Lord's motive was something else again.[18]

The Cross and the Switchblade was published on February 28, 1963, five years to the day that Dave had been thrown out of court at the Michael Farmer trial. Even after seeing the book in print, Dave and the Sherrills had no inkling that it would become the publishing phenomenon that it did, selling 11 million copies in its first ten years.

That miraculous success was driven in part by ever-increasing media coverage of Teen Challenge's work in the city in the months before and after its publication. In 1961, the *New York Times* had run a series of short interviews with Dave, and in the summer of 1963, a *Good Housekeeping* article presented Teen Challenge as a cutting-edge solution to the national scourge of drug addiction,

THE CROSS AND THE SWITCHBLADE

with a story that was essentially a condensed version of *The Cross and the Switchblade*. Both introduced the ministry to a broad secular audience, and helped generate widespread excitement about the story of its founding.

Christian churches and other ministries also did their part to fuel the book's success, purchasing copies to distribute to their congregations, or as evangelism tools. Dave was back in the *New York Times* after Clement Stone personally purchased 100,000 copies—a move that not only allowed the Brooklyn center to distribute the book for free, but landed it on the best-seller list as well. Stone mailed a copy to every Assemblies of God pastor in the country, and to many others. In the wake of sudden demand to keep readers informed about the ministry's progress, Dave began publishing *The Cross and the Switchblade Magazine*, sent bimonthly to subscribers and donors, which featured testimonies from students in the program, updates on the ministry, and editorial articles on a variety of religious and social topics. The magazine was edited by the well-known evangelist Leonard Ravenhill, who also co-wrote one of Dave's many follow-up books, *Twelve Angels from Hell*.

Dave's popularity grew along with the book's. After it hit the best-seller list, Dave said:

Suddenly I was considered a drug expert. I was on network television and radio. The speaking invitations came in faster than I could turn them down. I had to have three telephone lines installed in my office to handle all the calls, and four secretaries just to handle the flow of correspondence. People started stopping me on the street to ask me questions. At home we had to go to an unlisted telephone number for the first time in our lives. In short, I was no longer a private person.[19]

He appeared on network television with several top-name personalities—Art Linkletter, Mike Douglas, Virginia Graham—and on the *Tonight Show* and *Today Show*. He held crusades across the nation, and eventually around the world. A series of crusades in Brazil in 1972, for example, sparked the founding of dozens of Teen Challenge centers there. When Dave's picture was featured in an article on Teen Challenge in *Life*—the same magazine where pictures of hurting teenagers had inspired his first trip to New York City—Dave knew that God had brought everything full circle.

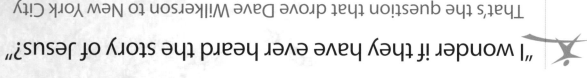

✈ "I wonder if they have ever heard the story of Jesus?"

That's the question that drove Dave Wilkerson to New York City to try reaching the seven teens on trial for murder in 1958.

GOING HOLLYWOOD

But God wasn't done with *The Cross and the Switchblade* yet.

Over the next few years, Dave and Bernard Geis received many offers to buy the book's movie rights, many of them quite lucrative. Early in this process, Dave decided that he would sell the rights only to a Christian producer, and only one who would promise to cast a Christian actor in the lead role. The right moment came when Dick Ross, a producer who had worked with Billy Graham, called to arrange a meeting with Dave and Bernard. He promised to produce a film that churches could use, and to stay away from depictions of sex and violence, while keeping the essential core of the story intact. His choice for writer and director was Don Murray, a former actor who had starred opposite Marilyn Monroe in *Bus Stop* and written and starred in the Christian-themed films *The Hoodlum Priest* and *Childish Things*. The lead role would be played by the famous singer Pat Boone.

Dave had met Pat before, when Pat had tried to buy rights to the script himself. Dave had asked him then if he was a Christian, and Pat answered, "Well, Dave, all I can say is that I'm trying." Pat had seemed right for the part in so many ways, and Dave and Gwen started praying for him to come to know Jesus. Three years later, when Dick Ross told Dave who he had in mind for the role, he added, "Pat asked me to pass a message on to you. He said, 'Tell Gwen and David that I have experienced the last two chapters of their book.'"[20]

Dave and Nicky Cruz spent two days with Don Murray, helping him rewrite the first draft of the script. Dave himself wrote the sermon in the film's climactic scene, largely from memory. When Pat Boone arrived on location in New York City, Dave walked him around to some of the rough neighborhoods and introduced him to gang members and drug addicts. As Dave recalled in *Beyond the Cross and the Switchblade*:

Of course, Pat had on his famous white buck shoes, and he looked pretty Hollywood. We stopped right in the heart of "Little Korea" in the Bronx. Word soon spread— "Hey, the cat himself is here, Pat Boone." They mobbed us, and to my surprise Pat used the occasion to preach Christ...On the second day I took Pat to the rooftops, into dark basement rooms where kids stuck dirty needles into their veins. A few minutes later Pat said he could never be the

▷ **THE CROSS AND THE SWITCHBLADE MOVIE**, directed by Don Murray and starring Pat Boone and Erik Estrada as Dave Wilkerson and Nicky Cruz, opened in 5,000 theaters in 1972. It has since been dubbed into more than 30 languages.

same again. "For me, this is going to be more than a movie, David. I see it as the greatest spiritual challenge of my life."[21]

The actor chosen to play Nicky Cruz was Erik Estrada, a former gang member himself, who would later find fame in the TV police drama *CHiPS*—the film was his first big break in Hollywood. In his autobiography, *My Road from Harlem to Hollywood*, Estrada said that his Christian grandmother was especially excited that he had landed the role of "the switchblade."[22] The musical score for the film came from the veteran Hollywood composer, and born-again Christian, Ralph Carmichael.

Ken Curtis, the associate producer, decided not to hold an advance press screening, fearful of the harsh New York City film critics. His fears turned out to be unfounded, as the reviews from New York were among the best in the country. The day before the film's release, Christian reporter McCandlish Phillips wrote a full-page article for the *New York Times* on the financial difficulties of getting the film produced and distributed, and the next day, critic Howard Thompson gave it a rave review:

> "The Cross and the Switchblade" prompts two questions as it shows how a street minister brings two New York City gangs to Christ. Is it convincing? And how hard does it hit? Answers: convincing and hard enough. I liked it.[23]

The film instantly met with popular success as well. It opened in 5,000 theaters across the country, including 42 in the New York metro area, and set first-week box office records in 40 cities. It was eventually dubbed into more than 30 languages and played on 16-mm film to packed church audiences around the world. Reports came of literally thousands of people accepting Christ after watching Pat Boone deliver Dave's powerful sermon.

The only unfortunate note was that the film's spiritual impact could not be matched by a financial reward. Dick Ross had formed a small production company in his own name and shot the movie for only $600,000, a feat that led Don Murray to call it "the miracle film, because it's a miracle that it ever got made."[24] But heavy distribution costs overwhelmed the small company. Soon Dick Ross & Associates was bankrupt, and a new company called Gateway Films, owned by the American Baptist Convention, struggled to earn back the denomination's investment. In another hard blow, Bernard Geis Associates—which was in charge of distributing royalties to Dave and the Sherrills—also declared bankruptcy after the film's release. Dave had planned to donate his share to the ministry, and later admitted to feeling very angry about the loss. He even considered a lawsuit, but he came to see God's hand in the circumstance:

> In many ways I think the Lord was protecting us at Teen Challenge by not having too much money come in as the result of our own efforts. . . . At the very last of *The Cross and the Switchblade* we said that the Holy Spirit was in charge here.
>
> If He really was in charge, he had to be in charge of our financial life, too.[25]

Pat Boone on Teen Challenge

Shortly after finishing work on *The Cross and the Switchblade* in 1970, **Pat Boone** reflected on what it had meant for him to play the role of David Wilkerson:

"The fifteen years of my professional career have led me to this point. Everything I've done thus far has been to prepare me for this. I don't know what's going to happen to me after this film, but it's the deep conviction of all of us that this is the most important thing we've ever done. We have a sense of destiny, partly because we are addressing ourselves to the real and growing problem of drug addiction. But there's more. This film is about changed lives. It's about people who are made new, literally rescued from addiction. It's about miracles, the kind you read about in the Bible, relating people directly to God and turning them around. It's not a Sunday school lesson; it's a real experience about real people." 🖉

[Source: *The Cross and the Switchblade* DVD special features (Vision Video, 2003)]

DÝKA A KŘÍŽ — David Wilkerson — spolu s Johnem a Elizabeth Sherrillovými
DAVID WILKERSON · DAS KREUZ UND DIE MESSERHELDEN
DAVID WILKERSON · KORSET OG SPRINGKNIVEN
Krzyż i sztylet — DAVID WILKERSON
CRUCEA ŞI PUMNALUL — WILKERSON — Vida
LA CRUZ Y EL PUÑAL · WILKERSON — Vida
НА ЖИВОТ И СМРТ
La croce e il pugnale — DAVID WILKERSON
A Cruz e o punhal — David Wilkerson
na život i smrt — Dejvid Vilkerson

> " It's the message of the cross and dependence on the Holy Spirit that makes Teen Challenge unique. "
>
> — Rev. Jim Cymbala, The Brooklyn Tabernacle

The Son With No Hope
Victor Torres

Victor Torres's parents moved to New York City from Puerto Rico in the 1940s, searching for prosperity. What they found was a rough Brooklyn neighborhood that lured their young son into gangs and drugs.

"Injecting a needle into my veins was a great thrill," Victor says, "but even greater was the feeling of being high. Nothing bothered me then." But Victor soon decided that he didn't want to be a drug addict for the rest of his life. He spent two weeks at the Metropolitan Hospital in New York City kicking heroin, but 24 hours after leaving the hospital, he was using again.

For the next five years, Victor sank deeper into the abyss of drug addiction. He would detox at the hospital, only to start using heroin all over again. One

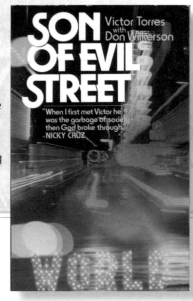

night at home, he injected too much and passed out. "As I woke," he recalls, "I saw my mother and sister standing over me crying."

"My son is dead," his mother screamed when she saw the needle in his arm. Victor stumbled out of the room, trying to drown out his mother's words: "When are you going to get hold of yourself? When are you going to realize that someday you will die from an overdose?"

Victor responded, "I'm tired of hurting you. I want to change, I don't know the way. There's nothing that will change my life."

Victor's mother found Christ at a storefront church called John 3:16, and she began to pray for her son. In 1963, Victor met David Wilkerson and Nicky Cruz at a street outreach. He entered the new Teen Challenge program at 416 Clinton Avenue and struggled with withdrawal pains for three days.

On the third day, Victor recalls, "I walked through the chapel door and knelt in the middle of the floor. 'God, if you are real, please, please change me. Take this desire from me. I'm tired of life. I want to change, but I don't know how.'" At that moment, Victor felt his desire for drugs being replaced with a new sense of joy and peace. He went on to graduate from the Teen Challenge Training Center in Rehrersburg, Pennsylvania.

Victor and his wife Carmen have since pioneered several ministries, including the "Jesus House," a small home for troubled teens that grew into New Life for Youth, with three sites and 100 beds. They also founded New Life Outreach International Church in Richmond, Virginia, which has received commendations from two governors for its help to hurting people.

[Source: *The Cross and the Switchblade Magazine*, Sept.-Oct. 1965]

‹ Victor's autobiography, written with Don Wilkerson in 1977, is titled *Son of Evil Street*.

Teen Challenge's Home Church
Rev. Jim Cymbala senior pastor
The Brooklyn Tabernacle

In the early 1970s, Jim and Carol Cymbala started their ministry at a struggling church on Atlantic Avenue in Brooklyn, called The Brooklyn Tabernacle. They had heard Dave Wilkerson speak and knew Teen Challenge was nearby, so they invited the men's program to attend the church, which had fewer than 20 members.

Over the years, as people with addictions came to The Brooklyn Tabernacle, Jim referred them to Teen Challenge. Together with Don Wilkerson, the Cymbalas rented the Baptist Temple in downtown Brooklyn for monthly rallies on Saturday nights. Carol developed her music ministry there, directing a small choir. One night, when *The Cross and the Switchblade* movie was screened, the crowd overflowed the auditorium and downstairs space, and hundreds more waited outside for a late-night showing.

Today, more than 8,000 people worship at The Brooklyn Tabernacle on Sundays, making it one of the largest churches in Brooklyn. The choir that Carol started in the 1970s has 300 members and has won multiple Grammy awards. Jim says, "The Wilkersons, Nicky Cruz, and Sonny Arguinzoni helped build this church into what it is today."

"God adapts," Jim says, "but the principles are always the same. It's the message of the cross, repentance of sin, and dependence on the Holy Spirit. This is what makes Teen Challenge unique—it adheres to Scripture but adapts with the Holy Spirit to the needs of people today."

"Teen Challenge is where the theological and spiritual meet the practical and routine, and then … the miraculous happens! You see this when all the components of the program come together - devotions, chapels, Bible classes, prayer, work, and personal responsibilities - to achieve the outcome of a changed life."

— Tim Culbreth, Executive Director, Teen Challenge, Hot Springs, Arkansas
Volunteer at Teen Challenge Brooklyn, summers of 1981, 1983

In the Footsteps of His Parents
David Yerry

For **David Yerry**, the path out of addiction began when his parents became Christians. Before coming to Christ, they had been alcoholics, and young David followed their example, getting caught in a cycle of drinking and drug use. When he saw his parents' restored lives, however, he wondered if he should try the Teen Challenge program they told him about.

He walked through the doors of the Brooklyn center in 1978, smoking a cigarette. It would turn out to be his last one.

After graduation, David served with his wife as a missionary in France, then earned a Business degree from St. Paul Bible College. He currently serves as the Director of Administration for the Billy Graham Evangelistic Association.

Dave Yerry (right) is pictured above with Franklin Graham (left), President and CEO of both Samaritan's Purse and the Billy Graham Evangelistic Association.

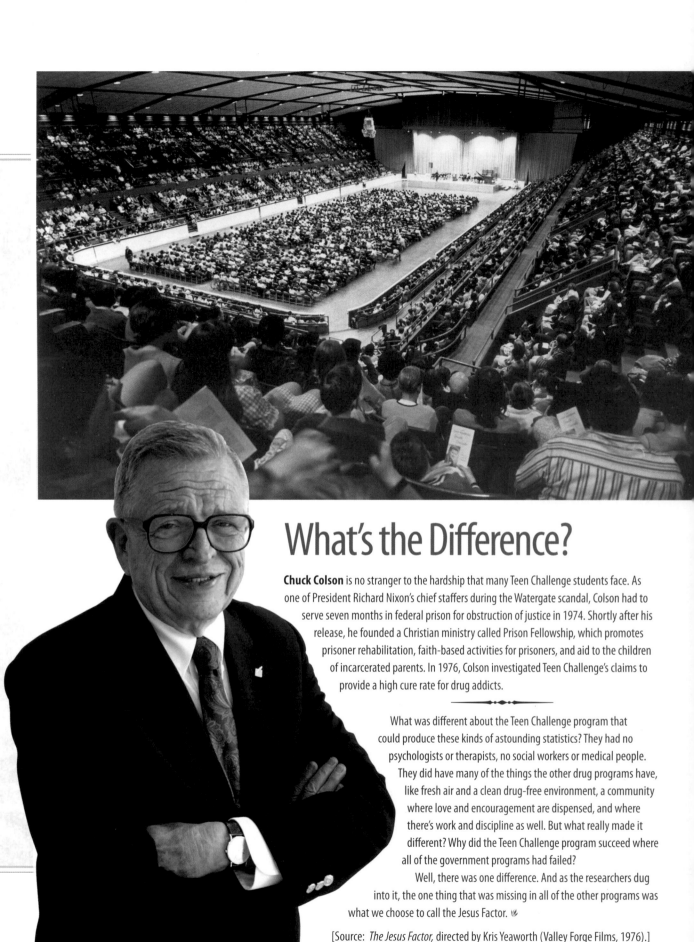

From the earliest days of Teen Age Evangelism and Teen Challenge, Dave spent much time travelling, not only to raise financial support, but also to spread the word about God's work in Brooklyn. In 1961, the same summer that the first crew of volunteers moved into 416 Clinton Avenue, a new Teen Challenge center opened in Chicago. Three years later, centers had sprouted up in Boston, Dallas, Philadelphia, San Francisco, and Los Angeles. (For more on how these centers got started, see the next chapter.) Dave took a hands-off approach with the new centers, preferring to let God's work flow unimpeded, but he willingly offered his time, and sometimes sent workers to help the new ministries.

As Dave travelled the country, his popularity as a speaker and consultant grew, and after publication of *The Cross and the Switchblade* in 1963, he became a man in high demand. His ministry platform expanded beyond New York City, as he led a series of Youth Crusades in several cities across the nation in 1967. At the same time, he noticed that the drug epidemic was spreading from the inner cities to suburbs and small towns. In his writing and speaking tours, Dave turned his attention to the nationwide drug problem, and to other large-scale social issues in America.

In 1971, Dave turned over the operation of Teen Challenge in Brooklyn to his brother Don, moved to Texas, and continued his ministry with a new organization called World Challenge. He did not stay away from New York City forever, though. In 1986, God called him back to the city where he had been called 30 years earlier. He founded the Times Square Church in Manhattan. Dave continues to support Teen Challenge, though he no longer holds a leadership position in the organization.

> **❯ FOUNDER OF PRISON FELLOWSHIP MINISTRY**
> In 1976, Chuck Colson investigated Teen Challenge's claim to provide a high cure rate for drug addicts. He concluded that the "Jesus Factor" was the key to Teen Challenge's success at helping young people find freedom from addiction.

What's the Difference?

Chuck Colson is no stranger to the hardship that many Teen Challenge students face. As one of President Richard Nixon's chief staffers during the Watergate scandal, Colson had to serve seven months in federal prison for obstruction of justice in 1974. Shortly after his release, he founded a Christian ministry called Prison Fellowship, which promotes prisoner rehabilitation, faith-based activities for prisoners, and aid to the children of incarcerated parents. In 1976, Colson investigated Teen Challenge's claims to provide a high cure rate for drug addicts.

What was different about the Teen Challenge program that could produce these kinds of astounding statistics? They had no psychologists or therapists, no social workers or medical people. They did have many of the things the other drug programs have, like fresh air and a clean drug-free environment, a community where love and encouragement are dispensed, and where there's work and discipline as well. But what really made it different? Why did the Teen Challenge program succeed where all of the government programs had failed?

Well, there was one difference. And as the researchers dug into it, the one thing that was missing in all of the other programs was what we choose to call the Jesus Factor. ❧

[Source: *The Jesus Factor,* directed by Kris Yeaworth (Valley Forge Films, 1976).]

<　NATIONAL YOUTH CRUSADES, 1967
Dave Wilkerson addressed the nationwide drug problem,
and other large-scale social issues in America.

VERIFYING SUCCESS

Under the direction of Frank Reynolds in the mid-1960s, the Rehrersburg center began to keep records on the men who had completed the program, in an attempt to measure its effectiveness. An article in the Religion section of *Time* magazine in 1964 was the first to report the claim that 80% of the men who graduated from Teen Challenge went on to live drug-free lives. The article also noted that about 50% of the men who entered the program did not complete it, but the statistics were still overwhelming, especially compared to government-sponsored drug rehabilitation programs, which only saw a 5-15% success rate. Dr. Catherine Hess, who initiated the nation's first methadone program in New York City, summed up the grim reality of most secular programs in 1976:

> One thing that concerns us more than anything in the gamut of treatment is the low cure rate. In the hospitalization called detoxification, the cure rate is about 1%. And for those that go to a therapeutic community, which we say is a drug-free kind of treatment, we find that the cure rate is about 10%. This is discouraging, when we have a problem as big as it is today.[26]

By 1973, Teen Challenge's claims had caught the attention of the federal government, which set out to establish their validity. Dr. Hess, who was then serving as the Narcotics Advisor to the Secretary of Health in Pennsylvania, headed up the government's research team, which was supported by a grant from the National Institute on Drug Abuse, part of the Department of Health, Education, and Welfare.[27] The study took three years to complete and focused on the 366 men who had either dropped out or graduated from the Teen Challenge program in 1968. 64 graduates of the Farm (97% of all graduates for that year), along with 122 dropouts, were given a 100-question interview by the National Opinion Research Center at the University of Chicago and required to submit a urine sample. 87% of them were former heroin addicts, half had been addicted to other drugs as well, and the average length of addiction was five years. Nearly half had tried secular programs before coming to Teen Challenge.

The results of the interviews and drug testing astounded the skeptics and believers alike. The urinalysis confirmed that 67% of the graduates were completely clean of every drug, including marijuana, and 92% were in good to excellent health.

Another impressive statistic was the rate of employment. Only 50% of the Teen Challenge inductees had held a steady job, but 73% of the graduates were employed and self-supporting, and 72% had gone on to further education. Dr. Hess's conclusion was a resounding endorsement. "There is no question in my mind," she said, "that the Teen Challenge program is the most successful one that I have ever seen."[28]

Blessing at the Methadone Clinic
Canzada Edmonds

By the age of 40, **Canzada Edmonds** had been a drug addict for two-thirds of her life. She started with alcohol in junior high and progressed to heroin and crack. She also used methadone, which didn't cure her addiction, but did bring an unexpected blessing: a staff member at the methadone clinic told her about Teen Challenge.

Canzada remembers herself as the most unruly, undisciplined woman in the program. But this, too, was a blessing in disguise. While in the laundry room serving out a punishment, she prayed seriously for the first time, and God answered.

Today, Canzada is the founder and director of the Divine Exchange Program in Washington, D.C. Among other things, it provides faith-based support groups for methadone patients. ✍

<　DR. CATHERINE HESS, who founded New York City's methadone program, led a research project on Teen Challenge, which was funded by the federal government's National Institute on Drug Abuse. The study determined that between 67 and 86% of Teen Challenge's graduates were living drug-free five years later, and that 92% of them were in good health.

But Teen Challenge's astounding statistics have also attracted many doubters. The 1964 *Time* article noted that Dave Wilkerson was hurt by critics in the Christian community, but that he had little concern for skeptics from the secular medical establishment. The article quoted a dismissal from Dr. Robert Baird of New York City's Haven clinic:

> Sure, he'll cure a few who are motivated by a religious fervor. But what's he going to do—turn every addict in the country into a minister?[29]

Dr. Baird's suggestion was not far off the mark—Dave would have loved to see every Teen Challenge graduate become a pastor. The 1976 National Institute on Drug Abuse study found that 57% of Teen Challenge graduates took up leadership positions in their local churches, 45% attended a Christian college, and 22% entered full-time ministry.

Researchers have found, in fact, that the chances for a Teen Challenge graduate's success can usually be linked to his religious attitudes. In the 1976 NIDA survey, 56% of the dropouts considered themselves "very religious" or "somewhat religious." Of the graduates, only 23% called themselves "religious" before they started the program, and 39% even described their religion as "none." Don Wilkerson gave an explanation for this disparity:

> The truth is, it is easier to start from scratch than to overcome religious opinions. And some guys never do get detoxed from religion; they would rather be right and stay in the hell that they have made of their lives, than be willing to be wrong and come into the kingdom.[30]

Over the next 30 years, even as Teen Challenge programs have grown and changed, its statistics have remained remarkably consistent, confirmed by several independent studies. In 1994, Dr. Roger Thompson, head of the Criminal Justice Department at the University of Tennessee, concluded that 67% of graduates from Teen Challenge Chattanooga were living drug-free.[31] 88% told him that Teen Challenge was the most beneficial treatment program they had tried, and 92% said the program had a positive impact on their lives.

In 1999, Aaron Todd Bicknese at Northwestern University surveyed graduates of three of the largest Teen Challenge centers in

^ PRESIDENT GERALD FORD AND DON WILKERSON
Gerald Ford was the first U.S. President to show support for Teen Challenge. He met with Don Wilkerson in 1976.

the USA. Bicknese found an 86% success rate after three years for these graduates, and successfully defended the results in his dissertation, *The Teen Challenge Drug Treatment Program in Comparative Perspective.*[32]

The government and independent researchers have a variety of explanations for Teen Challenge's ability to change lives—the residential aspect of the program, the length of stay, and the strict discipline, to name a few. But perhaps the most convincing explanation is found in the title of a 1977 book by David Manuel, later made into a film with Charles Colson, which explored the key to Teen Challenge's success: *The Jesus Factor.*

WHY SUCH FAILURES IN DRUG & CORRECTIONAL PROGRAMS?
WHAT'S · MISSING?

T · H · E

J·E·S·U·S
FACTOR

DAVID · MANUEL

> Don Wilkerson called the secret of Teen Challenge's success "The Jesus Factor," a phrase which became the title of David Manuel's 1977 book about the ministry.

∧ Caprice Scott now serves as a missionary in Romania, along with her husband and daughter.

Pack my bags; I'm going home!

Caprice Scott

Caprice Scott worked full-time for Teen Challenge Brooklyn in the 1980s. All day, she counseled and prayed with women struggling with drug addiction. But she didn't spend her free time simply relaxing. Instead, she volunteered in a ministry that touched dozens of unseen lives.

Caprice attended the Challenge Center Community Church, a congregation that Teen Challenge helped start in 1987. A group of women who had found Christ through the church wanted to show God's love to their community. So together with Caprice, they showed up as volunteers at a local hospital to work with babies with AIDS. The hospital staff was shocked—in those early days, many volunteers were afraid even to visit AIDS patients.

The work was also heartbreaking, since most of the babies did not live past age 2. But the women knew how desperately they needed the love, touch, and soothing voices that the nurses could not provide.

A few months into the work, Caprice met a 6-year-old boy named Marty. His social worker suspected that Marty had contracted the virus through sexual abuse. He had lived most of his life in foster homes, and now that his body was withering away, he rarely had visitors.

Caprice visited daily, and brought remote control cars to play with. She also told Marty about the love of Jesus. One night, he woke screaming, begging someone to call Caprice. When she arrived, Marty said, "I wanted you to pray; it hurt so bad."

Hours before he died, Marty told Caprice, "Pack my bags; I am going home." Caprice's ministry wouldn't be remembered by many grateful recipients in this life, but she had no doubt about her reward. ❧

The Writing on the Wall

For 15 years, **Ralph Rodriguez** developed a reputation as a scheming, hard-hearted addict, who would rob anyone for drug money. He was shooting heroin in an abandoned building in Spanish Harlem when he saw two words spray painted on the wall: "Jesus Saves," along with a telephone number. Ralph called the number and learned that Cosmos, a graduate of Teen Challenge, had painted it. Cosmos brought him to Teen Challenge that same day.

Ralph was tired of his old life, but he struggled in the program. He dropped out, got hooked on heroin again, and spent seven months in jail before returning with a new attitude. A year later, he had earned a new reputation, as a passionate Christian who would seize every opportunity to share the love of Jesus.

After graduation, Ralph attended art school on a full scholarship. He shared the gospel with teachers and classmates, and every assignment he completed featured a Bible verse. Then came the biggest test of Ralph's life, the discovery that he had AIDS. But as his physical health deteriorated, he grew even stronger in spirit, and from his hospital bed, he witnessed to doctors, nurses, patients, and visitors.

His mother had one final request: "My son was dead for so many years, but Teen Challenge brought him back alive. Will you hold his funeral at Teen Challenge?" More than 400 people crowded into the Brooklyn chapel that day in 1987, to pay tribute to Ralph's compassion and deep love for his Savior. ❧

My soul thirsts for God, for the living God. When can I go and meet with God? My tears have been my food day and night.
PSALM 42:2-3

‹ Sketch by Ralph based on Psalm 42:2-3

TODAY'S NEW MIRACLES

The miracles of fifty years ago still have the power to inspire those who pass through Teen Challenge as students, staff members, and volunteers. *The Cross and the Switchblade* book still enjoys tremendous readership, but some mistakenly draw the conclusion that it represents what is still happening today at the Brooklyn center. Though the heart of the ministry is still evangelism and discipleship, the majority of Teen Challenge's efforts today are focused on drug addiction and other life-controlling problems.

In a 1971 interview with CBS News, Dave Wilkerson noted that "Teen Challenge became primarily a drug prevention program, an inpatient care center, because we found we couldn't just go out and say, 'Jesus loves you.' They said, 'Well, Jesus loves me, but you'd better help me quick, or I'm going to take an O.D.'"[33]

One reason for this shift in focus was the sharp decrease in gang activity since the 1950s. Teen gangs still exist in New York City, but they are not nearly as prevalent as they were when Nicky Cruz's Mau Maus roamed the streets.

Crime among young people, as well as the overall number of drug addicts, was rising steadily when Dave Wilkerson first travelled to New York, but had leveled off by 1963. Crime rose again in the late 1960s and kept rising for over 20 years, fueled in part by the explosion of crack cocaine in the 1980s.

For the past several years, however, New York has had the lowest overall crime rate of any of the ten largest cities in America.[34] A variety of factors have contributed to this decline, including Mayor Rudy Giuliani's crackdown on crime and quality-of-life issues in the 1990s. Another important element has been the growth and spread of churches in the city, a process in which Teen Challenge has eagerly played a role. The Teen Challenge choir and ministry teams visit more than 100 churches per year in the New York metro area, and the ministry is supported by hundreds more, from virtually every denomination.

In the early 1970s, Teen Challenge held monthly rallies at the Baptist Temple in downtown Brooklyn. The Brooklyn Tabernacle partnered with Teen Challenge to sponsor these rallies and connect new converts to a church home. Those who said they had a drug problem were referred to Teen Challenge, and the others to Brooklyn Tabernacle. In this way, Teen Challenge helped the church grow, until

⌃ CLASSES AND DISCUSSION GROUPS Teen Challenge students participate in daily classes, where they learn Biblical principles to establish a new lifestyle of following Jesus. Support groups provide both encouragement and reality checks.

Activities vary widely within each individual Teen Challenge center, but always include worship, prayer, counseling, and work.

attendance at its building on Atlantic Avenue had maxed out. Today, Brooklyn Tabernacle is one of the largest congregations in the city, with more than 8,000 worshippers on Sunday, and renowned for its Grammy-winning choir.

But as much as things change, they also stay the same. Hospital detoxification units and drug rehab centers in New York City see about 65,000 admissions per year,[35] and there is no shortage of addicts who are seeking to change their lives. From time to time, new drugs become popular—like LSD in the 1960s, Ecstasy in the 1990s, and crystal meth today—but the majority of those coming to Teen Challenge in Brooklyn still struggle with heroin and cocaine.

The Brooklyn center has two separate residential addiction recovery programs, for men and women, each with a capacity of 20 students. The men typically spend 4 months in Brooklyn before transferring to the Farm in Rehrersburg, Pennsylvania for 8-10 months of additional training, while the women spend their entire 12-16 months in Brooklyn.

All Teen Challenge students take classes on Christianity, where the emphasis lies not only on Bible study and memorization, but on practical living skills. Course titles include "Anger and Personal Rights," "Growing Through Failure," and "Love and Accepting Myself."

A typical day for a Teen Challenge student also involves morning prayer, weekly chapel services, choir practice, individual and group counseling, and work projects, which for women in the last phase of the program may involve outside employment.

❮ TEEN CHALLENGE RESIDENTIAL PROGRAMS nationwide use the same classroom curriculum. It features courses with titles such as "Love and Accepting Myself," "Obedience to God," and "Anger and Personal Rights."

45

> ### AFTER SCHOOL PROGRAM
> Every day after school, children receive love, attention, and help with their school work from Teen Challenge volunteers and staff.

Visiting speakers present monthly seminars on topics relevant to recovering drug addicts and new Christians, such as Sallie Culbreth's "Committed to Freedom" series for victims of sexual abuse—a major topic of concern, since approximately 90% of the women and 75% of the men at Teen Challenge have suffered from sexual abuse in childhood. Outside guests are always invited to these seminars, and Teen Challenge staff are on hand during business hours to provide phone counseling and referrals to other ministries.

In 1999, under the leadership of Executive Director Dave Batty, who wrote much of Teen Challenge's course materials as the National Curriculum Coordinator, the Brooklyn center started an After School Program for elementary school children. The primary goal of the program, which has about 25 regular attendees, is to give young students a safe place to spend time after school, help improve their academic performance, and inform them of the dangers of alcohol and drug abuse. The After School Program features academic tutoring, computer training, physical activities, and field trips. Young volunteers also play an important role in Teen Challenge's Rock the Block summer evangelism events, which stage Christian music concerts and worship services in public parks throughout Brooklyn.

The After School Program for elementary school children is a safe place to spend time and improve grades.

SUMMER EVANGLISM OUTREACHES
New York City area Teen Challenge centers partner in conducting Rock the Block street and park outreaches throughout the summer. Here a group of students from Teen Challenge in Sand Hills, North Carolina presents a human video drama.

Teen Challenge offers all of its services at no cost, and is completely funded by donations from individuals, churches, and businesses. The Brooklyn center takes no money from the federal, state, or local government. Its most formidable challenge is keeping staff salaries competitive with other service-oriented jobs, but through God's grace, Teen Challenge has consistently managed to recruit well-qualified staff members for this difficult but rewarding form of ministry. With seven buildings on its campus, six of them more than a century old, maintenance and upkeep is also an enormous expense. The Brooklyn center is currently engaged in The Freedom Campaign, a $2.7 million fundraising endeavor that has already accomplished a renovation of the kitchen and bathrooms at 444 Clinton Avenue and hopes to see the complete renovation of the original house at 416 Clinton in the next few years.

^ BROKEN LIVES RESTORED
The original Teen Challenge center at 416 Clinton Avenue in Brooklyn, New York, continues to serve as a place of healing for young men.

Hello God,
I don't know if you know me—
I don't know you, but I want to.
I want you to take away the pain
in my life.

— prayer of a new student
inviting Christ into his life.

The story, of course, is far from finished.

Each day new chapters are being written in the transformed lives of youngsters all over New York.

And who's in charge here?

The Holy Spirit is in charge.

As long as He remains in charge, the programs will thrive. The minute we try to do things by our own power we will fail.

— Excerpt from the Epilogue in *The Cross and the Switchblade*

A Tight Schedule

At the heart of the Teen Challenge program is its rigorous daily schedule, which encourages students with life-controlling problems to discipline themselves in new habits. Activities vary widely within each individual Teen Challenge center, but always include worship, prayer, counseling, and work. Printed below is the schedule for a typical day at the Teen Challenge men's program in Brooklyn:

6:30 AM	wake-up
7:00	help prepare breakfast
7:45	eat breakfast and clean up
8:30	group devotions and prayer
9:00	class on Christian living
11:00	personal study time
12:00 PM	eat lunch
12:45	group counseling session
1:30	work detail with maintenance crew
4:30	personal counseling session
5:00	eat dinner and clean up
5:45	choir practice
7:00	chapel service
8:30	free time, eat snacks and make phone calls
9:30	personal devotions
10:00	lights-out

∧ **VICKIE GAINES** entered the Teen Challenge program in 2001. Top left, before coming to Teen Challenge. Top right, her graduation from Teen Challenge. Vickie also graduated from Teen Challenge International Ministry Institute in Jacksonville, Florida and returned to work at Teen Challenge Brooklyn for four years.

< In addition to restoring the lives of teens and adults, Teen Challenge also brings young children back to secure Christian homes. Pictured above is the dedication of a child whose father is a student at Teen Challenge. Both father and mother were baptized in the same service.

"What characterized the beginnings
of many Teen Challenge centers across the nation
were people called by God who responded
with simple steps of obedience.
Miracles of deliverance and transformation
soon followed, and continue today."

CHAPTER 2 - *The USA Story*

This means that anyone who belongs to Christ has become a new person.

The old life is gone; a new life has begun!

2 CORINTHIANS 5:17

(NEW LIVING TRANSLATION)

^ **PICTURE BANNER AT TOP OF PAGE:** This 900+ voice choir, made up of Teen Challenge students and graduates from across the nation, sang for the Assemblies of God national "2000 Celebration," in August 2000 at Indianapolis, Indiana. The national choir gave the crowd a taste of heaven with "Can You Believe What the Lord Has Done?" and other worship songs.

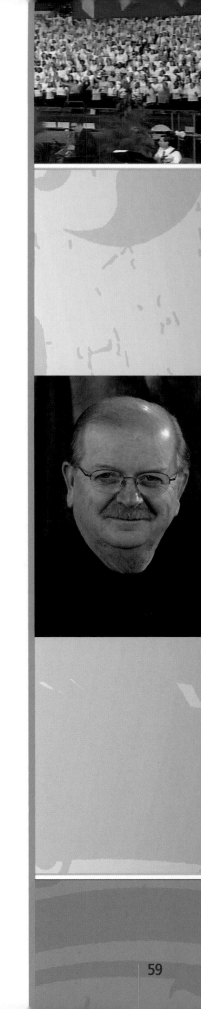

Dear Reader,

Like many of our Teen Challenge students, my former life without Christ is nothing to be proud of. In the 1960s, America was in turmoil. Hippie culture, antiwar demonstrations, and the free love movement were in full swing, and marijuana and psychedelic drugs like LSD were everywhere. My life got caught up in that whirlwind, as I immersed myself in the experimental drug culture. I was on a course to destroy my marriage, my family, and everything else. I am so thankful I had a Christian wife who never stopped praying for me. Betty and I have been married for 45 years now, and have seven grandchildren.

During those turbulent years, Teen Challenge was spreading its influence across the country without my knowledge. After I accepted Christ into my life in 1969, Betty and I attended a rally in Sacramento, California, which featured a young preacher named Dave Wilkerson. He challenged the audience to lay down their addictions and take up Christ. Men and women streamed to the front and tossed cigarettes, pornography, marijuana, and other drugs onto the floor. I was amazed, but little did I know how intimately I would become involved with this powerful ministry.

Teen Challenge has come a long way since the days of Dave Wilkerson's anti-drug rallies, and we owe much to his vision and spirit. In the early 1960s, Teen Challenge ministries sprang up in Chicago, Los Angeles, San Francisco, Boston, Dallas, Detroit, Seattle, and many other cities. Today there are more than 200 Teen Challenge centers across the U.S. They vary in size and scope, and they work with men, women, families with young children, and teenagers. Some of the newest Teen Challenge centers are Spanish-speaking, and others help graduates re-enter society. In 2007, Teen Challenge centers across the country ministered to more than 1.5 million at-risk youth and adults through street outreaches, prison meetings, community events, and mentoring programs.

The spiritual needs of our nation are constantly changing. When Dave Wilkerson first hit the streets of New York City, teen gangs were a major concern, but heroin addiction soon took center stage. By the late 1960s, marijuana and psychedelic drugs had reached suburban communities. In the 1980s, crack cocaine became the drug of choice, and thousands of addicts died of AIDS. Today, methamphetamine addiction is a nationwide scourge, which has infiltrated even the smallest rural areas. The need for Christ's love, and for ministries like Teen Challenge, has never been greater.

Throughout its history, Teen Challenge has helped thousands of drug addicts find the freedom that can only come from Christ. But we are poised to make an even greater impact on the millions of drug users in America today. As you read about these miracles, remember that God is transforming lives at Teen Challenge at this very moment. And He will continue to do so long into the future!

In Christ,

Mike Hodges, *President*
TEEN CHALLENGE USA

GROWING INFLUENCE

By the time Frank Reynolds had firmly established a successful Christian discipleship program for drug addicts in Rehrersburg, Pennsylvania—largely through a process of trial and error—Teen Challenge centers had sprouted up in dozens of cities across the nation.

The spread of Teen Challenge across the U.S. started in Chicago in 1961, under the leadership of Paul Bredesen and Devore Walterman and a group of college student volunteers including Mike Zello and Ed Tedeschi. Over the next three years, Teen Challenge centers were also founded in Los Angeles, San Francisco, Dallas, Boston, and Philadelphia. Dave Wilkerson assisted some of these efforts by travelling to meet with community leaders, and by sending workers from Brooklyn to help pioneer the new ministries.

This sudden growth of Teen Challenge centers was not the result of any grand strategic plan, but rather ordinary people responding to God's call with simple steps of obedience. Miracles of deliverance and transformation soon followed, and continue even today. From the very beginning, these centers saw the most broken and desperate drug addicts transformed by faith into completely different people. Filled with hope and compassion, many of these new graduates responded in turn to God's call to become full-time workers for Teen Challenge.

The new centers varied widely in their philosophies and approaches to addiction recovery. For example, some worked exclusively with teens, while others took in an older population. Some worked only with women, others with men. Some were located in the heart of the inner city, while others served small towns and rural areas. Some became involved in planting new churches.

But all of the Teen Challenge centers shared a few distinctive traits. First, all of them were built on a foundation of evangelism and outreach, the efforts of Christian workers to share the gospel with people on the street and find those who needed help. Also, as the centers grew, all found ways to expand their ministries to include long-term discipleship for drug addicts. Graduates were strongly encouraged to get involved in a local church, as a setting for continued spiritual growth.

> First home of Teen Challenge in Chicago, Illinois.

Students in ministry

Many of the young men and women who come to Teen Challenge have lost their dreams, but God gives them new hope and a new purpose for their lives. Teen Challenge students earn practical experience in ministry by traveling on missions trips, sharing their testimonies, performing in dramas and choirs, and taking part in community outreaches. The students pictured here are on a missions trip to Guatemala.

∧ The Teen Challenge in Morrow, Arkansas, was the first center in the nation to provide a long-term residential recovery program for juvenile boys aged 13-17.

Another shared priority for the centers was the importance of work—from manual labor, to academic work in the classroom, to practical ministry experience. Steve Reynolds, Frank's son, who served as Dean of Education at the Farm in Rehrersburg, explained the importance of developing good work and study habits among recovering addicts:

> More important than anything we can formally teach them during their eight months here are the habits of responsibility that we try to instill in them—being on time for their classes, getting their homework done, coming under the authority of their teachers, making the best use of their study and classroom time ... to God's glory. If we can teach them these things, then we've given them something that will be of great value to them, whether or not they go on to better their education.[1]

And most Teen Challenge graduates did pursue further education. According to the National Institute of Drug Abuse study in 1976, 72% continued their schooling, through high school equivalency exams, colleges, and seminaries. Because Teen Challenge programs also gave students practice serving others in a variety of ministry situations, a large number went on to hold leadership positions in their churches—57%, according to the NIDA survey—and 22% entered full-time ministry.[2]

Teen Challenge centers operated as independent religious charities, relying on donations from individuals and churches. But as the ministry grew in size and influence, state and local governments began to show an interest in various types of partnerships.

∧ Pat Robertson (center), President of the 700 Club, with Jerry Nance (left), President of Global Teen Challenge, and Dave Batty (right), then Executive Director of Teen Challenge Brooklyn, New York.

Pat Robertson was already working in inner-city ministry to the Bedford-Stuyvesant section of Brooklyn in 1958 when Dave Wilkerson first came to New York City. Pat belonged to a fellowship group that included Harold Bredeson, a pastor who became good friends with Dave and connected him to John Sherrill, the *Guideposts* editor who helped Dave write *The Cross and the Switchblade*.

In 1959, Pat moved to Virginia to begin his television ministry, and in the following years invited Dave Wilkerson, Nicky Cruz, and many others at Teen Challenge to appear as guests on his TV programs.

"I saw the humble beginnings of Dave's ministry in New York City," Pat says, "and it was a dangerous setting with all the violence in the gangs. It's beyond calculation, the lives that have been touched and changed, who in turn have touched and changed many more. The impact is enormous. Really, it's God's work." ✐

[Source: Personal interview with Jerry Nance and Dave Batty, June 3, 2007.]

> **FILM EVANGELISM** Showing *The Cross and the Switchblade* and other Teen Challenge films on the streets, in parks, and other community settings has been an effective way to present the miracles of changed lives through the power of Jesus.

In the early 1970s, the state of Pennsylvania asked the Rehrersburg center to conduct training sessions on drug prevention for public school teachers. Frank Reynolds produced a film with Don Wilkerson called *Our High Society,* about the national drug problem, and Teen Challenge staff used it to give presentations at more than 250 public high schools, to an estimated 300,000 students.

In California, a state notorious for opposing drug rehab programs that incorporated religion, the Oakland Guidance Department for high schools asked Teen Challenge director Ken Shaw to spend two days a week counseling students with drug problems—and gave him liberty to speak about Jesus. In Chicago, Thurman Faison used ward leaders and block associations in politically organized neighborhoods to spread the word and raise funds for his Teen Challenge center. And in Washington, D.C., Mike Zello conducted Bible studies and chapel services at federally funded rehab centers.

But perhaps the most dramatic Teen Challenge story in the 1970s took place in Cincinnati, Ohio. Ken Bagwell, a local TV producer, helped to found the center there in 1972, after seeing the powerful effects of drugs on the city's young people. In April of 1974, Ken was brutally beaten with a baseball bat by a 14-year-old boy. He fell into a coma and died from his injuries two years later. His death was a tragedy mourned by the entire city, and it led to calls from local advocates to open up Teen Challenge as a court-approved option for juvenile drug offenders. The judicial system allowed director Jim Grey and other staff to counsel these juveniles, and gave them freedom to share their faith. In 1976, the Cincinnati Teen Challenge broke ground on the Teen Challenge Ranch and Kenneth Bagwell, Jr. Youth Home, a facility that houses 30 residents.

"Drugs did not provide an answer to my problems— they just messed me up more."

— Dan Todd
Teen Challenge Student
Washington, D.C.

KEN BAGWELL, JR., who helped pioneer Teen Challenge in Cincinnati, Ohio, in 1972 served as the Executive Director until his death in 1974, the result of being brutally beaten with a baseball bat by a 14-year-old boy in a local park.

NEW LEADERSHIP

In the years following the publication of *The Cross and the Switchblade* (1963), most Teen Challenge centers were affiliated with local Assemblies of God churches. Dave Wilkerson had started his ministry as an AG pastor, though a wide variety of other churches offered support as well.

In November 1972, Frank Reynolds received the following letter from T.E. Gannon:

> Brother Reynolds, I have a proposition to make to you. We now have 52 Teen Challenge Centers, plus these centers have 78 additional outreaches called satellites. These include coffeehouses, Sunday schools for ghetto children, and other ministries initiated by the Centers. At this time, we are feeling a need of a [National] Headquarters Department to coordinate all this ministry, as well as develop a pilot program at Evangel College to train Teen Challenge leaders. After seeking the Lord, we feel you should move to Springfield, [Missouri] and become the first National Teen Challenge Representative.[3]

Frank was a natural choice for the position. Not only had he established Teen Challenge's signature discipleship program; the Rehrersburg center had flourished under his leadership. The enormous success of the program he created at the Farm made Frank's decision to leave and take up the office of National President very difficult. But the miraculous nature of that success convinced him that God could do powerful work anywhere, and that following the path He had set out was more important than staying. He moved to Springfield, Missouri with his family on June 15, 1973.

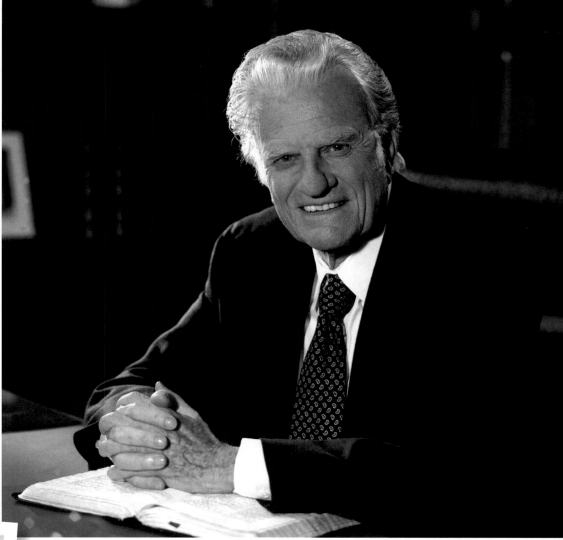

"I've believed in this ministry since its very beginning. And I continue to support it. I consider it a real privilege to endorse this work. Thank God for Teen Challenge!"

— Rev. Billy Graham

FRANK REYNOLDS served as the first President of the Teen Challenge USA organization from 1973-1987, helping to establish a national structure that could serve the growing number of Teen Challenge centers across the nation.

FORGING AHEAD

The mission of Teen Challenge is to help those with life-controlling problems become mentally sound, emotionally balanced, socially adjusted, physically well, and spiritually alive.

The 52 Teen Challenge centers Frank was charged with coordinating included addiction recovery programs for men and women, programs exclusively for adolescents, and a wide variety of community outreach programs. Though there are four times as many Teen Challenge centers operating today, the balanced variety of their services remains much the same as in 1973.

In the early 1970s, drug abuse swept through America as never before, and calls for help in setting up Teen Challenge ministries came from every region. *The Cross and the Switchblade* book sold millions of copies in the ten years after its publication, and the movie version released in 1971 continued to raise awareness about drug addiction, inspiring many young adults to work at Teen Challenge.

Recognition of Teen Challenge's effectiveness quickly spread beyond the Christian community. In 1971, the U.S. government invited a team of Teen Challenge workers

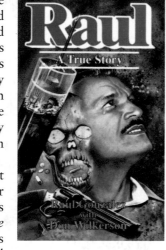

to travel to Vietnam to work with soldiers who were caught up in drug addiction. Mike Zello, who led the team, worked closely with the military to develop a new drug education program.

Frank's role as President was sketchily defined at first. He aimed simply to help develop new Teen Challenge centers, dozens of which were taking root on their own, and to encourage existing centers, in his words, "to apply a more structured and finer quality of operation."[4] He began to build an official network of Teen Challenge centers, which could all access ministry resources from the same central hub and share ideas with one another.

A major turning point in these efforts took place in 1976, when Don Wilkerson hosted a national Teen Challenge conference in New York City. Directors of Teen Challenge centers from across the country attended, and Dave Wilkerson gave them a personal tour of locations where scenes from *The Cross and the Switchblade* had taken place, including 416 Clinton Avenue and the Fort Greene Projects. Most importantly, the directors saw firsthand the discipleship program's structure and the way it flowed into the program at the Farm in Rehrersburg, Pennsylvania.

Many centers were not yet that far along in their development, but their directors were able to catch the vision for more effective ministry through what they saw working in Brooklyn and Rehrersburg, an important first step to national standardization. Teen Challenge centers across the nation adopted a mission statement developed by Ed Howe, Executive Director of Teen Challenge in Chicago. Teen Challenge's mission, which remains the same today, is to help those with life-controlling problems "become mentally sound, emotionally balanced, socially adjusted, physically well, and spiritually alive." The holistic approach outlined by the statement established a stable, unified vision for Teen Challenge nationally.

Vietnam

In 1971, the U.S. military invited a team of 18 Teen Challenge staff and graduates to Vietnam to provide drug prevention training for soldiers fighting in the war. Led by Devore Walterman, director of Teen Challenge San Francisco, the team included Don Hall, Mike Zello, Raul Gonzalez, Neal Washington, and others who shared their testimonies of how God helped them become drug free.

In his autobiography, Raul Gonzalez shares his experience as part of these Drug Education Field Teams.

"Every morning at 5:00 a.m. we were up, giving drug education classes, which most always turned into witnessing opportunities. We also went from company to company speaking with soldiers, encouraging them to seek the Lord. . . .

"As our mission concluded we were drained but exhilarated. The spiritual hunger of the men was beyond anything I could have ever expected. Their frankness about their drug problem, and the openness to the Lord, were also remarkable."

The military was so pleased with the work, Raul and others were asked to lead similar teams to Bangkok, Thailand, Japan, and Diego Island, not only to help the soldiers who were addicted to drugs, but the families of military personnel as well. ❧

[Source: Raul Gonzalez with Don Wilkerson, *Raul: A True Story* (Raul Gonzalez Ministries, 1989)]

❮ **THE CROSS AND THE SWITCHBLADE** has influenced tens of millions of people over the past 45 years. In addition to appearing as a book, movie, and DVD, a comic book version was created shortly after the book gained national prominence, targeting children with the positive message that Christ offers a better life than drugs, gangs, or violence.

One year after the 1976 national conference, Frank hired Dave Batty to fill the newly created position of National Curriculum Coordinator. Over the next 20 years, Dave wrote the *Group Studies for New Christians* and *Personal Studies for New Christians* classroom materials on a variety of practical topics—for example, "How Can I Know I am a Christian?" "Love and Accepting Myself," "Anger and Personal Rights," and AIDS— which are still used in Teen Challenge programs nationwide and around the world. Later, as the Executive Director of the Brooklyn center (1997-2007), Dave continued to write educational resources that were distributed worldwide, starting with "Enabling: Are you offering the wrong kind of help to your loved ones?" a resource for the family members of drug addicts. Dave currently serves as the Chief Operating Officer for Global Teen Challenge, where he is working to make the Teen Challenge staff training resources and student discipleship curriculum compatible with a variety of cultures around the world.

> **REGINALD YAKE,** Executive Director of Teen Challenge Training Center, Rehrersburg, Pennsylvania, 1973-1987.

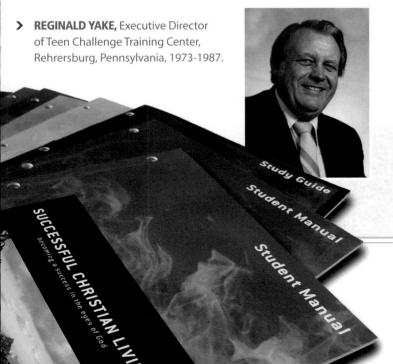

> President Ronald Reagan pictured here with Dennis Griffith, Executive Director of Teen Challenge of Southern California

Another component of the Teen Challenge program involved teaching former drug addicts how to develop a Bible-based work ethic. Rev. Reg Yake, who took over as director of the Farm after Frank, described how this vocational aspect of Teen Challenge's programs had been introduced:

A number of years ago, a student who was about to graduate asked if the Farm could help him find a job. What sort of work had he done in the world?

"Well, when I was in Sing Sing, I worked in the kitchen, and when I was in Chilicothe (the state penitentiary in Ohio), I worked on the farm, and when I was in Lexington, I worked at the bake shop."

Had he ever had a job outside of prison? "Yeah, for two weeks, but I can't remember what it was."

So the Farm incorporated into its program a division that would concentrate on the practical aspects of learning how to work, and for the completion of which a certificate would be granted, that graduates might show to prospective employers.[5]

President Ronald Reagan on Teen Challenge

"Not only does Teen Challenge help our young people deal with their substance abuse, but it also gives our kids something to live for — a relationship with God, a healthy self-esteem, and a direction in their lives that finally leads somewhere.

"I speak from more than 20 years of knowledge of the organization when I tell you that the Teen Challenge program works. It's effective — it's literally changing lives of young Americans from every walk of life. The government can't do it alone no matter how hard it tries. It's going to take the all out effort of concerned citizens like you and me to help turn the tide of drug abuse among kids. And the good news is that together we can and will do it."

Teen Challenge staff quickly discovered that the popular image of drug addicts and drug dealers as lazy or unwilling to work was a myth. The truth was that many addicts, constantly faced with the threat of losing their supply, would work incredibly long hours and go to ever more desperate lengths to keep up their expensive habits. Many Teen Challenge graduates today look back with regret on thousands of dollars earned through hard work, but squandered on drugs—dollars that could have been spent on family, houses, cars, or college educations. Work programs at Teen Challenge centers may not earn much of that money back, but they focus the former addict's energy in a productive direction, and lay the foundation for a work ethic that will last a lifetime.

Many Teen Challenge graduates have gone on to become successful leaders—pastors, teachers, and business owners. Arizona graduate Patrick Flyte is now a medical doctor. Many graduates have become leaders in Teen Challenge across the nation, while others have pioneered similar ministries reaching drug addicts with the hope of new life with Jesus Christ.

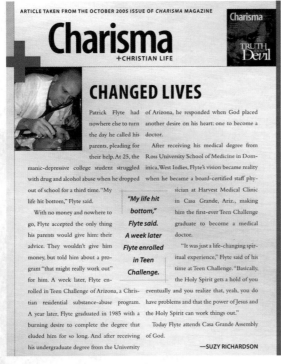

ARTICLE TAKEN FROM THE OCTOBER 2005 ISSUE OF *CHARISMA* MAGAZINE

Charisma
+CHRISTIAN LIFE

CHANGED LIVES

Patrick Flyte had nowhere else to turn the day he called his parents, pleading for their help. At 25, the manic-depressive college student struggled with drug and alcohol abuse when he dropped out of school for a third time. "My life hit bottom," Flyte said.

With no money and nowhere to go, Flyte accepted the only thing his parents would give him: their advice. They wouldn't give him money, but told him about a program "that might really work out" for him. A week later, Flyte enrolled in Teen Challenge of Arizona, a Christian residential substance-abuse program. A year later, Flyte graduated in 1985 with a burning desire to complete the degree that eluded him for so long. And after receiving his undergraduate degree from the University

"My life hit bottom," Flyte said. A week later Flyte enrolled in Teen Challenge.

of Arizona, he responded when God placed another desire on his heart: one to become a doctor.

After receiving his medical degree from Ross University School of Medicine in Dominica, West Indies, Flyte's vision became reality when he became a board-certified staff physician at Harvest Medical Clinic in Casa Grande, Ariz., making him the first-ever Teen Challenge graduate to become a medical doctor.

"It was just a life-changing spiritual experience," Flyte said of his time at Teen Challenge. "Basically, the Holy Spirit gets a hold of you eventually and you realize that, yeah, you do have problems and that the power of Jesus and the Holy Spirit can work things out."

Today Flyte attends Casa Grande Assembly of God.

—SUZY RICHARDSON

∧ After graduating from Teen Challenge Arizona, Patrick Flyte attended medical school and became a medical doctor.

As more Teen Challenge centers were started, Frank Reynolds found himself resolving more disputes between Teen Challenge centers and government agencies. For example, Herb Meppelink, director of Mid-America Teen Challenge in Cape Girardeau, Missouri, became embroiled with the U.S. Federal Wages and Standards Department over the student work component of the program.

To resolve the issue with the Mid-America center, Frank met with Senators Stuart Symington and Thomas Eagleton of Missouri, and shared his vision for Teen Challenge.[6] He used an article Herb Meppelink had written to explain the importance of work detail in addiction recovery. The senators were impressed, and within weeks, the bill that had outlawed recovery programs from requiring patients to work for free was changed. And just in time — similar legal questions soon arose in Michigan and Pennsylvania, but this time, with federal law on his side, Frank helped the Teen Challenge centers resolve them quickly.

Many other Teen Challenge centers faced strong opposition from community members and local zoning boards when trying to purchase property for a new ministry location. Teen Challenge's opponents most often expressed the attitude that drug addicts in the neighborhood would drive down the value of real estate.

President George H.W. Bush on Teen Challenge

"Your services have aided many in learning how to lead productive and happy lives, while still others have benefited from your programs on how to avoid serious problems.

"I share your belief that it is vital that we teach our young people about the importance of adhering to traditional values, the dignity of work, acceptance of personal responsibility, love for one's neighbor, and respect for the Creator. I commend you, for helping to instill such values and for reminding young people that humility and resolve lead to patience and strength. These virtues, by their nature, build self-worth and dignity. Keep up the good work."

"My life was changed on September 11, 1975, in Teen Challenge at Harrisburg, PA. I entered an atmosphere filled with the presence of God and He broke the chains holding my life. When I cried out to God, the weight of sin, addiction, and shame were literally lifted off of my shoulders. I am forever grateful."

— Greg Hammond

now serves as Chief Operating Officer of 27 Teen Challenge centers in Florida, Georgia, Alabama, Missouri, Iowa, and Nebraska

President George W. Bush on Teen Challenge

George W. Bush visited Teen Challenge in Colfax, Iowa when he was running for President. After his election, he has continued to speak about Teen Challenge, championing its success.

"Too many young people have already lost their lives, and too many others have suffered serious injury for us to ignore the problems of juvenile alcohol and drug abuse. Programs such as Teen Challenge work to change people's lives by changing their hearts. I commend you for your work with young men and women who are addicted to drugs and alcohol.

"Let us bring to all Americans who struggle with drug addiction this message of hope: The miracle of recovery is possible, and it could be you."

"I believe in the great work of this organization. A government-funded research project concluded that Teen Challenge has the highest success rate in helping people move from substance abuse, off substance abuse."

John Ashcroft, former United States Attorney General

NATIONAL ACCREDITATION

As Frank spent more time working with government agencies, he began to focus his attention on the issue of accreditation. Several state governments, like Michigan's, began to require Teen Challenge centers, and all counselors within them, to earn licenses granted by the state. Frank met with state officials in Michigan, and pointed out the Constitutional problems with such requirements. Since Teen Challenge focused on the broad issue of Christian discipleship rather than the narrow problem of drug addiction, and since the source of change within every recovery program was Jesus Christ, Frank saw that requiring counselors to undergo licensing based on a separate philosophy made little sense. In his view, the state of Michigan wanted to license Christians to preach the gospel, an obvious infringement on religious freedom. Eventually, the Michigan legislature agreed to an alternative licensing system.

Despite individual victories of this kind, Frank still felt a pressing need to develop national standards for Teen Challenge centers. For a guide, he looked to the medical community, whose services are accredited through an internal review process rather than by the government. Teen Challenge, he saw, needed a similar internal accreditation system. The first standards were drafted in the early 1980s, and were first implemented by the Teen Challenge center in Chicago.

Snow Peabody and Herb Meppelink, the next two Presidents of Teen Challenge USA, took accreditation to a new level, by requiring all Teen Challenge centers to meet a series of standards developed by Teen Challenge leaders from across the nation. The standards include adequate staff training, financial accountability, and safe physical conditions for the residents. In 1989, Doug Wever became the first National Accreditation Coordinator to oversee the process, a position now held by Doug Lance.

Another high-priority issue facing Teen Challenge as it expanded was a

One of the easiest places to find drug addicts is in local jails and prisons, and many Teen Challenge centers lead ministries there. Addicts who are convicted of drug-related crimes can often be probated to Teen Challenge programs. Pictured here is Harley Cox, Executive Director of Eastern Appalachian Teen Challenge in Roanoke, Virginia, on his way to interview a potential new student. ❧

^ **FIRST FIVE TEEN CHALLENGE USA PRESIDENTS** pictured here with Dave Batty, who served as the first Teen Challenge National Curriculum Coordinator from 1977-1997. Presidents and their years in that position (left to right) Frank Reynolds 1973-1987, Snow Peabody 1987-1992, Dave Batty, Wayne Keylon 1996-2000, Herb Meppelink 1992-1996, and John Castellani 2000-2006.

> Teen Challenge Jacksonville Leadership Institute in Jacksonville, Florida, is one of several schools which train Teen Challenge graduates to serve as staff in this ministry.

chronic shortage of well-trained staff. To help address this need, in the early 1990s, centers in Florida and Los Angeles developed separate Teen Challenge Ministry Institutes (TCMI), to provide training for graduates who felt a call to continue working for Teen Challenge. Since then, several other centers have started staff training schools as well.

Even with these new training schools, however, the national ministry was constantly threatened with a shortage of staff. In response, Teen Challenge in Florida established the Emerging Leaders Program in the spring of 2006. The ELP identifies students who have expressed a desire or call to enter the ministry, and begins training them during the last six months of their residential programs.

Even with the proliferation of Teen Challenge centers across the nation, it became clear that the drug epidemic was too large to be dealt with through recovery programs alone. Dr. Jimmy Lee, the founder of Teen Challenge in Chattanooga and Nashville, Tennessee, developed a support group ministry to equip local churches to become more effective in helping people with life-controlling-problems. Dr. Lee called his program Living Free, and used it to provide the church with practical tools for outreach. Living Free trained lay people within the church to lead support groups for people struggling with addiction and other problems. Coupled with the ongoing support network of the local church, Living Free helped many to successfully address their life-controlling problems and addictions without entering a recovery program like Teen Challenge. Today, Living Free is used worldwide by churches and Teen Challenge to bring hope to thousands of people struggling with overwhelming problems.

> "There is no better place for Christian discipleship and a transformation of one's life than at Teen Challenge. It is intense and purposeful. This is why I love this ministry."
>
> — **Rev. John Harper,** Teen Challenge graduate
> Illinois State Teen Challenge Director

‹ **LIVING FREE** Dr. Jimmy Lee developed the Living Free support group ministry as a means of helping local churches minister to those whose lives are damaged either by their own problems or a dysfunctional family member. Many Teen Challenge centers also use Living Free as a part of their ministry.

"JUST SAY NO" IN TENNESSEE

❯ President George W. Bush with Dennis Griffith, Executive Director of Teen Challenge of Southern California. In 2003 President Bush appointed Dennis to serve on the White House Advisory Commission on Drug-Free Communities.

Shortly before he retired as President of Teen Challenge USA in 1987, Frank Reynolds had the opportunity to meet with First Lady Nancy Reagan. She had heard of Teen Challenge's high success rate, and decided to visit the center in Chattanooga, Tennessee as part of her nationwide "Just Say No" drug prevention campaign. She met personally with Frank, to interview him and gather information about the reasons for the program's success. Frank still remembered the experience vividly twenty years later, as he wrote his autobiography:

"One of the security guards asked me how long my appointment was planned for. I replied, 'As long as she wants to talk to me.' He swore and said, 'I am so tired—and she never gets tired.'

"I looked up then as a tiny little woman, about five feet tall, entered the room. He was right! She was a bundle of energy, yet relaxed with me and appeared to have all the time in the world."[7]

After the interview, Mrs. Reagan took a tour of the facility, met with several former addicts one-on-one to offer words of encouragement, then addressed all of the residents and staff as a group. At the end of the day, Frank recalled, "I sent up a 'thank you' to God that the president of our nation had such a wife!"[8]

In the last 20 years, Teen Challenge has continued to attract the attention of national political leaders as they see its effectiveness in helping young men and women find real, lasting solutions to their addictions. President George W. Bush has been a longtime supporter of Teen Challenge. In 2003, he appointed Dennis Griffith, Executive Director of Teen Challenge in Southern California, to serve on the White House Advisory Commission on Drug-Free Communities. That same year, Bush also invited Teen Challenge graduate Henry Lozano, who had pioneered a Teen Challenge center in his hometown of El Centro, California, to attend the State

of the Union address as an honored guest. In his speech that night, Bush said, "Our nation is blessed with recovery programs that do amazing work. ... Tonight, let us bring to all Americans who struggle with drug addiction this message of hope: The miracle of recovery is possible, and it could be you."[9]

Though many national and local politicians endorse Teen Challenge, programs nationwide are still primarily funded through private donations. For many centers, raising the necessary funds continues to present a significant challenge. Some centers have developed extensive work programs in order to achieve financial sustainability.

❯ The young children of drug addicts are often unseen victims of addiction. Many Teen Challenge centers offer practical help, training, and counseling for the family members of those in the residential recovery programs. Teen Challenge centers in San Jose, California (pictured above) and Fort Worth, Texas were two of the first to provide a structured program where drug addicted parents could bring their children into the program with them.

BE IT KNOWN:
These Are NEUTRAL GROUNDS
Guarded by Angels through the Power
of the Holy Spirit by Direct Order
of Jesus of Nazereth. therefore:
NO Weapons, Drugs, Tobacco, Profanity,
Gambling, or Fighting Allowed.

∧ **GANG WEAPONS SIGN**   When Dave Wilkerson came to New York City in 1958, teen gangs were already on the decline because of the growing drug epidemic. However, in Los Angeles today, teen gangs are still a major problem. The city of Los Angeles spends over $80 million a year in programs to reach out to 463 gangs with approximately 40,000 members. Teen Challenge targets these teens with special ministry. As the sign at the edge of the property indicates, Teen Challenge in Los Angeles operates a safe haven for all young people regardless of their gang affiliation.

The particular issues faced by Teen Challenge centers across the nation vary widely not only by region, but also year by year. Dave Wilkerson focused his efforts on teen gang members in the early 1960s. Even at that early stage, however, drug addiction was eroding the foundations of many gangs. Within a few years, Teen Challenge's ministry had shifted to focus on addiction recovery. But gangs never fully died out. In Los Angeles, for example, gang activity for the past twenty years has been just as dominant as it was in 1950s-era New York.

By the 1970s, another shift in Teen Challenge's strategy became necessary, as the drug epidemic that had long plagued urban areas made its way to the suburbs, and into more affluent households. Dave Wilkerson responded to this new trend by holding youth rallies in many cities throughout the U.S., targeting his anti-drug message at the teens he called "goodniks . . . because they had so many of the good things our society has to offer."[10] He also pioneered new ministries in

New York City, such as coffeehouses, aimed at a more educated population than the original Teen Challenge street rallies. Dave viewed this new audience up close when he attended the first service at Catacomb Chapel, a ministry Ann Wilkerson and Fay Mianulli had started in Greenwich Village:

Teen Challenge was entering an entirely new atmosphere. These youngsters weren't slum kids. They hadn't dropped out of school and a lot had gone through college. They knew about the Bible, some of them had read it, and a few had even studied it.

These teen-agers had strong feelings about God—they were angry at Him! They blamed Him for everything distasteful about their lives, for every bruise, for every confusion. And they came to the chapel to argue with anyone who didn't feel the same way![11]

Teen Challenge in New York City branched out into full-fledged campus ministry in the early 1970s, when Faith Brown was appointed to oversee Seekers fellowship groups at NYU and Bronx Community College. Today, the Seekers (which are now independent of Teen Challenge) have chapters on 30 high school and college campuses in the New York City area.

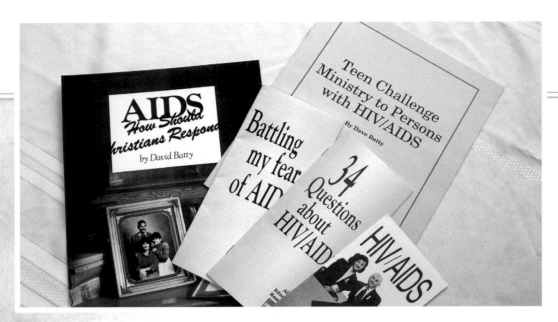

In the 1980s, mainline heroin use began making a comeback in major U.S. cities, accompanied by a new and especially addictive drug—crack cocaine, which could be smoked for an instant high, and which gained popularity among even the very wealthy. More deadly than the drugs themselves, however, was the new killer that stalked beside them.

The earliest statistics are disputed, since the virus was not properly diagnosed at first, but between 1980 and 1995, more than 350,000 Americans died from diseases triggered by AIDS.[12] The rates of HIV infection in the USA have plummeted since then, but the virus has still claimed more than half a million lives in the USA, and millions more worldwide. The homosexual community and needle-sharing drug users were especially devastated in the 1980s. Teen Challenge centers saw literally hundreds of residents die, both during the course of residential programs and shortly after graduation.

Teen Challenge USA responded by producing curriculum to educate students about the dangers of the HIV virus, and to correct the many common misconceptions about it. Teen Challenge staff members responded individually by developing ministries for AIDS patients and their loved ones. For more personal stories about Teen Challenge students and staff dealing with AIDS, see Ralph Rodriguez and Caprice Scott's testimonies in the previous chapter.

In the 1990s, a high-priority issue for many Teen Challenge centers was sexual abuse. Internal surveys showed that approximately 90% of women and 70% of men in Teen Challenge programs had suffered from sexual abuse—evidence of a strong and alarming connection between childhood trauma and later drug addiction.[13]

◁ **COMMITTED TO FREEDOM**
Sallie Culbreth, a survivor of childhood sexual abuse, first presented her seminar *Committed to Freedom* in 1992, at the Teen Challenge center in Hot Springs, Arkansas. Its curriculum, which has since been used at Teen Challenge centers and retreats across the country, offers Bible-based resources to help survivors confront and move beyond their past abuse.

Donna's Story

In the following testimony, taken from the Committed to Freedom Ministries website (www.committedtofreedom.org), a woman named Donna describes the pain and confusion of sexual abuse, and the hope that God provided her through Sallie Culbreth's ministry.

Betrayal. It was the theme of my childhood for thirteen years.

Sexually abused from ages five to eighteen by my stepfather, I was systematically *betrayed*, unloved, and discarded.

When I was nine, charges were brought against my stepfather and I was placed in a foster home. I had to testify against him in court, but he was found innocent. The judge ordered me back home to my mom and stepfather. I felt *betrayed* by the legal system.

By the time I was twelve, my mom regularly let my stepfather rape me. She used me to keep peace in the family, but also viewed me as "the other woman." I felt *betrayed* by my mother.

My siblings thought I was the favored child. They pressured me to ask my stepfather for privileges on their behalf. The cost? Sex with him. I felt *betrayed* by my siblings.

When I was thirteen, I told the pastor of my church about the abuse. He did nothing except bring the situation before the elders. The only discipline my stepfather received? He could no longer teach Sunday School. I felt *betrayed* by my church.

At age fifteen, I told a teacher at my Christian school. He told me I needed to pray. When the abuse continued, he told me I did not have enough faith. I felt *betrayed* by my teacher.

Through all of this, I had an eating disorder, experimented with drugs and sex, and had a nervous breakdown. I *betrayed* myself.

Where was God? I felt *betrayed* by Him, too.

This strong sense of betrayal messed with me in profound ways. Years after the abuse ended, the damage haunted every facet of my life. I found myself wounded and crippled, wondering why I was targeted as the one to be unworthy, unloved, disposable, and abandoned.

Then God brought *Committed to Freedom* into my life. I learned to exchange the lies from my stepfather, mother, siblings, pastor, and teacher, for the truth that I am loved, included, empowered, and cherished. The spiritual tools I gained because of *Committed to Freedom* have provided me with ongoing healing and growth.

I am not where I once was. I am continually traveling on this road to freedom, and I do not travel alone. I hold the hand of a fellow abuse survivor, Christ, who gently leads me to truth, hope, and a future.

The Uncaged Project
Soul Strategies to Rise Above a Wounded Childhood
by Sallie Culbreth

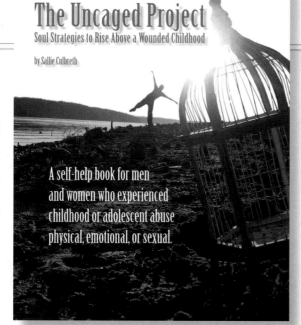

A self-help book for men and women who experienced childhood or adolescent abuse physical, emotional, or sexual.

In 1992, Sallie Culbreth, a survivor of childhood sexual abuse at the hands of a Christian minister, developed a series of seminars and curriculum for abuse survivors entitled *Committed to Freedom*. She led the first seminars at the Teen Challenge in Hot Springs, Arkansas, where her husband Tim served as Executive Director. She now leads dozens of events every year at Teen Challenge centers and other venues across the country. Through her organization Committed to Freedom Ministries and her 2006 book *The Uncaged Project*, she has helped hundreds of men and women with life-controlling problems confront the painful memories of their past.

TEEN CHALLENGE
Survey
on
Marijuana Use

May 1997

Since the early 1960s, marijuana has been used widely by both teens and adults. A 1997 survey of Teen Challenge students across the nation found that 97% had used marijuana, usually before experimenting with other drugs. 29% of those surveyed smoked their first joint before age 13; and more started using marijuana at age 13 than any other age group. One of the students surveyed used marijuana for the first time at age 3, at the invitation of her older brothers. 72% of students indicated that marijuana had served as a gateway to harder drugs, such as heroin, cocaine, or other similar drugs.[14]

In the late 1990s, party drugs such as Ecstasy and ketamine captured the attention of many teens, college students, and their parents, in part because of a few highly publicized overdose deaths. But a much more destructive drug waited in the wings—methamphetamine, or "crystal meth," which spread through the South and Midwest like wildfire in the early 2000s. The drug has the same addictive qualities as crack cocaine, but is cheaper to obtain since it can be manufactured locally. Teen Challenge centers in large cities

> **STAY SHARP** This interactive video presentation is a new resource that reaches today's young generation and challenges them to wholesome, drug-free lives.

< **THE UNCAGED PROJECT**
This study guide can be used for personal or small group study to address issues of physical and sexual abuse, and help victims take steps toward freedom and wholeness.

on the East and West Coast still work primarily with heroin and cocaine addicts, but throughout most of the nation, crystal meth has eclipsed them both, and its victims grow ever younger.

As part of its strategy to fight these new threats to teens, Teen Challenge of Florida produced a multi-media program in 1998 entitled *Stay Sharp*, which featured the testimony of Ray Gomez, a young man who had shot and killed his mother while high on LSD. Mark Romano, now Executive Director of the Bay Area Teen Challenge in Tarpon Springs, Florida, pioneered this program. The *Stay Sharp* DVD is now in its third edition, and features a national appeal. The interactive presentation has been shown at youth group meetings, public and private schools, after school programs, and YMCA camps.

The teen drug addicts that Dave Wilkerson first encountered in 1958, if they are still alive, are now in their sixties. Today a new generation of teens is also caught up in drug addiction, but its members are not necessarily responding to the same methods that have been successful in past decades. Teen Challenge continues to innovate and explore new strategies of connecting to today's troubled youth. The Internet offers many opportunities for communicating with the online generation, as do DVDs and interactive videos. Video games and the Internet offer their own forms of addiction as well, which Teen Challenge's ministry and the gospel stand ready to help young people overcome.

Stay Sharp

THINK ABOUT IT®

Today Teen Challenge is one of the nation's largest privately funded drug recovery ministries, with locations in nearly every state. Teen Challenge does not promise any quick fix for life-controlling problems. "Certainly we cannot claim a magical cure for dope addiction," Dave Wilkerson wrote in 1962. "The devil which hides in that needle is so deadly strong that any such claim would be folly."[15] Today the typical student will stay at least 12 months in the program, and many centers do not celebrate graduations until at least a year later. Many of those seeking help today also come from dysfunctional family backgrounds, which only adds to the difficulty of successfully returning to society.

The specific challenges have changed enormously over the years, but Teen Challenge's answer to them remains the same. Teen Challenge leaders recognize that preventing addiction and other life-controlling problems is a process that must start at a young age, and that Christ alone holds the key to prevention and cure. This message of hope, from the very beginning, would not be confined to America alone, and would quickly become a worldwide movement.

> "Drug addicts and alcoholics are no longer the only ones with extreme problems. Teen Challenge is creating new ministries that will allow us to impact our culture in a greater way than ever before."
>
> — Jack Smart, Executive Director
>
> Mid-America Teen Challenge Training Center, Cape Girardeau, Missouri

On the following pages, you will read testimonies which represent the tens of thousands of people across America who have experienced miracles in their lives through Teen Challenge. Entire chapters could be written about any one of these brief stories, and in fact, many of them have already been published as books.

But even if all the biographies were complete, they could not tell the whole story of lives changed by God at Teen Challenge, since many of the individuals who experienced these miracles went on to inspire thousands of others—husbands and wives, parents and children, strangers and friends. Many Teen Challenge graduates develop a special compassion for others caught up in addiction, and become advocates for bringing new addicts to Teen Challenge to experience God's transformation. Every day, new miracles like those you are about to read continue in more than 200 Teen Challenge ministry locations across the USA. ❦

NOTES ON CHAPTER 2

1. David Manuel, *The Jesus Factor* (Plainfield, NJ: Logos, 1977), p. 43.

2. Catherine Hess, *Research Summation: H.E.W. Study on Teen Challenge Training Center Rehrersburg, PA* (Springfield, MO: Teen Challenge USA, 1976).

3. Frank Reynolds with Joan Kruger, *Is There a God?* (Lenexa, KS: 3CrossPublishing, 2006), p. 99-100.

4. Reynolds, p. 106.

5. Manuel, p. 70.

6. Reynolds, p. 111.

7. Reynolds, p. 93.

8. Reynolds, p. 94.

9. George W. Bush, "State of the Union Speech," 29 January 2003; transcript accessed at http://www.cnn.com.

10. David Wilkerson, *Beyond the Cross and the Switchblade* (Old Tappan, NJ: Fleming H. Revell, 1974), p. 121.

11. David Wilkerson and Leonard Ravenhill, *Twelve Angels from Hell* (Old Tappan, NJ: Fleming H. Revell, 1965), p. 148.

12. For a set of official government statistics, see, for example, Centers for Disease Control and Prevention, *HIV/AIDS Surveillance Report*, vol. 17, revised edition, June 2007; accessed at http://www.cdc.gov/hiv.

13. Dave Batty interview with Sallie Culbreth, Founder and CEO of Committed to Freedom ministries.

14. *Teen Challenge Survey on Marijuana Use,* (Springfield, MO: Teen Challenge USA, 1997).

15. David Wilkerson with John and Elizabeth Sherrill, *The Cross and the Switchblade* (New York: Bernard Geis, 1962; Jove Special Sales Edition, 1993), p. 165.

"I believe that God is calling Teen Challenge

to become a premier discipleship training program that graduates

chemical-free passionate followers of Jesus Christ.

I believe God wants to call scores of Teen Challenge

graduates to full time ministry."

Rev. Joe Batluck, President
Teen Challenge Training Center
Rehrersburg, Pennsylvania

Manuel Baerga

Capitol Heights, Maryland

NORTHEAST REGION

Massachusetts

A Voice in His Head

Rodney Hart

Rodney Hart stole to buy drugs, but also for the thrill. At age 14, he stole a taxicab, and drove his friends around until it ran out of gas. After high school, he worked for a landscaping company, where he would scope out wealthy houses by day and rob them at night. He even stole from churches, since they made easy targets.

After moving out of his parents' house, Rodney slept in subway stations, constantly drunk or high. Even when sober, he believed the spirit of the Indian chief Geronimo had possessed him. Eventually, he was locked in a mental institution and heavily sedated.

 "You haven't been free for a long, long time.

And you are dying. Your soul is dead."

One day, while looking out the window at a tractor harvesting crops, Rodney thought, "If only I could be free again. I'm dying in here." From inside himself, he heard another voice: "You haven't been free for a long, long time. And you are dying. Your soul is dead."

His brother Glenn helped him get into Teen Challenge in 1975. As Rodney entered the program, he saw a sign in front of the building: "If any man be in Christ, he is a new creation." Rodney scoffed—he didn't believe it.

To show his disdain, he snuck a bag of dope into the program. He showed it to his roommate, a former heroin addict, but watched in horror as he flushed the bag down the toilet. Rodney wondered if maybe the sign was right—this crazy man definitely was a "new creation!"

Alone in their room, the roommate led him in a simple prayer: "Jesus, let me know you're real. Amen." Rodney wasn't sure if anything had changed, but later in a chapel service, he heard another voice in his head: "I'm here with you, Rodney. This is where you can find me." He prayed, "Jesus, I give my whole heart to you. Please forgive me of my past. Take my whole life, and make me a new creation."

God answered that prayer in a major way. After graduating from the Farm in Rehrersburg, Rodney worked with Teen Challenge and similar ministries in Texas, Boston, and Paraguay, South America.

Today Rodney serves as the Executive Director of Teen Challenge New England, which oversees ten centers and more than 300 students. Rodney and his wife, Lynn, have been serving Teen Challenge together for the past 28 years. ❧

[Source: Richard Omohundro, Jr. with David Hazard, *They Overcame* 2nd ed. (Brockton, MA: TCNE Publishing, 2003), p. 128-155.]

RHODE ISLAND

15 Months for God

Cathy Smith

For 15 years, crack cocaine transformed Cathy Smith from a loving mom and homemaker into a deceitful, selfish drug addict. She refused to drive her daughter to school, and she rubbed cocaine in her four-year-old son's mouth to numb his toothache, rather than taking him to the dentist. Her children grew to hate her, just as she hated herself.

One day, Cathy told a friend that her sister needed to escape from an abusive boyfriend. The friend gave her a booklet about Teen Challenge. When Cathy read about the 15-month program, she thought, "If I can get high for 15 years, then I can give God 15 months."

The program actually took 21 months, as Cathy slowly learned to let go of her past. It was a long road, but one that ended in a restored relationship with her grown children.

Today, Cathy is an Assemblies of God pastor, and is working toward a degree in Early Childhood Education. Every month, she coordinates Children's Church for the Teen Challenge graduation ceremony. ❧

Maine
A Long Hard Road
Peter Fabiano

Peter Fabiano grew up in a family of fifteen children with an abusive father. He started using alcohol and drugs at 9 years old, and tried to take his own life in his mother's basement. For the next 22 years, he tried to blot out the pain with anything he could find—pornography, sex, drugs, and money.

He didn't find the cure for his pain until Christmas Eve, 2000. Sitting in a crack house, he realized that God had something better for him. He entered Teen Challenge the day after Christmas, and gave his life to Christ two days later.

Peter took two years to complete the program. It was the hardest thing he had ever done, since it forced him to stop making excuses and deal with the condition of his own heart. But when he graduated, he thanked God that the journey had been so demanding, since it had prepared him for a future in ministry.

In 2007, Peter and his wife Shondi, also a Teen Challenge graduate, moved to Augusta, Maine to pioneer a new Teen Challenge center.

Vermont
From Broken To Humble
Chris Nichols

In July of 2005, the top floor of Chris Nichols' house, where his grandmother lived, caught fire. He tried desperately to rescue her, but Chris had recently stolen her credit cards and racked up a $10,000 debt, so she had locked all her doors. By the time firemen arrived, it was too late. Chris watched his grandmother die on his front lawn.

For the next month, Chris sank deeper into addictions that already controlled his life—alcohol, Ecstasy, and Oxycontin. All the good things in his life, including his job, his girlfriend, and his home, began to slip away.

Chris came to Teen Challenge a broken man. But through the program, God turned his brokenness into Christian humility. As he came to accept Christ's forgiveness, Chris began to see a larger purpose for his life.

Chris graduated in June of 2007. He coordinates Teen Challenge's Learning Center in Vermont, and is studying to become a pastor. His mother also became a Christian through his experience. Chris says, "Life today could not be better."

Rhode Island
A Prisoner's Repentance
Tabatha Mello

Tabatha Mello's mother was a heroin addict, so Tabatha spent her childhood in foster homes, moving from one abusive household to another. A loving family adopted her at age 7, but she couldn't stand their rules, and ran away five years later. She ended up back in the foster home system, continually running away and getting caught again.

Tabatha became a Christian at age 14, at a Bible study in a juvenile detention center. She went to church occasionally, but her young faith couldn't compete with the temptation of drugs. By age 19, she was hopelessly addicted to heroin and cocaine.

At a church service in 2001, Tabatha felt an overwhelming desire to repent and let God take control of her life, but she had no idea how. The next day, she overdosed on heroin, and landed in prison for 6 months. She thanked God for the strict sentence, though, because there in jail, she finally surrendered her whole life to Jesus.

After her release, in January of 2002, Tabatha entered the Teen Challenge program, with nothing but prison clothes on her back. Over the next year, she learned to forgive the many people who had hurt her, and to embrace God's forgiveness for herself. She also answered God's call to enter the ministry. At age 22, she earned her full credentials as an Assemblies of God pastor.

Tabatha now works on staff in the Teen Challenge women's home in Providence, Rhode Island. Her husband Jonathan leads the Teen Challenge Drug Awareness Team in Brockton, Massachusetts.

NEW HAMPSHIRE

Todd Sheehan
Tomorrow Too Late

The turning point in Todd Sheehan's life came the morning of October 20, 2003.

"Death was made very real to me," Todd says, "as I held my lifeless girlfriend. Dead of an overdose of heroin and cocaine. That night we had been talking about changing our lives, and we decided that tomorrow was a good place to start. Tomorrow we would make a change. Tomorrow we would seek help. The tragic reality is that we put things off until tomorrow and tomorrow never comes."

Todd tried a secular rehab, but two months later he was back where he started—in the same bedroom where his girlfriend had died. For the first time in his life, he cried out to God. The next day, his mother told him about a new Teen Challenge center that had opened in their hometown.

Todd graduated in 2005, and plans to become a minister. "My faith is no longer in a bag of dope or a bottle of pills," he says. "My faith is in God."

NORTHEAST REGION

Philadelphia, Pennsylvania

From Philly to the Dakotas
Mike Gilmartin

At age 27, Mike Gilmartin didn't need more reasons to throw his life away. He was broke, his marriage was in trouble, and he couldn't control his cycles of depression and binge drinking. Then his best friend, his wife's brother Mark, was murdered in a random attack.

Mike snapped. He stormed into a Bible study at a local church and demanded an answer to the question that tormented him: "Where is my brother-in-law?" Rather than arguing with him, pastor Kenneth Fornicola befriended Mike and told him about Teen Challenge in Philadelphia.

Mike graduated in 1989 and today serves as the executive director of Teen Challenge in South Dakota. His son-in-law Nathan Lloehr, also a Teen Challenge graduate, is the dean of men. 🌿

[Source: Corinne Scott, "Teen Challenge of the Dakotas Restores Broken Lives," *Living Stones News* 27 June 2006.]

Syracuse, New York

Full-Blooded Onondaga
Eddie O'Brien

As a full-blooded Onondaga Indian, Eddie O'Brien inherited a proud heritage. But on his 40th birthday, he didn't feel proud. He had blown a full scholarship to Colgate University because of his drinking, and dropped out of a dozen rehab programs. He came to California homeless, and turned to prostitution to pay for his booze and an apartment.

Eddie woke up from his birthday party feeling sick. As he looked at empty bottles and photos of his gay lifestyle, he heard God say, "Eddie, I did not create you for this!" He walked away, never to return, and found a bed at the Los Angeles Rescue Mission. Counselors there recommended Syracuse Teen Challenge.

Eddie eventually graduated from the Teen Challenge International Ministry Institute in Jacksonville, Florida. He now works as an intern at Syracuse. 🌿

Rehrersburg, Pennsylvania

Double Addiction
Kennon Baker

Kennon Baker had two addictions, one for drugs and another for crime. He loved the rush of breaking into houses in his family's upscale Atlanta neighborhood. Over time, his crimes grew more serious—he dealt illegal firearms and was arrested for assaulting his girlfriend.

When Kennon was arrested on felony burglary charges, his parents gave him an ultimatum: enter a Teen Challenge program or serve a long prison term. So he joined the program, planning to breeze through just enough to impress the judge at his next hearing. But a week later, something disrupted those plans. A counselor shared a verse from Romans about the mind of a sinful man, and Kennon heard as if it had been written for him, tears streaming down his face.

Kennon finished the program at the Teen Challenge Training Center in Rehrersburg, then moved on to the TCMI staff training school in Florida, then back to Rehrersburg to work in the Teen Challenge ministry. 🌿

REHRERSBURG, PENNSYLVANIA

A Dirty Farm Story

Melvin Martinez

In the book *The Jesus Factor*, published in 1977, writer David Manuel relates a story told to him by Hank Garling, a Pennsylvania farmer who managed the dairy farm at the Teen Challenge Training Center in Rehrersburg, along with his wife Betty. Hank's story is about a Teen Challenge student named Melvin Martinez, who helped someone out of a dirty situation.

⬥

Well, there are so many [stories], if you really sat down and thought about them. But one does come to mind—about the time we lost a calf in the barn. She was gone for two days, and we couldn't find a trace of her. Plumb disappeared.

Well, sir, at the far end of the barn there's grating that runs across the width of the barn just inside the doors. Under that grating is the manure pit, and what we do is scrape all the manure down to the far end of the barn, lift that grating and scrape it into the pit. When the pit fills up, then we get the little loader-tractor down there and push her out to where we can load it on the spreader. Pretty efficient system.

Finally, after two days of looking and not finding her, one of the students, a great big fellow named Melvin, gave out a holler. "She's down here in the manure pit!" And everybody took off for the far end of the barn to see.

Well, sir, she was completely buried. Had her head stuck up to breathe, but it was buried, too. All there was showing was two little holes in the manure at the tip of her nose. It was only the grace of God that Melvin happened to spot her at all. What happened was that the cows had kicked the grating loose as they walked over it, but while it was open, the calf had fallen down in there. Then one of the guys, seeing the grate out of place, had put it back, without noticing her down there.

Why Melvin, he didn't think anything about it; he just jumped down in there and pulled her out, as easy as you please. And you know, today that's a part of his testimony. He tells it and then says that that's the way Jesus reached down and rescued him like a lost calf, from the muck and mire of sin. ❧

[Source: David Manuel, *The Jesus Factor* (Plainfield, NJ: Logos, 1977), p. 134-36.]

Ivette Mastrobuono

A Teen Challenge Romance

Ivette Mastrobuono lived through a nightmarish childhood in Puerto Rico, where her grandmother practiced the occult religion of Santeria. She left home at 16, pregnant and alone, and moved to New York City.

In New York, she found the Times Square Church, pastored by David Wilkerson. She grew as a Christian there, but struggled with alcohol, drugs, and promiscuity. Shortly after her cousin died of an overdose in 2002, she entered Philadelphia Teen Challenge. She transferred to New Haven for the second phase of the program, where she met a counselor, Nicholas, who would later become her husband.

Ivette couldn't stand Nicky at first—in her own words, "he was too pushy and too intense." She gladly received lectures and homework from any pastor but him. To make matters worse, Nicky seemed to be picking on her.

In her prayers, Ivette asked God, "What is wrong with this man?" But when her heart began to stir, she understood. Then she prayed, "God, if this is the man you have for me, you have to show me—because I can't find anything I like about him!"

In time, God convinced her, and as Ivette neared the end of her program, the two got permission to date, under strict supervision. According to Ivette, "I felt like I couldn't even look at him without getting in trouble!" After graduation, she flew to Argentina for a missions trip, and when she returned, Nicky was waiting at the airport to drive her home. Ivette almost didn't get in the car, she was so nervous about not getting permission first.

In 2004, Pastor Rodney Hart married the couple, in a ceremony to which every one of New England's Teen Challenge centers were invited. Since then, the Mastrobuonos have worked as missionaries for Teen Challenge in El Salvador and Honduras. Last year, they became directors of the Teen Challenge men's home in Newark, New Jersey. ❧

NORTHEAST REGION

Factoryville, Pennsylvania

Book of Wisdom
John Orzechowski

John Orzechowski grew up going to church and played guitar in a Christian band. But as a teenager, he questioned the existence of God in a world of suffering, and became an atheist.

Drug use came easily after that, as he decided to have as much fun as possible in his short, meaningless life. At age 15, after trying alcohol, marijuana, LSD, painkillers, and Ecstasy, he started injecting heroin.

> "If he is real, then he can reveal himself to me, and I would believe. If not, I would die with my addiction."

John realized right away that heroin addiction would destroy his life. But he resisted going to the Teen Challenge juvenile boys program, since he had already tried Christianity as a child. So he made a deal with God: "If he is real, then he can reveal himself to me, and I would believe. If not, I would die with my addiction."

God did reveal himself, in an unexpected way. At Teen Challenge, John discovered the Book of Ecclesiastes, and saw that its writer had struggled with the same feelings of meaninglessness he had. John wasn't struck with a lightning bolt of belief, but slowly his heart began to change. Two months into the program, he recommitted his life to Christ.

John now attends Southeastern University, studying the Bible and English. He has spent his last three summer breaks at the Teen Challenge center in Swaziland, Africa, where he works with orphans with AIDS. ❧

Buffalo, New York

A Timely Visit
Cory James Connell

Cory James Connell had used cocaine since the age of 12. He decided to get help when a group of Teen Challenge students gave a presentation on life-controlling problems at his church in Myrtle Beach, South Carolina.

Cory had many ties to his hometown that would make a long-term program difficult, but he prayed that God would make a way. Within a week, he had managed to get out of his apartment lease, leave his job, and with the help of his church, get on a bus to Buffalo Teen Challenge.

A few years after his graduation in 2002, Cory earned a degree in International Community Health from Elim Bible Institute, and completed an internship as a medical missionary to the Philippines. He now works on staff at Teen Challenge in Buffalo, NY. ✍

Rural Ridge, Pennsylvania

A Brighter Future
Brian Hamilton

Brian Hamilton experimented with marijuana and cocaine in college, but he still managed to excel in his studies and sports. He could pitch a 90 mile-per-hour fastball, won an academic scholarship, and played drums in a local band. After school, he took a management position at an electrical engineering firm.

His drug use never got in the way of his success—until he tried heroin. By the age of 34, Brian had lost his wife and daughter, his job, and his house. All told, he had spent nearly half a million dollars on drugs.

After trying several secular rehabs, Brian had nearly lost hope. But at Teen Challenge, he found an even brighter future than the one he'd had before. Four years after graduating from the program, he has returned to his wife and family, earned a better position at the same company, and bought a new home. Even better, he has a new relationship with God. Brian volunteers with several ministries, including two worship bands and the outreach Connecting Business Men to Christ. ✍

> By the age of 34, Brian had lost his wife and daughter, his job, and his house.

From Exploitation to Empowerment
Jane Christiansen

Jane Christiansen was a heroin addict with a label—hopeless. She had turned to a psychologist for help, and after 5 minutes of counseling, he ordered her, "Out!" of his office, claiming she was hopeless. Her lawyer stood before the Municipal Court and told the judge, "I refuse to represent my client any longer on the grounds that she is hopeless." He picked up his briefcase and walked out of the courtroom, leaving her there alone.

Her new public defender told Jane how she could identify with her, because she, too, came from a background of addiction. Jane asked, "What about the craving that drives me back to heroin no matter how many times I kick?" The lady responded, "You'll never be cured of that, but we'll teach you how to live with it."

Sick and in jail, she came across a Bible placed by the Gideons. She started reading, and for the first time heard God's message of salvation. A short time later, two women from Philadelphia Teen Challenge helped her enter the program. A few days later, during one of the chapel services, the speaker invited those forward who needed their sins forgiven. Jane was one of the first to the front. "As I prayed, I experienced exactly what I had read in that Gideon Bible in jail—Jesus washed away all my sin. By the time I stood to my feet I was free, completely set free! That craving for drugs was gone."

In that same chapel at Teen Challenge Jane received the call of God to full-time missionary service. After graduation and Bible college, Jane worked for Global Teen Challenge, helping to establish centers in Spain, Lithuania, and Serbia. She has also worked with several other ministries on five continents. Jane is currently the director of "God 4 Girls," a new ministry that provides education, Bible training, and vocational skills to young girls who have been sexually exploited and trafficked. God 4 Girls has so far established bases of operation in the Congo and northern Mexico. ✍

NORTHEAST REGION

West Babylon, New York

A Family Program
Danielle Poulson

Danielle Poulson was upset when her mother first entered Teen Challenge. In her mind, it was an admission that their family had failed. But five months later, addicted and with nowhere to live, she decided to give Teen Challenge a try herself.

Danielle bucked against the strict restrictions of the program at first, but eventually decided to surrender her life to Jesus. She graduated soon after her mother did, reconciled and ready to start a new life. Danielle graduated from Evangel University in 2005, and is now attending Assemblies of God Theological Seminary to become a chaplain in the US Marines. ☙

WEST BABYLON, NEW YORK

A Musical Romance
Marc & Denise Oliver

Before coming to Long Island Teen Challenge, Marc Oliver felt he had never completed anything. First he had to leave the Marines on a medical discharge, then he dropped out of college. God brought him to Teen Challenge, he was sure, just so he could finish something and move forward in life. He completed the program, then stayed on as a driver and a leader in the men's travelling choir.

Denise Corbett graduated from Long Island Teen Challenge in 1995, and later became the women's program supervisor and choir director for both men and women. She often prayed that the Lord would give her a godly husband. As she saw Marc more often around the choir, she began to think about him. At the same time, Marc sought counsel from director Jimmy Jack about his growing feelings for Denise.

On May 7, 2004, during Teen Challenge's annual banquet, Marc knelt in front of students, staff, pastors, and guests, and asked Denise to be his wife. They were married a year later, in a music-filled ceremony. ☙

Athens, West Virginia

The Old College Try
Michael "Dusty" Small

Dusty Small loved high school, hanging out with friends and playing sports, but college just made him lonely and depressed. He spent his first semester drinking, failed his classes and dropped out of college. Loneliness continued to follow him into the working world, until a co-worker introduced him to methamphetamine. The drug soothed his pain at first, but before long, despair crept back in.

To make money, Dusty learned to manufacture crystal meth. He studied harder and found more success in his criminal career than he ever had at academics. He wasn't invincible, though. He was serving his third jail sentence in 2003 when a pastor told him about Teen Challenge.

In the program, Dusty discovered a relationship with Christ that took away the feelings of loneliness and inadequacy. Two years later, he decided to give college another try. He now attends Zion Bible College in Rhode Island, where he was recently elected Class President. ✺

From Nightmare to Miracle
Jacqui Strothoff

When Jacqui Strothoff found heroin, all of her problems seemed to melt away. The sexual abuse from childhood, the abusive marriage at age 16, the miscarriage that left her sterile, the suicide attempts—everything was replaced by peaceful silence.

In reality, her nightmare had just begun.

The needle robbed her of everything she loved, including a boyfriend who died of an overdose in bed beside her. She and a friend buried his body secretly, for fear the police would take their stash. Eventually she confessed the crime, but it didn't take away the cravings or the voices in her head. She sat in her apartment shooting speedballs, a combination of cocaine and heroin, hoping after each one that she wouldn't wake up.

But that wasn't the end. When her teenage brother stopped by to check on her, she offered him a hit. He shot up and immediately began convulsing. When the paramedics arrived, he was already dead, and Jacqui was screaming for God.

At the funeral, Jacqui could hardly look at her family. Her father introduced her to a man named Frank, who said, "God told me if you turn your life over to him, he'll raise you up and use you." Jacqui didn't believe it, but she pretended for her father's sake. Frank led her in a prayer for forgiveness, then gave her a book about a Teen Challenge graduate. As she read it, Jacqui wondered if the same miracle could happen to her. She called the number on the back for New Life for Girls, a program started by a Teen Challenge graduate. The woman who answered the telephone said, "We've been praying for you! Frank told us you would call."

The first time Jacqui prayed with the women at New Life for Girls, she felt a burning in her stomach. The women said, "That's the Holy Spirit!" Jacqui figured the program must be a cult, but decided to give it 24 hours. In a chapel service the next day, she raised her hand to praise God, and suddenly fell on her back. Strange words came pouring from her mouth, and for the first time, her whole body felt pure.

> "God told me if you turn your life over to him, he'll raise you up and use you."

Over the next year, Jacqui devoured Christian teaching. She would sneak out at night, hide under the organ in the chapel, and read her Bible until dawn. She didn't understand much, and what she did understand seemed unbelievable—that Jesus could love and accept someone so rotten. But she knew her experience was real.

Her mother, who had forbidden the family to see her, brought everyone to Jacqui's graduation in 1975. Jacqui attended Twin Oaks Leadership Academy, then Southwest Missouri State for a degree in social work. With her husband Bob Strothoff, a Teen Challenge graduate, she travelled the country leading seminars on sexual abuse.

On their first anniversary, Jacqui learned that she was pregnant. "I just love the way the Lord timed it," she says. "It was as if to say, 'Don't worry about what people have said can never happen in your life.'" Today Jacqui serves as the Executive Director of three Teen Challenge women's programs in New England. ✺

Maryland

The Dealer
Manuel Baerga

Unlike most heroin addicts, Manuel Baerga got rich from drugs. With his brother, he ran a large distribution network in New York City and Miami. Once, on a trip through North Carolina, Manuel was arrested with 10,000 pounds of marijuana and $100,000 in cash, but he skipped bail and adopted a new identity. When he was arrested again in Maryland, he pulled a gun on the police, and this time there was no escape.

In jail, a volunteer from Teen Challenge gave him a leatherbound Bible. Not interested, Manuel gave it to another inmate. A few days later, that inmate became a Christian and witnessed to him. Soon Manuel was reading the Bible every night, too. When he fell to his knees and asked God for help, he felt free for the first time in 15 years.

Against his lawyer's advice, Manuel pled guilty to every charge, certain that God wanted him to tell the truth. Prison officials had noticed his changed life, though, and wrote letters to the judge asking for mercy. Manuel received seven years, but served only two before being released to Teen Challenge. When reunited with his wife Laura, he found that in his absence she had become a Christian, too.

Today, Manuel serves as the Executive Director of Teen Challenge in Maryland, and as the President of Hispanic Evangelical Ministers. ❧

∧ (Top left) Manuel Baerga and his wife, Laura.
(Top right) Manuel with kids participating in a summer outreach.

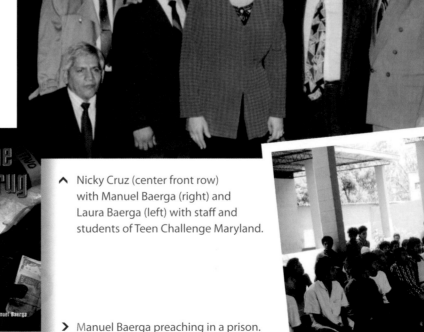

∧ Nicky Cruz (center front row) with Manuel Baerga (right) and Laura Baerga (left) with staff and students of Teen Challenge Maryland.

Inside the Miami Drug Cartel
by Manuel Baerga

❯ Manuel Baerga's autobiography.

❯ Manuel Baerga preaching in a prison.

NORTHEAST REGION

Newport News, Virginia

Back on the Fast Track
Colby Thomas

Colby Thomas smoked marijuana with his older brother at age 11, and by 14 was trying mushrooms, Ecstasy, cocaine, and prescription pills. Two years later, he stole his brother's Jeep for a drug-fueled joyride, and flipped it. None of his friends inside were hurt, but Colby found himself facing a year in jail. Instead, the judge recommended Teen Challenge.

Colby, who had done time at several juvenile detention centers, expected to have to fight at Teen Challenge. He was surprised to find everyone so friendly, even if they were rough around the edges. He developed deep friendships with many fellow students, in addition to a new relationship with God.

Colby had fallen so far behind in school, he wasn't sure he could catch up. But Teen Challenge prepared him for the GED test, which he passed, and today, at age 21, he studies kinesiology at Thomas Nelson Community College. When he graduates, he will be a nationally certified personal trainer. Colby's wife, Heather, is a senior at Old Dominion University. ❦

> Colby, who had done time at several juvenile detention centers, expected to have to fight at Teen Challenge.

> **DISCOVERING NEW LIFE**
> The daily Bible classes build a foundation for students learning to live in a new relationship with Jesus Christ.

Garrison, New York

Journey Out of Despair
Beth Greco

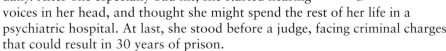

Beth Greco, Director of the Walter Hoving Home for women, knows firsthand what despair feels like. She tried cocaine for the first time when she was 9 years old. Before dropping out of college, she was using drugs daily. After one especially bad hit, she started hearing voices in her head, and thought she might spend the rest of her life in a psychiatric hospital. At last, she stood before a judge, facing criminal charges that could result in 30 years of prison.

Beth came to the Walter Hoving Home, in her own words, "as a last-ditch effort." There, she found the love of God, the only thing that could fill the deep hole of despair in her life. Her family relationships were restored, and for the first time, she began to have good dreams about the future.

After completing the program, Beth returned to federal prison to serve the remainder of her reduced sentence. Afterward, she returned to the Hoving Home to work as a counselor.

Beth, along with her husband Tim and son Jason, are involved in many other community groups, such as the Salvation Army. The local Lions Club voted Beth their Lion of the Year for 2007. ❦

"I am now living for Christ and am so joyful!

Never did I think life could be so abundant!

Thank God for Teen Challenge."

Coty Dodd
Teen Challenge Graduate

Coty Dodd

Alabama

SOUTH REGION

Columbus, Georgia

An Inspired Father
Dr. A.J. Aspinwall

Dr. A.J. Aspinwall came to faith in Christ through his son, a graduate of the Teen Challenge Training Center in Rehrersburg, Pennsylvania. Dr. Aspinwall decided that his hometown, Columbus, Georgia, needed a similar center. Together with Rev. Tom Owensby, a Baptist pastor, he began sharing his vision at local churches and door-to-door.

The ministry started with a crisis hotline at an Assemblies of God church, which Rev. Owensby manned by himself. In 1987, the Women's Center opened in Columbus, Georgia, and came under the umbrella of Teen Challenge in 1988. Today, with a new facility purchased in 2005, the Women's Center has a capacity of 60 residents. The crisis hotline also continues—though now with many more counselors. ❧

Columbus, Georgia

Second Chance
Lori McKee

Lori McKee entered the Teen Challenge Women's Center in Columbus on the very first day it opened its doors. A few weeks later, she was back on the street using drugs.

But God didn't give up on Lori. Neither did her Christian brother—he kept praying that she would find the help she needed. Eleven years later, Lori came back to the Columbus center and completed the program. She has devoted her life to helping other women discover the freedom she found in Jesus. She has worked at Teen Challenge in Columbus, Georgia, and more recently served as Director of the Teen Challenge women's program in Milwaukee, Wisconsin. ❧

 "God didn't give up on me"

— Lori McKee

Nothing Short of Perfection
Robert Gleason

When Robert Gleason came to the Vero Beach Juvenile Boys Teen Challenge, he could see that the program wasn't perfect. But he also saw staff members devoting their lives to something bigger than themselves. Robert graduated from the program at age 16, determined to share the perfect love of Christ he'd found.

Now, at age 21, he serves as a missionary, doing construction work for the House of Hope orphanage in Zacapa, Guatemala. Despite differences in culture, many boys at the orphanage endure the same struggles he did as a teen—and they respond eagerly to his message of God's perfect plan for their lives. Robert is also working to start a prison ministry, a mountain outreach, and a Christian evangelism program at a government-run orphanage. ❧

Fort Lauderdale, Florida

"You're Trying to Brainwash Me!"
Katrina Engle

Katrina Engle first heard the gospel at a Baptist church, where her parents sent her while they recovered from Saturday night hangovers. She would come home and preach to them about the evils of beer and cigarettes, sermons that fell on deaf ears. She was too young to realize they were also using drugs.

Her dad was arrested on a gun charge, and suddenly Katrina's friends at school and church shunned her. So she found a new set of friends, kids she could party and get high with. But they brought more problems than they solved—Katrina got pregnant and miscarried, her boyfriend died of AIDS, and soon she was in and out of rehab centers. "They wanted to take away the anesthesia," Katrina recalled. "But who would take away the pain?"

After Katrina threatened to commit suicide at age 18, her friend Inez helped her find Teen Challenge. At first, she rebelled against the staff who confiscated her cigarettes and rock music. "You people are trying to brainwash me!" she shouted. A counselor replied, "Yeah, we are trying to wash the bad out and the good in." She soon came to respect the Teen Challenge staff, many of whom had similar stories to her own, and she allowed God to change her life.

Today, Katrina and her husband Roger serve as missionaries in La Moskitia, Honduras, where they run a home for abused, sick, and malnourished children. ✺

Lakeland, Florida

An Emerging Leader
Jennifer Austin

When Jennifer Austin was a junior in high school, her parents discovered her heroin use and brought her to Teen Challenge. In the program, Jennifer saw hope for the first time. She had been addicted for five years—a huge portion of her young life—but saw that Christ could bring her contentment without a drug.

Jennifer graduated in December 2005 and enrolled in the very first class of the Teen Challenge Emerging Leaders Program. The ELP is a six-month training program designed to raise up new leaders at Teen Challenge centers around the world.

Jennifer now attends Southeastern University, where she studies criminal justice and social services. She plans to use her training to help young people who face the same struggles she did. ✺

JACKSONVILLE, FLORIDA

Jason Bingham

Teen Challenge Jacksonville Leadership Institute

The Teen Challenge Jacksonville Leadership Institute (TCJLI) is a two-year training program designed to prepare former Teen Challenge students to take up staff positions at centers around the world. But TCJLI has touched the lives of more than just Teen Challenge graduates.

In July 2003, Jason Bingham left his home in Buffalo, New York, with $400 in his pocket. He hated the person he had become, after years of chasing after money and sex, so he left behind everyone he knew. Within weeks, he was homeless on the streets of Jacksonville, Florida.

Desperate, Jason went to the nearest church for help. The pastor there prayed for him and gave him food. While Jason sat in the church parking lot after a morning service, a van full of TCJLI students pulled up, and invited him to lunch.

At the TCJLI center, Jason saw a joyful group of men and women singing worship songs, and heard testimonies of changed lives that astounded him. At that moment, Jason says, "I wanted what they had." They made arrangements for Jason to enter the Teen Challenge program in Macon, Georgia on March 18, 2003, and a week later he gave his life to Christ. After he completed the Teen Challenge program, he attended the TCJLI staff training school and graduated in December 2005.

Jason never returned to Buffalo, but the broken relationships with his family have been restored. He now works as the Program Coordinator at Teen Challenge in Savannah, Georgia. ✺

⌃ Teen Challenge Jacksonville Leadership Institute in Jacksonville, Florida

SOUTH REGION

Louisiana
The New Kid
Erik Hill

Erik Hill learned at a young age that Christian ministry can be difficult. His father was a youth pastor, so his family often moved from town to town. Because he was always the "new kid," Erik was picked on and had a hard time making friends. To be part of the in-crowd, he smoked marijuana, and soon moved on to LSD, crystal meth, and a hopeless addiction.

Erik's dad helped him find Teen Challenge, and there his life changed. In the middle of a lesson, one of the teachers asked if he knew Jesus, and led him in prayer right there in the classroom. Erik has been a Teen Challenge teacher himself since 2003, and now has a son of his own. ❧

Hot Springs, Arkansas
Pure Hopeless
Bubba Davis

Bubba Davis grew up going to a small country church with his family. Many of his relatives worked in ministry, but Bubba had never experienced life with Jesus for himself. Instead, he spent all his time drinking with friends.

Bubba's father knew his son had an alcohol problem, but helped him find a good job. Bubba kept up a clean appearance for years, but eventually the drinking affected his judgment. He was fired, and soon he was living out of his pickup truck. "I thought of myself as pure evil," Bubba says. "In reality, I was pure hopeless."

It took a severe thunderstorm in August, 2000 to shake him from his stupor. While he sat helpless in his truck, two tornadoes passed close by, one on either side. When the storm stopped, Bubba knew that God had spared him. A week later, his dad brought him to Teen Challenge.

In the program, Bubba began to rebuild the solid foundation of faith his parents had given him as a child. He is married now, and works as a Teen Challenge work detail supervisor. ❧

Beyond Mathematics
Randy Neff

Randy Neff was an engineer who found it difficult to believe anything that wasn't proven mathematically. He couldn't understand, for instance, how anyone could believe in an all-powerful, loving God. He also couldn't understand why all the things that should make him happy—a successful career, money, sex—just didn't. Or why none of the treatment programs he tried could get his drinking under control.

Randy's wife was days away from kicking him out when she heard about Teen Challenge. She simply left the information packet on the kitchen table, and he made the call.

Randy had never had a roommate before, so living with 16 strangers at Teen Challenge was a harsh adjustment. But he came to see that through faith, he could love even the most difficult people, and have a relationship with God, something he had been seeking for years without knowing it.

Randy now serves as the Assistant Executive Director of Teen Challenge South Texas. ❧

Morrow, Arkansas
More Than Just an Act
Russell Henry

Russell Henry was a drug addict by the age of 13. The lifestyle came naturally, since his parents were addicts, too. When a court ordered him to the Teen Challenge Ranch for boys in Morrow, Arkansas, at age 15, he saw it as a "get out of jail free" card. He decided to pretend he was doing well there.

Before long, his act turned into the real thing. In a chapel service, he felt the crushing shame of his sin, and Christ's enormous sacrifice on the cross. Instead of toying with the staff, Russell became eager to learn from them, especially as he felt God calling him into ministry.

Russell earned his GED in the program, and through a staff member's contacts entered a six-month missionary school. During a mission trip to India, he met his wife. Both of them attend Mt. Zion School of Ministry in Grantville, Pennsylvania. Russell says, "I thank God for that little ranch in the middle of nowhere." ✦

Greensboro, North Carolina
The Broken Chain
Wayne Duesberry

Wayne Duesberry used sedatives, LSD, cocaine, and speed, sometimes all at the same time. But crack cocaine was the worst—it prevented him from keeping a job and destroyed his marriage. Eventually, Wayne decided that death was better than a life of misery. He tried to hang himself with a chain, but incredibly, the chain broke. Wayne sank even further into depression—he couldn't even succeed at killing himself!

But he would soon thank God for that broken chain. In 1998, his sister took him to Teen Challenge, in Greensboro, North Carolina, where he learned of Christ's love and forgiveness, and how to forgive himself for past mistakes. Today, Wayne serves as the intake coordinator at Greater Piedmont Teen Challenge. ✦

 Wayne decided that death was better than a life of misery. He tried to hang himself with a chain, but incredibly, the chain broke.

FT. WORTH, TEXAS

A Better Mom
Pamela Auzza

CELEBRATING FIFTY YEARS OF MIRACLES
50
ANNIVERSARY CELEBRATION
TEEN CHALLENGE INTERNATIONAL

Pamela Auzza's mother was impossible to please. She would get drunk and beat her daughter, then send her to the bedroom alone. Pam grew up feeling ugly and worthless. It would be many years before she learned Psalm 27:10: "When my father and mother forsake me, then the Lord will take care of me."

Later in life, Pam had five children of her own, and she vowed not to put them through the same trauma. But addiction made that impossible. When she went to prison, and Tobias and Tanisha were taken away from her, Pam had to admit it—she had chosen drugs over her children. When she entered Teen Challenge, the hardest truth to confront was that she had become a bad parent.

But not for long. In 2002 Pam graduated from Teen Challenge in Fort Worth, Texas, and returned to work on staff. She has reconciled with her children, and keeps in touch with her six grandchildren as well. ✦

SOUTH REGION

Warrior, Alabama

Cheerleader for Christ
Coty Dodd

On the outside, everything in Coty Dodd's high-school life seemed perfect. Her cheerleading squad won a national championship, and Coty was featured on the cover of *American Cheerleader Magazine*. She graduated with honors and won a college scholarship.

On the inside, though, Coty felt lost and insecure, constantly trying to please everyone. She took barbiturates and crystal meth to cope. Shortly after arriving at college, everything fell apart—she dropped out and entered the first of several rehab programs. Four years later, she was living out of her car, driving from one drug house to the next.

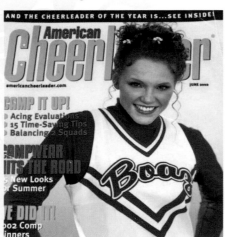

Coty eventually ended up in jail, a stay that turned out to be a blessing. After two months, she took the opportunity to enter Teen Challenge, and there met Jesus Christ for the first time. Where there once was fear and confusion, she was filled with peace and security. Coty says, "The intimacy with Him cannot be expressed in words, but can only be experienced one on one."

Coty still lives in Alabama, where she is currently working toward a ministerial license. ❧

✶ "The intimacy with Him cannot be expressed in words, but can only be experienced one on one."

Oxford, Alabama

Mighty Man
Matthew Poole

The only things that could make Matthew Poole happy at age 19 were drugs and money. He stole from everyone he knew, including his mom. As Matt puts it, "I had the mindset of a child, and I did childish things."

At Teen Challenge, Matt met mature Christian believers who showed him a better way of life. He called them "mighty men," a reference to King David's elite soldiers. After he accepted Christ himself, Matt reconciled with his family and graduated from Teen Challenge in 2004.

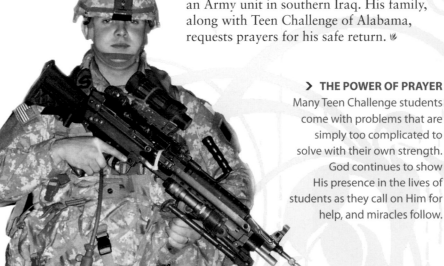

In early 2008, Matt left his wife Jessica and week-old daughter Mckenzie to join an Army unit in southern Iraq. His family, along with Teen Challenge of Alabama, requests prayers for his safe return. ❧

> **THE POWER OF PRAYER**
> Many Teen Challenge students come with problems that are simply too complicated to solve with their own strength. God continues to show His presence in the lives of students as they call on Him for help, and miracles follow.

Carthage, North Carolina

A Late Relapse
Bob Abt

Bob Abt thought he had his old cocaine addiction under control. He had a wife and two kids, a job with the fire department, and his own remodeling business—along with a strong Christian faith. He hadn't done drugs in eight years.

When his back started to hurt and doctors couldn't explain it, Bob took cocaine to ease the pain. Within a year, he was planning life around his daily hit. He lost his job, his house, and his wife, who filed for divorce. At wits' end, Bob resolved to call his pastor and do anything he said. Pastor John recommended Sandhills Teen Challenge.

The first thing Bob did after graduation from the Farm was re-marry his wife. He started a new business, bought a house, and is now putting his son and daughter through college. ✒

Savannah, Tennessee

Answer to Unprayed Prayers
Kristy Lewis

By all rights, Kristy Lewis should have gone to prison for a long time. She was arrested for selling crack cocaine, but as soon as her family raised the $37,000 bail, she was back on the street dealing. She and her husband smoked crack as well, and soon everything they owned was lost or sold. Eventually, Kristy found herself a convicted felon facing 8-12 years.

At her mother-in-law's urging, Kristy and her husband entered Tennessee Valley Teen Challenge in December of 2004. Together, they surrendered their lives to Christ and began to rebuild their marriage and life with their young son and daughter. Even after becoming a Christian in Teen Challenge, Kristy never prayed that God would keep her out of prison. After she graduated from Teen Challenge God gave her a special gift— her entire prison sentence was suspended. ✒

CROSBYTON, TEXAS

Tireless Workers
Chuck and Judy Redger

50 ANNIVERSARY CELEBRATION — TEEN CHALLENGE INTERNATIONAL — CELEBRATING FIFTY YEARS OF MIRACLES

As a college student in 1961, Chuck Redger had no idea that hearing Dave Wilkerson speak would change the course of his life. But Dave's speech a few weeks before he entered Central Bible College inspired him, and as a freshman, Chuck spent time with the first college students who had worked at Teen Challenge in Brooklyn the previous summer. In 1962, he became a volunteer himself.

For two summers, Chuck worked on a ministry team that conducted street services and evangelism at Coney Island in Brooklyn. The team handed out thousands of gospel tracts, one of them entitled "Chicken," to people from all over the city who came to Coney Island.

In 1964, Chuck and his future wife Judy helped another team of college students pioneer a Teen Challenge center in San Francisco. They worked mainly with young people in the Haight-Ashbury district who used LSD. Five years later, they returned to New York City to direct the Teen Challenge CURE Corps ministry, then went on to direct Teen Challenge centers in Texas, Colorado, and Utah.

Even today, 47 years later, Chuck and Judy are still breaking new ground in their ministry. In 2007, they moved back to West Texas to found a new Teen Challenge center in Crosbyton.

Chuck reflects that in its early days, Teen Challenge workers didn't have an advanced curriculum to work with or training in addiction recovery, but the Spirit of God gave them success. Today, he says, "we have the curriculum, nice buildings, we have training for staff. But it is still the anointing of God that gives the victory and changes lives." ✒

SOUTH REGION

Dublin, Georgia

A Long-Term Solution
John Shewman

John Shewman used alcohol and marijuana from a young age, but nothing consumed his life quite like crack cocaine. For five years, he tried every detox center and rehab program he could find, but to no avail. Finally, a social worker told him he needed a long-term program.

At Teen Challenge, John discovered what he really needed—a purpose in life. He saw that when serving God became his true desire, the Holy Spirit gave him power to overcome any temptation.

John now works as the Operations Manager at Teen Challenge Middle Georgia, giving back to the program that helped save his life. He and his wife Lynn recently celebrated their fourteenth wedding anniversary, an accomplishment John says "would not have happened without the intervention of Jesus Christ." ❧

South Carolina

Promise on the Kitchen Floor
Matt Rogers

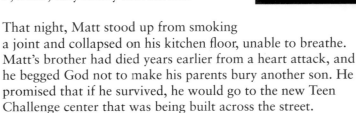

Matt Rogers paid dearly for his alcohol and marijuana addictions. First, they cost him a six-year career in the Marines, when he flunked a drug test. Then they cost him his 20-year marriage, his two children, and his health. And on March 9, 2007, they nearly cost his life.

That night, Matt stood up from smoking a joint and collapsed on his kitchen floor, unable to breathe. Matt's brother had died years earlier from a heart attack, and he begged God not to make his parents bury another son. He promised that if he survived, he would go to the new Teen Challenge center that was being built across the street.

When he woke up and caught his breath, Matt walked across the street and asked the Teen Challenge staff workers for help. A week later, he entered the program.

Matt graduated in February 2008 and currently attends the Teen Challenge Jacksonville Leadership Institute staff training program in Jacksonville, Florida. ❧

MIDLAND, TEXAS

A Match Made in Heaven
Scott and Shannon Reynolds

Scott Reynolds spent 17 years in what he called a "garbage lifestyle" of alcohol, drugs, and bad decisions. Once, he even spent time in a Japanese prison for smuggling drugs. He entered Teen Challenge in Muskegon, Michigan in 1991, and found a relationship with Christ that set his life on an entirely different path.

At the age of 28, Shannon had been through five rehab programs and several long prison terms, but she was still a full-blown crack addict. In 1998, a court ordered her into Teen Challenge of Chattanooga, Tennessee. The program was difficult, but Shannon found that in Christ, she had a constant friend in times of trouble.

Near the end of the program, Shannon prayed that God would help her find a husband, preferably a Teen Challenge graduate who shared her passion for the ministry. Today, Shannon Reynolds serves as the Women's Program Director for Teen Challenge in Midland, Texas, where her husband Scott is the Executive Director. ❧

Mount Vernon, Oklahoma

Finding Love in the Right Places

Jill Everitt

Jill Everitt just wanted someone to love her—she couldn't see that God and her family already did. So as a teenager, she started drinking and taking crystal meth, and she fell into a hurtful relationship.

Eventually, Jill ran away from home. The police picked her up in Alabama, and her mom and grandpa drove her straight to the New Lifehouse Teen Challenge center for adolescents.

Jill knew she needed help, but this wasn't how she'd planned to get it. She resisted the program, and God, at first, but when she opened her heart to Him, she found that miracles happened.

First, she was delivered from her crystal meth addiction without any withdrawal symptoms. Then God changed her heart, convinced her to end her destructive romantic relationship, and restored the loving relationship with her family.

Jill returned home in time to attend her high school graduation. She is currently working toward an Early Child Development degree, and hopes someday to open a day care facility with her husband Jason. 🌿

Bayamon, Puerto Rico

A Little Child Will Lead Them

Pepe

Instead of going to school, 8-year-old Pepe spent his days in front of a grocery store, earning change helping people carry bags to their cars. What the customers didn't know was that Pepe's mother used his money to buy drugs.

Eventually, the store manager reported Pepe to the Social Services Department, and he was sent to the Teen Challenge children's home. He arrived with a hostile attitude, rebellious and constantly cursing. Within a few weeks, he was smiling, singing in chapel services, and ministering to others.

Pepe's 11-year-old brother came to Teen Challenge a short time later. His mother found help at another rehab program and, with the help of Teen Challenge and a local church, accepted Christ into her life. When she regained custody of her sons, they came home to a completely new mother, in love with Jesus rather than with drugs. 🌿

CHATTANOOGA, TENNESSEE

"Is This a Joke?"

Tammy Etheredge

Tammy Etheredge first heard about Teen Challenge while she sat in a jail cell, "nowhere to look but up." She had lost everything to drugs—the business she started, the farmhouse she owned, even her church friends. Still, when her family told her the program would take 12 to 15 months, she said, "Is this a joke?"

Tammy arrived at Teen Challenge in June 2000, scared and uncertain. Staff members talked to Jesus as if they knew him, and students prayed for impossible things, like healing and deliverance from addiction. Tammy thought about leaving, but within a few days, her physical sickness and craving for drugs had disappeared. Now she wondered, "Is this for real?"

Not long after, while watching a videotaped sermon with other students, Tammy gave her life to Christ. Through the Teen Challenge Group Studies for New Christians classes, she learned to take control of destructive thoughts, and peace replaced the turmoil in her heart.

After graduation, Tammy worked for Women at the Well, a ministry similar to Teen Challenge, then returned to Teen Challenge Chattanooga as a live-in counselor. 🌿

"You must seize the opportunity of a lifetime

during the lifetime of that opportunity."

Steve Hill

Teen Challenge Graduate

MIDWEST REGION

Steve Hill

Cape Girardeau, Missouri

MIDWEST REGION

Minnesota

From Meth to Life
Brad Schmidt

When Brad Schmidt went on binges with crystal meth, he wouldn't sleep for three or four days. But getting high and restless didn't make him more productive—he was jobless and living out of his car. Soon he was in jail, too, and social services took away his baby daughter.

Social workers told Brad that since he was addicted to meth, there was no hope for change. But in 2001, that hope came, in the form of Minnesota Teen Challenge. He found in Jesus Christ a path to a much better life. Today, the same social workers who said there was no hope invite Brad to speak to their clients. More importantly, he holds a steady job as a carpet-cleaner, and his daughter is back home. ✿

Minnesota

"Is This Worth It?"
James Tribble

James Tribble spent 20 years bound to heroin and crack cocaine, addictions which cost up to $1500 per day. The steep price forced him to rely on a dangerous gang lifestyle, where he received a nearly fatal stab wound. As he sat in a pool of his own blood, James asked himself, "Is this really worth it?"

Teen Challenge was the sixth treatment program James tried, and the one where he found freedom. Today he serves as a licensed minister at a local church and on staff at the Minnesota Teen Challenge men's program. ✿

MINNESOTA

Everything and the Kitchen Sink
Vivian Hernandez

Vivian Hernandez sold anything for crack cocaine—furniture, family heirlooms, stolen jewelry. Once, she literally tried to sell the kitchen sink.

Vivian used crack to forget about the relentless series of tragedies in her life. After her parents passed away, her only brother died of a heart attack at age 25, news she received on her honeymoon. She did drugs with her husband, then he committed suicide at age 36. As Vivian's addiction progressed, she was harassed by violent loan sharks, who burned her with an iron.

But her greatest struggle would come after she gave her life to the Lord at Teen Challenge. On a trip to the health clinic, Vivian discovered that she was HIV positive. She realized that after losing everything else, she might also lose her life. Either God didn't love her, she decided, or he was preparing her for a more incredible life than she could imagine.

Twelve years later, the pure joy on Vivian's face shows just how incredible it has been. Her physical and emotional health have been restored, as has her relationship with her daughter, who recently graduated from college.

Vivian worked at Teen Challenge in Brooklyn for 11 years as a counselor, teacher, and intake coordinator. She now serves as the Life Skills Manager for the Bowery Mission Women's Program in New York City. ✿

Cape Girardeau, Missouri

The Power of a Name
Steve Hill

Over the years, Steve Hill lost many friends to drugs. One was stabbed to death for failing to pay off his supplier, two died while driving drunk, and another killed himself in jail. Steve knew it was only a matter of time before he was on that list, too.

When his father died, Steve got high on pills and stayed that way until the funeral was over. All the while, he ignored his grieving family members. "My heart was sealed," he wrote later, "a heart of stone."

All of that changed on October 25, 1975, when Steve got sick from heroin. As his body went into convulsions, he could feel death coming. It scared him more than anything else ever had, and suddenly he wanted to live.

For three days, he lay helpless in bed. Then his mother invited a Lutheran minister to visit and tell him about Jesus. The sound of that name brought hope, and Steve began to shout it aloud—"Jesus! Jesus!" His convulsions stopped and a sense of peace flowed through him.

The name of Jesus also helped keep him away from his old lifestyle. "Within weeks," Steve recalled, "I was separated from every drug pusher or user friend. It was as if the word 'Jesus' spoken in love and respect made them scatter."

Steve's problems weren't over, though. He still faced felony charges for selling drugs, and up to 25 years in jail. But with the help of a merciful judge, he was transferred to Outreach Ministries of Alabama, and from there to Mid-America Teen Challenge in Cape Girardeau, Missouri.

After graduating from the program and from the Twin Oaks Leadership Academy in Texas, Steve and his wife Jeri worked as Teen Challenge staff workers, then as youth pastors and evangelists, helping to plant churches in Argentina, Spain, and Russia. From 1995 to 2000, they were key leaders in the famous Brownsville Revival in Pensacola, Florida, which saw the gospel preached to more than 3 million people.

Since those dark days at death's door in 1975, Steve has reached millions through stadium rallies, televised messages in 150 countries, and his autobiography, *Stone Cold Heart*. He currently pastors the Heartland Fellowship Church in Dallas, Texas. ❧

[Source: Stephen Hill, *Stone Cold Heart* 4th ed. (Dallas, TX: Together in the Harvest Publications, 1995), pp. 41, 46.]

ST. LOUIS, MISSOURI

An Expert Quitter
DeVon Wilson

For DeVon Wilson, quitting was a hobby. The moment hard times came, he would give up on his goals and fall back into drugs and alcohol. After he dropped out of two colleges and failed to stay clean to join the military, his childhood friends gave up on him. When he stopped spending time with his kids, his family gave up on him, too.

The only person who kept any faith in him was his mother. Even when he stopped coming home for holidays, she persisted in inviting him to church. When DeVon went to jail, his mom visited and gave him a brochure about Teen Challenge. As he left to join the program, DeVon was suprised to hear his cellmate say, "God is going to bless you and change your life!"

In the program, DeVon discovered many more people who believed in his abilities. Through Scripture and the class curriculum, he came to see how much God loved him, and found ways to destroy his self-defeating attitude.

DeVon completed the program in 2005 and went back to college, making the Dean's List his first two semesters. He now has a full-time job, an apartment of his own, and a restored relationship with his children—and he loves to go home for family gatherings. DeVon also works as a mentor, both at his workplace and at the Teen Challenge center in St. Louis. ❧

MIDWEST REGION

Kansas City, Missouri

God's Work in Progress
Amber Harris

As a teenager, Amber Harris lived with her mom, a drug user, and on weekends visited her dad, an alcoholic. By age 14, she was drinking and using any drug that might give her satisfaction. In June of 2007, at age 16, Amber lost her mom to cancer, and she drank more heavily to cover up her fear and pain.

Amber's dad tried to lay down rules when his daughter moved in, but he worked long hours, and when they fought, she ran away. He sent her to an outpatient rehab, and Amber pretended to get better. But when she was hospitalized with alcohol poisoning, they both knew she needed a permanent change.

Amber hadn't grown up going to church, so Teen Challenge was the first place she learned about God. She accepted Christ into her life on September 5, 2007, and was baptized three months later. The Teen Challenge program guided her through the grieving process for her mom, and taught her ways to show God's love to her dad, by letting him be a loving parent.

Amber knows she still has a long road ahead, but also knows that when problems come, she won't have to turn to drugs or alcohol. The Bible verse that gives her strength is Isaiah 41:10: "Don't be afraid, for I am with you. Do not be dismayed, for I am your God. I will uphold you with my victorious right hand." ❦

Muskegon, Michigan

The Pastor's Kid
Greg Henderson

Growing up as a pastor's son, Greg Henderson never guessed he would be a slave to anything. He accepted Christ at age 14, sang in the choir, and taught Sunday school. That was before he tried crack cocaine, a bondage that held him for 20 years.

Greg walked away from his wife, two sons, and a successful restaurant business. He still went to church, but prayed for God to let him die.

One Sunday, a group of visiting Teen Challenge students gave their testimonies—one was a former cocaine addict Greg knew. He could see how her life had changed, and decided to try Teen Challenge for himself. He soon experienced God's transformation in his own life and discovered a new reason to life. Greg graduated in September 2007, and plans to follow in his father's footsteps. ❦

SOUTH DAKOTA

No Safety Net
Josh Verley

When Josh Verley came to Teen Challenge in South Dakota, he was using nine different prescription drugs—amphetamines, sedatives, antidepressants, and more. He had taken medication for ADHD since the second grade.

Mike Gilmartin, the director at Teen Challenge, told him they would all have to go since the center had no psychiatrist to administer drugs. Josh would have to try living without them, or go to prison for forging prescriptions. "Are you people serious?" Josh said. "I can read the Bible in jail. I need somebody to give me a new pill."

If he couldn't be medicated, Josh thought, at least he could nap and watch TV. But he was surprised to find his days at Teen Challenge filled with activities—wake-up at 6 AM, then prayer time, chores, and classes. In the afternoons, he worked at Rainbow Play Systems, making playground equipment. "It was a shock to be expected to work," he said, "and to shave."

A month into the program, Josh invited Christ into his life. Gradually, he learned to live without the false security of medication. For the first time, he could stay awake longer than a few hours, and he couldn't escape from reality. Most importantly, the Teen Challenge staff wouldn't entertain his excuses—he had to take responsibility for his actions and rely on God.

Josh graduated Teen Challenge in South Dakota, and then enrolled in the re-entry program at Teen Challenge of the Midlands in Omaha. ❦

[Source: Corinne Scott, "Teen Challenge Is Making a Difference for Prescription-Drug Addict," *Living Stones News* 22 May 2005.]

Peoria, Illinois

Under the Circumstances
Joe Shinkey

Throughout his life, Joe Shinkey let circumstances define his actions. One of his sisters died in a car accident, and his father turned to alcoholism. Joe took advantage of his father's absences to defy his mother's authority and experiment with drugs. He smoked marijuana in high school and crack cocaine in college. He dropped out and found a full-time job to support his habit.

Then, in March 2004, Joe found his father on the couch, dead of an overdose. His grief was another excuse to lose control. One night, after a five-day crack binge, he fell asleep at the wheel and crashed head-on into an SUV.

Neither driver was seriously hurt, but the accident exposed Joe's addiction to the rest of the family. His sister urged him to try Teen Challenge.

Joe dropped out after just a week, but nine months later, with no other hope on the horizon, he returned. His first night back, at an Easter service, he felt God's power deliver him from addiction, a moment he called his "Damascus experience."

After graduation, Joe took another full-time job, this time to pay for a missionary school called the Rockford Master's Commission. He now sees the circumstances of his life, including the Teen Challenge program, as preparation for this ministry. In 2007, as part of his schooling, he travelled with a missions team to China. ✵

Evansville, Indiana

The Youngest Criminal
Thelma Clay

Thelma Clay didn't know she had shot and killed her sister. She hadn't even known her father's gun was dangerous, since she was only 4 years old.

Nevertheless, her parents sent her away for a year. When she returned, Thelma had no idea why the family didn't seem to love her anymore. So she grew bitter and disobedient. She got pregnant at age 14, started selling drugs, and soon became her own best customer. Heroin would hold her in bondage for over 20 years.

In 2004, Thelma faced 20 years of prison time for dealing. But the judge was a Christian woman, who could see that Thelma wanted something better for her life. She sentenced her to 5 years, and after the first year allowed her to transfer to the new Grace House Indiana Teen Challenge.

Thelma knew that this was where she needed to be, and she soaked up the program's teaching about humble reliance on God. She graduated in the spring of 2007. ✵

∧ Those who have been forgiven much have a special love for Jesus.

"Are You Ready Yet?"
Lonnie Richardson

One night, Lonnie Richardson woke up and heard God ask: "Are you ready to come serve me yet?" With tears in his eyes, Lonnie answered, "Yes, but I can't. I'm trapped." His life up to that point had included running away from home, stays in juvenile detention centers, and a year of prison. He wasn't locked up now, but he was drowning in an endless round of parties.

A few days later, a pastor came to visit and asked Lonnie if he was ready to change his life. Lonnie said yes, and the pastor helped him enter Teen Challenge. After several months, the Lord began to deal with his heart, showing him that his lifestyle would never bring a sense of purpose or meaning. Lonnie prayed simply, "Lord, use me."

After graduation, Lonnie attended Bible college and returned to Teen Challenge as a staff member. Five years later, he is still on staff, married with two children, and pastoring a church in southern Ohio. ✵

MIDWEST REGION

Cleveland, Ohio
God's SWAT Team
Dave Austen

As a SWAT team member, Dave Austen knew the importance of weapons and armor. He maintained his equipment, practiced with it, and kept it up-to-date. When it came to his spiritual life, though, he was showing up to a fight unarmed.

As a young man, Dave lost his teenage brother to a freak accident and grew angry with God. He left the church, stopped seeing his Christian friends, and poured himself into his career. His drinking increased, his marriage failed, and he burned out at work. Finally, he retired early, at the rank of Assistant Police Chief.

When he found Teen Challenge, Dave saw it as the last hope to salvage his life. There he was able to focus entirely on letting go of his anger and letting Jesus become leader of his life. Just before graduating in January 2007, Dave wrote, "Today I wear a different kind of armor and carry a weapon that doesn't need a holster, the Word of God." ❧

Milwaukee, Wisconsin
The Bible Reading Program
Shana Stark

After high school, and a few stints in juvenile detention for truancy, Shana Stark became a full-time drug addict. She worked during the day, partied at hotels all night, and woke up with different men each morning. When she felt depressed, she kept herself knocked out with sleeping pills.

Shana's sister was dating a Christian man, and they invited her to a Bible study. Shana didn't pay much attention to the discussion, but after that point, she constantly wanted to read the Bible. She would get high with friends, then pull out her Bible and ask God to speak. "As crazy as it sounds," Shana says, "whatever we would read would be right on track. God was meeting us where we were at."

When Shana entered the Teen Challenge program, she could hardly read. But months of memorizing Scripture improved her skills, and soon she could understand all types of writing. Shana now works for a ministry in inner-city Nashville with her husband Matthew. ❧

KENTUCKY

From Dropout to Teacher
John Burns

John Burns turned to street drugs as a teenager, as a way of rebelling against his parents. He dropped out of high school and spent the next ten years caught up in addiction.

At Teen Challenge, John struggled at first with the classes. What kept him going was the loving support of staff, and his newfound prayer life. Over time, the words of the Bible began to make sense, and John felt their truth washing away the corruption and delusions in his mind. Slowly, God helped him put the pieces of his broken life back together.

After completing the program, John enrolled in a three-year Youth Challenge Bible Institute in Pennsylvania, then Central Bible College in Springfield, Missouri, where he earned a bachelor's degree in Bible. "Only through God," John says, "could a person who was a high school dropout, burnt out on drugs, achieve that goal."

John serves as Assistant Director at Kern County Teen Challenge in Shafter, California, along with his wife Rachel and four children. He now teaches the same classes God used to change his life as a Teen Challenge student. ❧

^ John Burns, doing what he loves best, teaching Teen Challenge students in the classroom.

North Dakota

Chased by Monsters
Keelan Opp

Keelan Opp raced down the road, high on crystal meth. He thought he was being chased by police, but they were only "meth monsters" in his mind. In a panic, he swallowed his entire stash, over nine grams of methamphetamines. He woke up in the hospital several days later.

Keelan thought his brain was destroyed for good, but after a few weeks at North Dakota Teen Challenge, he could feel his mind and body being restored. Keelan says, "I would recommend to anybody who has a little of piece of them that wants to live a drug-free life to contact Teen Challenge, so they can be set free just like I was." ✿

Kingman, Kansas

A Birthday Decision
LeAnne Moffett

On her 18th birthday, LeAnne Moffett had to make a choice: leave Teen Challenge, or stay and graduate from high school. A year earlier, she hadn't wanted to travel from her home in Dallas to Main Place Youth in Kansas. Instead of taking her to school as usual, her dad simply drove the opposite direction. When they arrived seven hours later, staff members informed LeAnne that she would be staying at this Teen Challenge adolescent center for a year.

LeAnne was shocked at first, but knew her parents were justified. Her life in Dallas had become chaotic, with the wrong crowd, drugs, and destructive behavior. In time, she came to see their tough decision as God's intervention. By the time she was old enough to leave, she knew where the Lord wanted her. He had repaired her relationship with her family and given her ambition for the future.

LeAnne received a full scholarship to college, and earned her degree in Mathematics from the University of Texas in 2007. She is currently applying to law schools. ✿

KENTUCKY

Nothing to Offer
Mary Beth Barnes

Mary Beth Barnes attended church for over 30 years, but she never felt that she could trust God in the midst of turmoil. She had a college degree in Music Education and held several good jobs, but when difficulties arose, she turned to alcohol and drugs. They only made her problems worse, and soon she was living on the streets.

In August of 2003, alone in a jail cell, having lost all of her worldly possessions, friends, and dignity, Mary Beth cried to God in desperation. She prayed, "God, I have nothing to offer you except Mary Beth, and right now that's not saying a lot." At once, she felt at peace, as God assured her that was all He wanted.

Mary Beth recommitted her life to Jesus Christ and entered the Priscilla's Place Teen Challenge program in Louisville. The Bible memory verse she clung to for inspiration was Psalm 139:7-8 "Where can I go from your Spirit? Where can I flee from your presence? If I go up to the heavens, you are there; if I make my bed in the depths, you are there."(NIV) She saw that even in the dark times of her life, God had always been there, pursuing her soul.

Mary Beth currently works in administration at the Central Baptist Church of Chattanooga, Tennessee. She teaches a class at the Chattanooga Teen Challenge called Celebrate Freedom, which helps men and women find the same peace in Christ she did. ✿

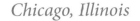

MIDWEST REGION

Chicago, Illinois

Life-Saving Forgiveness

Jim Dycus

Jim Dycus worked as a pimp on the streets of Chicago in the early 1970s. But even that lucrative criminal career wasn't enough to pay for his $300-a-day drug habit. He started holding up drugstores, and during his third robbery, a policeman shot him in the arm. Before his eyes, Jim saw the faces of everyone he'd let down, including his three estranged children.

After a nine-month prison term, Jim tried hard to change. He went through a secular rehab program, but the cravings kept coming back—as did nightmares about his mother, who had jumped in front of a train ten years earlier. Finally, he checked into Teen Challenge, just to get off of the cold Chicago streets.

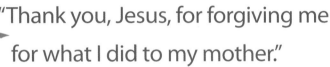

"Thank you, Jesus, for forgiving me

for what I did to my mother."

Jim was shocked to find a group of men just like him— tattooed, rough-looking, with track marks on their arms— smiling and praying for each other. The next morning in a chapel service, he heard one of the students pray, "Thank you, Jesus, for forgiving me for what I did to my mother." Jim felt his heart melt at the words. Then the center's director, Ken Schmidgall, asked him, "Do you want Jesus to forgive you for what happened to your mother?"

Immediately, Jim fell to his knees and recited a prayer of confession. He invited Christ into his life on that day in 1972, and never used an illegal drug again.

Less than two years later, Jim married his wife Barbara, a Salvation Army Captain whom he heard preach at a meeting. Jim and Barbara went into ministry together, running Sunday school and divorce recovery seminars that attracted hundreds of people to the Belmont Assembly of God in northwest Chicago.

Jim has been on staff at Orlando Calvary Assembly of God in Winter Park, Florida for the past 23 years. He oversees the missions, homeless, and benevolence ministries, which include a rescue program for prostitutes. ☙

[Source: John W. Kennedy, "Transformed: Jim Dycus' New Lease on Life," *Pentecostal Evangel* 10 April 2005, pp. 25-29.]

OMAHA, NEBRASKA

To Catch a Thief

Brian Swails

Brian Swails came to Teen Challenge at age 18 to avoid a five-year prison sentence. He had only been to church a couple of times in his life. Now, he was praying every day, asking God to make Himself real to him.

And God answered. One day during prayer, Brian felt peace rush over him. The Bible at last made sense, and its words seem to pop off the page at him.

Five months into the program, while Brian was studying a class assignment called Counterfeit Christianity, he felt suddenly guilty for a crime he had committed before entering Teen Challenge—stealing money from an ATM machine in Iowa. He sensed God telling him to make restitution.

A few months later, Brian transferred to the Teen Challenge re-entry program in Omaha, and he told the director about the stolen ATM money. Together, they decided to travel to Des Moines and meet with the bank president.

Sitting in the president's office, almost sick from nervousness, Brian handed over $150. "I'm sorry for what I did," Brian told him, "and I ask you to forgive me." The president was astonished, and spent the next 45 minutes asking questions about Brian's faith and Teen Challenge. As he walked out of the bank, Brian says, "It felt like someone had lifted a 400-pound weight off my chest. It was like total freedom!"

The bank president reported Brian's confession to the police, but no criminal charges were filed against him. After that day, Brian says, "I wake up every morning and think, 'Oh boy, what's God going to give me today?'" ☙

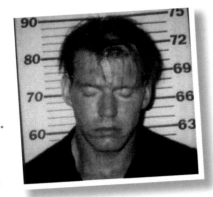

Colfax, Iowa

The Boxing Preacher
Brian Schroeder

Brian Schroeder took steroids to enhance his skills in the boxing ring. After high school, he put that size and athleticism to use—as a debt collector for drug dealers, to support his crystal meth addiction.

During stretches in jail, Brian would call his father, a minister, and ask him to pray. His father mentioned Teen Challenge, and a short time later, Brian met an inmate who was a Teen Challenge student, so he decided to apply.

He was quickly sidetracked, though, by his dealer's new illegal escort service. On one job, Brian drove to Wal-Mart with a prostitute to try out stolen credit cards. Sitting in the store's parking lot, he felt God's presence like a glass of water pouring down from heaven. He turned to the woman with him, and out of the blue she said, "I gave my life to the Lord when I was thirteen years old."

God's spirit seemed to fill the car, and for the next few hours, they felt their hearts soften. They decided to pack up and return to their families. But when they drove back to their hotel, all of their possessions and partners in crime were gone. During their absence, federal agents had raided the operation. Grateful for God's mercy, Brian entered Teen Challenge a few days later.

In the program, his family's years of prayers were answered. Brian grew in his relationship with God, and developed disciplines that would serve as a foundation for the rest of his life.

Brian met his wife Kirsten while working as a Teen Challenge intern, and in 2000 earned a license to minister at Celebration of Christ Church in Des Moines. He served as an associate pastor for two years, then felt called back to Teen Challenge, where he is still on staff. ✒

Learning to Listen
Sonny Oliver

When he came home from Vietnam in the late 1960s, Sonny Oliver was addicted to heroin. He tried rehabs, a mental institution, and drug programs in the jails where he served time, but eventually resigned himself to being an addict forever.

One day in his Chicago neighborhood, Sonny saw a rich-looking man he thought wanted to buy drugs. Instead, the man told him about Jesus, and invited him to Prevention House, a recovery center similar to Teen Challenge. After two months in that program, Sonny transferred to the Teen Challenge Farm in Rehrersburg, Pennsylvania.

At the Farm, Sonny's helpless attitude toward his addiction began to change, along with the rest of his lifestyle. Through Bible classes, he learned that God had a purpose for his life, and he began to hear God's voice through prayer. Through the staff, he learned how to respond to authority, and through their families, he learned what a healthy home life looked like.

When Sonny entered the Farm in 1970, he was functionally illiterate, but after graduation he earned a GED and a BA in Christian Education from Central Bible College. He returned to Rehrersburg and worked at Teen Challenge for 18 years, starting in the print shop. He also met his wife Priscilla, who was the choir director. Eventually, Sonny became the Training Center's Program Director, the first Teen Challenge graduate to hold that position.

Sonny and Priscilla now live in Lebanon, Pennsylvania and minister at a church called In the Light Ministries in nearby Lancaster. ✒

∧ PERSONAL EVANGELISM on the streets has long been an effective way to connect with those most desperately in need of help.

"My passion for Teen Challenge is found in changed lives.

I am convinced that the Lord has called Teen Challenge

to snatch as many lost people from the gates of hell as possible.

God has charged Teen Challenge to set the captives free.

It is a tough task that can only be done one person at a time."

Chris Hodges, President

Pacific Northwest Teen Challenge

WEST REGION

Robert Metcalf

Southern California

Graham, Washington

Career Mom
Laurie Clark

Laurie Clark left her four young children with others when she entered the Bernice Flaherty Home, a Teen Challenge program for women. When she graduated, she went back to being a single mom, a 24-hour-a-day job, and wondered how she would support them.

Fortunately, Laurie didn't leave God behind at the program. A friend suggested she consider babysitting, and Laurie said, "Are you crazy? I have four of my own!" But soon, several mothers, including a stranger at a car wash, were asking her to watch their children.

Laurie founded Arise Shine Daycare in 1997. She runs the fully licensed Christian daycare center out of her three-bedroom home, using prayer, Bible lessons, and songs about Jesus. ❧

Montana

Cousins in Christ
Gena Sorrell & Elisabeth DeRoche

Gena Sorrell and Elisabeth DeRoche met in their early twenties, as students at Teen Challenge. Gena was struggling with a 10-year methamphetamine addiction, and Elisabeth had dropped out of college after heavy drinking and an abusive relationship.

They had both grown up on the Flathead Indian Reservation in western Montana, but discovered they had even more in common—they were cousins! They became fast friends, and after graduation, worked together at Teen Challenge's Higher Ground coffee shop in Missoula.

After a string of drug-related deaths struck the reservation in 2004, Gena and Elisabeth both felt a burden for young people there. The next summer, they organized a four-day music and evangelism event at the powwow grounds in Arlee, Elisabeth's hometown. The "Rushing Wind" outreach to the Salish and Kootenai Tribes celebrated its third successful year in June, 2007. ❧

PORTLAND, OREGON

Not a "Functional" Addiction
Mike Cabrera

Like his mother, who raised a family on her own, Mike Cabrera learned to live as a functional alcoholic. He was happily married with two children, and held a good job in construction. He didn't shirk his duties at work, and he never had a problem finding co-workers to party after hours.

But on the inside, Mike was losing all hope and joy in life. His wife Sabrina noticed, and decided she couldn't watch his downward spiral any longer. With her help, Mike entered Teen Challenge, and there found an ultimate source of hope and peace.

Today Mike serves as a deacon and youth pastor, and volunteers with Teen Challenge on his days off. When it comes to his own family, he says, "My heart is filled with hope—to be the dad I never had to my sons." ❧

WEST REGION

WEST REGION

Los Angeles and San Diego, California

The Great Escape Attempt
Sal & Debby DiBianca

Sal DiBianca's girlfriend Debby didn't like Los Angeles Teen Challenge. Not only was Sal getting help for his cocaine addiction there, he had also quit smoking and drinking and having sex—surely he was being brainwashed! When she came to visit on Thursdays, Debby would sneak in alcohol and cigarettes and wear her skimpiest clothes. When Sal didn't respond to the sexual temptation, she accused him of becoming gay.

Finally, in a last-ditch effort to "rescue" Sal from his prison, Debby decided to burn down the Teen Challenge center. But God had a different idea. On her next visit, Debby heard the gospel message and accepted Jesus. Two weeks later, she was a Teen Challenge student herself, at the center in San Diego.

After they graduated in 1981, Sal and Debby married and entered the very first class at the Teen Challenge Ministry Institute. They currently serve as directors of Sandhills Teen Challenge in North Carolina, where they have been for more than twenty years. ❦

> In a last-ditch effort to "rescue" Sal from his prison, Debby decided to burn down the Teen Challenge Center. But God had a different idea.

LOS ANGELES, CALIFORNIA

God in the Parking Lot
Phil Cookes

Phil Cookes joined his first gang at age 5. From there, his life story reads like a rap sheet—robberies, beatings, counterfeiting, drug running, and a crushing heroin addiction.

While serving a jail term for drug possession, Phil sought help from a psychologist. As Phil poured out his heart about his addiction, the man just stared at him sadly. "I'm sorry," the psychologist said. "I truly don't know how to help you."

But God knew just what Phil needed. As a teenager, Phil had been caught and handcuffed in the parking lot of a church, before one of his many trips to juvenile hall. Years later, while on his way to commit an armed robbery, Phil ran into an old friend in that same church parking lot. His friend had been a drug addict, but had come clean after finding Jesus. He talked about the transformation in his life, and for the first time, Phil felt hope in his heart.

Today, Phil is the pastor of that very church. He graduated from Teen Challenge in 1984, then attended the Teen Challenge Ministry Institute. But even as he turned his life around, he never left his home turf. He now serves as the director of Los Angeles County Teen Challenge, where he leads a variety of outreach programs to drug addicts and those at risk.

Phil's proudest accomplishment has been to establish a park in his old neighborhood, where kids play basketball and other sports under adult supervision. All entrants are searched with a metal detector, and a sign on the fence reads, "These are neutral grounds by direct order of Jesus Christ."

Unlike the prison psychologist, stumped by the power of addiction, Phil has a ready answer for the hundreds of young people who have shared their desperation with him. When they ask, "How can I change?," he points them to his Savior. ❦

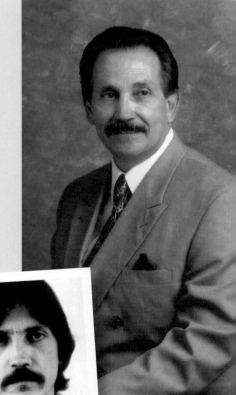

An Unthinkable Tragedy
Dennis Whitman

Dennis Whitman grew up a peace-loving boy in a violent household. His hippie friends and their drugs were an escape from his father's drunken rages. He started with marijuana, then LSD, and with it a "religion" that combined Buddhism with the drug-inspired writings of Timothy Leary.

Dennis was arrested for selling LSD in 1969, and he preached his message of chemically induced inner peace to other inmates. When he got out of prison, he was sad to find the hippie movement over, and he started dropping acid more heavily. But his real tragedy had yet to begin.

One night, Dennis snorted a bag of angel dust with his brother and slipped into a two-day hallucination. In the vision, he was fighting with his brother and stomping on pineapples. He awoke to discover his brother lying in a pool of blood, beaten and kicked to death. A few weeks later, Dennis was convicted of involuntary manslaughter.

To keep from going insane with guilt, Dennis returned to his Buddhist meditation, and he sang blues songs at full volume in the prison showers. He found two books in his cell and read them—*The Cross and the Switchblade* by David Wilkerson and *The Man in Black* by Johnny Cash. In his own words, "those two books planted the seed."

Dennis did most of his time in San Quentin, one of the roughest prisons in America, but God managed to find him there. Another prisoner gave him a Bible, and when he read it for the first time, Dennis says, "I felt like I was burning inside—I mean literally burning. It was an awful, scorching pain."

He invited Christ into his life, and after serving three years, went through the Teen Challenge program in San Francisco. The hardest part of his new Christian life was accepting Christ's forgiveness for his brother's death, an unthinkable event he has never stopped thinking about.

Today Dennis is married with five kids and directs the Teen Challenge center in Turlock, California. He volunteers as a counselor at San Quentin and gives presentations on drug education to schools. ✒

[Source: Chaplain Henry Howard, as told to Chaplain Ray, *Changed Lives in San Quentin* (Dallas: Acclaimed Books, 1986), pp. 119-45.]

Another prisoner gave him a Bible, and when he read it for the first time, Dennis says, "I felt like I was burning inside— I mean literally burning."

Rebuilding a Marriage
Michael and Jennifer Mallinson

50 CELEBRATING FIFTY YEARS OF MIRACLES
ANNIVERSARY CELEBRATION
TEEN CHALLENGE INTERNATIONAL

Michael Mallinson started using crystal meth and Oxycontin as a student at Chico State University. The effects were subtle at first, as he only got high on weekends, but soon he was using every day and skipping school. His girlfriend Jennifer followed in his path, lost her job, and was kicked out of her parents' house.

Michael and Jennifer got married, but their relationship was put to the test as Michael faced eight years in prison for drug charges. He realized it was time for real change, and convinced the judge to let him enter the Teen Challenge men's program in Sacramento. Ten days later, Jennifer entered the women's program in Yuba City.

Michael and Jennifer agree that the most important change that Teen Challenge brought to their lives was a relationship with Christ. But the program also helped restore and rebuild their marriage. They are now expecting their first child.

Jennifer says, "In Teen Challenge, I learned to be a follower, a leader, a friend, a wife, and a future mother. God used this program to transform my life!" ✒

Ventura, California

The Hardest Thing
Cindy Garife

Cindy Garife started using and selling drugs at the age of 13. She thought that life was behind her when she married her high school sweetheart, but he turned out to be abusive. When Cindy was eight months pregnant, he tried to kick her into having a miscarriage. Cindy knew she had to leave, but she knew only one way to make fast money—as a drug dealer.

Cindy spent the next few years in and out of jail, as she struggled to raise her two daughters, China and Crystal, on her own. During a mandated stay at a drug rehab center in Ventura, she heard a radio program that featured testimonies from girls at Teen Challenge. At around the same time, her brother entered the Teen Challenge program in Riverside, and he wrote letters encouraging her to do the same.

Cindy finally came to her senses in a prison where she saw mothers and daughters doing time together. She called her mom. "I'm ready to change," she said. "Please call Teen Challenge."

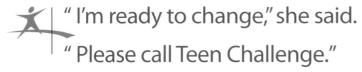

" I'm ready to change," she said.

" Please call Teen Challenge."

Cindy calls Teen Challenge "the hardest thing I ever did sober." But as difficult as the program was, she preferred going through difficulties with Jesus at her side over getting high alone.

After graduation, Cindy went to college, where she had perfect attendance and was elected class president. She worked as a medical assistant before going into ministry with her husband Jerry, who is the director of Tri-County Teen Challenge in Ventura. ❧

Shafter, California

Prayer at the Front Door
David Fogg

David Fogg started drinking and smoking pot to be popular in high school. By age 19, he had moved on to crack cocaine, and he didn't care about popularity. All he wanted was the drugs.

David's father came to see him in MacArthur Park, where he spent his days, and encouraged him to try Teen Challenge. David resisted at first, but in August of 1990, wounded and bleeding from a fight, he decided to give Jesus a try.

Director Jerry Garife met him at the door of the center, took his hands, and prayed for him. After a while, several Teen Challenge students joined in. David gave his life to Christ that day, and in the following months, he learned the basics of life again—how to work, take responsibility, and live with others.

David is currently the Vice President of the Burbank Association of Realtors. When not selling real estate, he and his wife work with addicts who are thinking about entering the Teen Challenge program. ❧

After School Program Success
Ismael Mojarra

Ismael Mojarra grew up in a gang-infested neighborhood of Santa Ana, California. At age 12, he came with his older brother to a pizza party sponsored by Teen Challenge.

Ismael was consumed with anger and fear, but the center helped him get his life on track. "I found a sanctuary here," he said in a 2006 interview with the Orange County Register, "and I accepted God in my life."

After high school, Ismael attended Vanguard University, where he studied psychology and math. His continued to volunteer with Teen Challenge, with the goal of becoming a high school principal in his old neighborhood. "I just want to bring myself to these kids," he said. "We let them know where we grew up, and that they can do it, too."

On May 16, 2007, at age 26, Ismael died in a car accident on Main Street in Santa Ana. More than 800 people attended his memorial service.

Dennis Griffin, the director of Teen Challenge Southern California, said, "Although his life was a short one, he made a huge impact for the kingdom and he will continue to be an inspiration. For such a young man, he was a giant in faith and was an encouragement to all who knew him." ❧

[Source: Scott Martindale, "Teen Outreach Worker Dies in Car Crash," *Orange County Register* 19 May 2007.]

⌃ TEEN CHALLENGE CASTLE The Teen Challenge in Riverside, California, is located on the grounds of the old Benedict Castle. The great room of the castle serves as the chapel where this student is praying.

WEST REGION

Tucson, Arizona

From Dump Truck to Doctor
Patrick Flyte

At Northern Arizona University, Patrick Flyte was just one of the guys, attending keg parties and smoking marijuana. After two years, though, he was flunking out, couldn't function in the classrom, and was diagnosed with manic depression. His parents offered to help, but only if he entered Teen Challenge.

Patrick hated the program at first, but soon realized that the staff wanted him to succeed. After graduating in 1984, he worked as a dump truck driver, then worked his way through the University of Arizona and Ross University School of Medicine in the Caribbean.

In 1994, Patrick became the first Arizona Teen Challenge graduate to earn an M.D. He now works as a family practice physician in Casa Grande, Arizona. ❧

Tucson, Arizona

The Girl Who Had It All
Victoria Ferriari

Tori never had trouble with drugs or alcohol. In fact, at age 16, she seemed to have the world on a string—she was class president, got good grades, and was dating the star of the football team. All of her friends were jealous.

But none of them knew what happened behind closed doors. Her boyfriend, Erin, was abusing her. It started with harsh words and insults, then a rape, then fistfights that Tori always lost.

Tori didn't always believe Erin's apologies, but she stayed with him anyway. She did believe it when he said that she was stupid and worthless, that no one else could love her. Erin falsely accused Tori's parents of abuse, and soon she was in foster care, bouncing from home to home as she lost her ability to cope.

Tori entered the Teen Challenge Springboard Home for Youth in Crisis in 1985, confused and afraid. She didn't think that anyone could love her, but that's what everyone at the home kept telling her. So did God, through the Bible verses everyone kept reciting. Ten days into her stay, she knelt at the altar during a church service and gave her life to Jesus.

After leaving Springboard, Tori made sure her next boyfriend was a godly man. Today, she and her husband Davide have two sons, Alfonso and Robert. In 2002, Rev. Victoria Ferrari became the director of the same home that showed her the love of Christ. ❧

> **HOME OF HOPE**
> This Teen Challenge center in Casa Grande, Arizona offers help and restoration to mothers and young children.

CASA GRANDE, ARIZONA

Meth Mom
Lindsey Tharan

At first, Lindsey Tharan thought that crystal meth would make her a better mother. She always had extra energy and was constantly cleaning her house. But she also locked herself in the bedroom to get high, leaving her two-year-old twin daughters to fend for themselves.

The truth didn't hit her until 2004, when she was arrested and lost her home. She realized her girls needed a better mom and a better life. A friend told her about Teen Challenge, and she entered the Home of Hope family center. There, Lindsey made her truly best decision as a parent— she dedicated her life to Christ.

Two weeks into the program, her daughters Hannah and Madison joined her. Their father accepted Christ a short time later, and in January 2007, Lindsey and Jeff were married. When Lindsey thinks of her girls growing up with a restored family, she says, "I can't wait to see what God has in store for their lives." ❧

> " I needed Jesus to bind up my broken heart …
> I had plans to be dead, but God had a different plan."

New Mexico
A Different Plan
Tiffany Jackson

Tiffany decided to kill herself at age 10. It was her fault, she thought, that her parents had divorced, and that they constantly fought over her custody. But Tiffany didn't succeed at her plan—that night, she fell asleep waiting for her mom to go to bed.

Instead, she turned to drugs, sex, and uncontrolled anger. At age 16, she was committed to a mental hospital. There she took depression medication, but it felt like a temporary fix. True healing had to come from another source, one that she discovered at Teen Challenge's Adolescent Center.

"I needed Jesus Christ to bind up my broken heart," Tiffany wrote while in the program. "You see, I had plans to be dead, but God had a different plan." ❧

Casa Grande, Arizona
Deacon's Daughter
Holley Lawson

Holley Lawson grew up in a church where her dad was a deacon and her mom taught Sunday school. She never accepted Jesus into her life, though, and as a teenager started drinking and smoking marijuana. Later, her husband introduced her to methamphetamine, and what started as a weekend habit grew into a six-year addiction.

Her husband eventually left her, and to cope, Holley used more crystal meth, this time injecting it intravenously. Even discovering that she was pregnant couldn't break the drug's hold. Finally, sitting alone in an Arkansas jail cell, she cried out for help.

Holley discovered the Home of Hope in Arizona, a Teen Challenge program for mothers with young children. She left her 8-year-old daughter Allie with her mother and entered the program with her baby son Ethan.

At Teen Challenge, Holley found a personal relationship with Christ for the first time. She also learned the discipline and parenting skills she needed to raise her two children. Holley now works part-time to support them, while attending Arkansas State University. ❧

A Bad Rap
Daniel Scott

Daniel Scott had a long rap sheet, for crimes he'd committed since age 13. Drug possession, disturbing the peace, breaking and entering, grand theft auto—the list was endless. He'd used alcohol, marijuana, cocaine, crystal meth, acid, and speed, and been caught with all of them.

After serving a year in the Arapaho County Jail, Daniel was picked up by federal authorities and taken to the penitentiary in Denver. There, he faced a minimum sentence of 15 years.

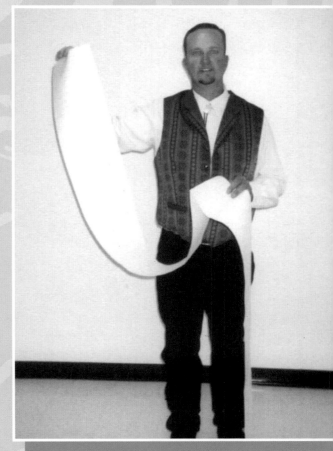

Fortunately, his mother was praying. She could see that the drugs were really his broken way of searching for God, and she sent him an application for Teen Challenge. When the federal judge asked what he had to say for himself, Daniel pulled out the application. The judge sentenced him to probation contingent on graduation.

Daniel's rap sheet didn't disappear right away, but at Teen Challenge, he filled many other kinds of sheets—with Scripture memory verses, classwork, and prayers. After graduation, he started his own successful business, Covenant Construction, with his wife Lisa. ❧

> Daniel Scott had a long rap sheet, for crimes
> he'd committed since age 13. Drug possession,
> disturbing the peace, breaking and entering,
> grand theft auto—the list was endless.

"Teen Challenge is a move of God
sweeping across the darkest corners of the nations,
harvesting multitudes of desperate and dying souls
held under the spell of addiction."

Greg Hammond

CHAPTER 3 - *The Global Story*

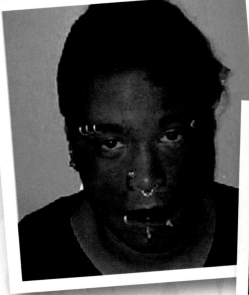

Anthea Groenewaldt

South Africa

Declare his glory among the nations,

his marvelous deeds among all peoples.

PSALM 96:3 NIV

Dear Reader,

It is my honor to be part of a ministry that reaches drug addicts around the world. More than 25 years ago, I began working with David Wilkerson and teaching at Twin Oaks Leadership Academy, a Teen Challenge staff training school in Texas. My wife Libby and I had the opportunity to meet many Teen Challenge graduates who are now powerful spiritual leaders in every corner of the globe.

Over the past 50 years, Teen Challenge has grown to include some 1,038 programs in more than 80 countries. These programs offer a total of 23,000 beds for boys, girls, men, and women who come to Teen Challenge looking for freedom from addiction and other life-controlling problems.

These programs offer an astounding variety of services, including residential addiction recovery, crisis centers, outpatient counseling, coffee houses, street rallies, youth programs, school presentations, child rescue operations, and more. In parts of the world where Christians struggle to find community, Teen Challenge has even helped to start new churches.

No other ministry to the hurting has such a worldwide impact. No other ministry has so much potential to make a difference in the lives of drug addicts. And no other ministry has seen the results of so many changed lives.

In all these years, and in all these countries, the Teen Challenge program has found success for just one reason: the Jesus Factor. There is no program, no procedure, no special person who can set a drug addict free like the power of Jesus. He alone is the agent of change in this ministry, the one who brings transformation to broken lives.

The United Nations reports that there are more than 200 million drug addicts in the world. Where some might see an enormous task with little hope of making a difference, Teen Challenge sees an unprecedented opportunity. We have the most committed leaders and workers in the world—and 23,000 students waiting to be trained. Our history has proven that we have a solution that works— one that can transform every last one of those 200 million lives.

A worldwide need demands a world-spanning vision. Global Teen Challenge has developed a strategic plan that focuses on five critical areas: staff training, sustainable funding, communication, operational standards, and new program development. Christians from more than 30 nations have given Global Teen Challenge standing invitations to start new centers in their homeland. As our second 50 years begins, we will continue to forge ahead as pioneers, finding fresh ways to integrate Teen Challenge's successful model into every language, culture, and nation of the world.

The challenges that lie ahead are daunting. But we serve a God who can make miracles happen. We know, because we have seen Him do it in the past! Truly, the best years for Teen Challenge are yet to come.

In Christ,

Jerry Nance, *President*
GLOBAL TEEN CHALLENGE

SPREADING THE WORD

From the moment it was published in 1963, Dave Wilkerson's dramatic memoir *The Cross and the Switchblade* became an international publishing phenomenon. Clement Stone, the insurance company president who had supported Teen Challenge's earliest efforts, bought a copy for every foreign missionary in the Assemblies of God denomination, and mailed thousands of books around the world. Several of these missionaries, who were excited to tell the story in more languages, in turn began the work of translating. In time, the book would sell more than 15 million copies in more than 30 languages worldwide.

At the same time, Dave received invitations to speak at churches and rallies around the world. He responded to the call with a series of international Youth Crusades. The messages he delivered in nations such as Canada, Holland, Germany, Puerto Rico, Brazil, South Africa, Australia, and Thailand were primarily evangelistic, intended to share the good news of Jesus Christ and not necessarily promote Teen Challenge. But many who attended these events, who had read of Dave's successes in Brooklyn, responded by starting the same type of outreaches in their home countries. Often, they took on the name "Teen Challenge." A single speech was sometimes all it took to inspire the founding of multiple addiction recovery ministries—as in Brazil, where dozens of independent Teen Challenge centers sprang up practically overnight, after Dave headlined a series of rallies in 1972.

Dave was not interested in serving as the international director of Teen Challenge so he decided to let growth take place organically, outside the confines of an official corporate structure. Dave explained the logic of this decision in his 1974 book *Beyond the Cross and the Switchblade*:

> We had developed a rather unusual method for expanding the work
> of Teen Challenge. We grew by encouraging independent ministries, so
> I encouraged other people to borrow our principles for use in their own
> local situation. Our role would be to advise, pray, and help raise funds.
> Beyond that, the work was up to the local Spirit-anointed churches in
> any community.[1]

Many of the new Teen Challenge centers would have little need for America's help in any case. Over the next decades, as the total number of centers grew to more than 1,000, they would discover for themselves the importance of fellowship and regional organization, and would eventually form the international ministry known today as Global Teen Challenge.

> ❯ **FILM MINISTRY** *The Cross and the Switchblade* movie has had great cross-cultural appeal around the world. Pictured here is Assemblies of God missionary Al Perna, who began working in 1971 as the training coordinator of Continental Teen Challenge, which included training volunteers to conduct the film ministry. Al later served as the associate director of Eurasia Teen Challenge, then as Eurasia Teen Challenge Director from 1985 to 1998.

 The international expansion of Teen Challenge began in Canada. The publication of *The Cross and the Switchblade* in 1963 resulted in rapid exposure to other countries around the world.

SPIRITUAL REVOLUTION IN BRAZIL

By David Patterson

The fall of 1972 will never be forgotten by the members of the Crusade Team accompanying David Wilkerson to Brazil. The Team included four associates and Pastor Carl Alcorn of Wichita Falls, Texas. These nationwide crusades were the first of their kind ever conducted in this nation. Missionary Evangelist Bernhard Johnson interpreted Mr. Wilkerson and his evangelistic association set up the crusades and arranged for follow-up.

These youth crusades were conducted in the largest gyms and auditoriums available. Cities included Belo Horizonte, Rio de Janeiro, Sao Paulo, Campinas, Porto Algere, Fortaleza, and Belem. In most cities thousands were turned away and people crowded into every available inch of space. At the conclusion of each service people were asked to stand and move back to make room for those who wished to respond to the invitation. More than 25,000 young people responded to the invitations. At Mr. Wilkerson's request they threw down on stage packs of tobacco, pills, marijuana, heroin, and all forms of drugs.

Governors and other key government officials not only attended the crusades but invited Mr. Wilkerson to meet with them privately to discuss ways and means to combat the growing drug problem in Brazil. The

David Wilkerson and Bernhard Johnson (Brazilian Crusade Coordinator) meet with laymen and ministers to discuss plans for Teen Challenge.

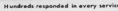

Hundreds responded in every service.

Every available inch of standing room was accounted for in this packed Brasilia auditorium.

9

∧ **REV. CHARLES RINGMA** established the first Teen Challenge ministry in Brisbane, Australia, in 1971. Before the Brisbane center opened, Rev. Ringma went on a four-month fact-finding trip, visiting Teen Challenge ministries across Europe and America. Teen Challenge soon began to spread across Australia. In 1975, Luis and Mary Santillon started a Teen Challenge coffee shop on Barkly Street, St. Kilda, in Victoria.

< **BRAZIL RALLIES BY DAVE WILKERSON**
In 1972 Dave Wilkerson conducted a series of crusades in 13 cities in Brazil with 250,000 in attendance. More than 25,000 young people responded to the invitation at the end of the services. The nation's leading magazine, *Manchete*, featured the crusades and carried a banner line reading, "God is the only solution to drugs in Brazil." These crusades served as a catalyst for many new Teen Challenge centers to be opened. Today there are more than 70 Teen Challenge centers in Brazil.

FOUR "BLOSSOMS" FROM DALLAS

In 1962, Howard Foltz was a young student at Southwestern Assemblies of God College in Waxahachie, Texas. Howard and his wife Pat felt a calling to street ministry, and they tried to get college students involved through Saturday night meetings at Bethel Temple in Dallas. These "Action Nights" involved, in Howard's own words, "confrontational, in-your-face" evangelism on the streets of Dallas. Few college students were interested, though, and no more than a handful attended for the first few months.

All of that changed in September of 1962. Dave Wilkerson visited Southwestern to preach at a chapel service, and in Howard's words, "he shut down the campus."[2] So many students responded to Dave's altar call and began praying for repentance, the college cancelled classes so they could spend the day in prayer. Suddenly, the campus was galvanized for the kind of street ministry that Dave had described. More than 100 students attended Howard and Pat's next Action Night, along with 50 church members from the Dallas area.

It quickly became clear that to retain the Christian converts who struggled with life-controlling problems, some form of long-term discipleship program was necessary. So in 1963, four married couples—Howard and Pat Foltz, Billy and Sue Burr, Eugene and Carolyn Hunt, and Irvin and Linda Rutherford—moved in together, pooled their salaries, and used the savings to start a Teen Challenge center in Dallas, Texas. As the ministry became established, they purchased an old rescue mission in downtown Fort Worth called the Door of Hope, which they used as a coffeehouse and outreach center, and later became a women's residential recovery program. Howard recruited workers from Bethel Temple and from his fellow college students at Southwestern.

Remarkably, the leaders of Dallas Teen Challenge had no idea that the trials and errors of their first few years mirrored those taking place in Brooklyn at the same time. Early in the planning stages, Howard approached Dave Wilkerson for advice, but Dave told him simply, "It's your program; God will show you what to do." As it turned out, the plans God had in store for this particular program extended far beyond just the Dallas-Fort Worth area.

In 1963, as the new Teen Challenge center was taking in its first residents, a Teen Challenge worker received a vision while praying for the ministry. She saw a fruit tree drop its blossoms into

˄ DAVE WILKERSON CRUSADE IN THE UK As word of the Teen Challenge ministry in New York City spread, Dave Wilkerson was invited to conduct rallies in countries throughout Europe and South America, as well as South Africa. Pictured here is one of Dave's first crusades in the United Kingdom. Often these events raised awareness of Teen Challenge in various countries, or served as catalysts for starting new Teen Challenge ministries where none existed.

a stream, and the petals float away in four different directions—a symbol she interpreted to mean that missionaries would travel to four corners of the earth. The vision proved to be powerfully prophetic, as one by one, the four couples who had founded Teen Challenge in Dallas responded to calls to the mission field. The Foltzes travelled to Europe, the Burrs to Africa, the Hunts to Latin America, and the Rutherfords to Asia—four separate continents. All told, more than 30 international missionaries, and counting, have received their calls to ministry while at one of the Dallas-Fort Worth Teen Challenge centers, either as a student or staff member.

˃ STREET EVANGELISM has always been a trademark of Teen Challenge ministries. As in New York City, young people were often recruited as volunteers to spread the word about Teen Challenge and the transforming power of Jesus Christ. Many of the tracts these volunteers handed out were written and published locally, just as they were in New York.

TEST RUN IN HOLLAND

When Howard and Pat sensed God calling them into missions, they assumed that they would simply relocate somewhere in Latin America and start another Teen Challenge center, but those doors did not open. Howard sought advice from the well-known veteran missionary Charles Greenaway, who told Howard that Christians in the Netherlands had been asking American missionaries to start a Teen Challenge center for that nation's growing population of drug addicts. Howard and Pat resigned from their positions in Dallas in 1968 and moved overseas the following year.

Teen Challenge's first "test run" in Europe was a small coffeehouse in The Hague. Like the coffeehouses started by Ann Wilkerson in Greenwich Village, it served free food and provided a safe atmosphere of music and conversation with Christian volunteers. Within a few months, hundreds of people in The Hague had heard the gospel, and as word of mouth spread, the coffeehouse venue grew so popular, workers had to wash dishes throughout the night to keep from running out of cups, plates, and silverware.

∧ **HOWARD FOLTZ AND DIETER BAHR** Howard Foltz (left) served as an Assemblies of God missionary to Europe and helped pioneer the ministry of Teen Challenge in Eurasia. He is pictured here with Dieter Bahr (right), who started Teen Challenge centers in Bitburg, Germany and in Luxembourg. The very first evangelical church in Luxembourg grew out of a Teen Challenge coffeehouse there.

The Holland coffeehouse became a catalyst that jump-started dozens of similar ministries across the continent. Christians throughout Europe travelled to the Netherlands to see the coffeehouse in action, and to seek Howard's advice about starting their own. Within two years, Teen Challenge coffeehouses had sprung up all across Europe. In Switzerland alone, 30 coffeehouse ministries started in one year, all using Holland as a model.

As popular and widespread as the movement was, however, the coffeehouse in Holland soon faced the difficult question that virtually every Teen Challenge ministry worldwide has to answer—what to do with the drug addicts and others with life-controlling problems, who had become Christians but needed help incorporating their new faith into their everyday lives? Howard and Pat knew that their ministry, like the Brooklyn and Dallas Teen Challenge centers before it, would soon have to add the residential discipleship ministry focus.

˅ Many Teen Challenge ministries around the world have started with street evangelism coupled with a coffeehouse ministry, a casual setting where people can be introduced to Jesus Christ. Though the coffeehouse ministry in the USA was short-lived, this method of outreach continues to be very effective in many countries today.

^ **COFFEEHOUSES** In Ethiopia (top) and Romania (bottom), Teen Challenge workers use this setting to share how Jesus has set them free from addiction and sin. Teen Challenge in Portugal uses its coffeehouses as a key part of the intake process for new students, and as a ministry to family members.

NICKY CRUZ RALLIES When Nicky Cruz met Christ through the ministry of Dave Wilkerson in 1958, little did he know that God would call him to a lifetime of evangelism. As Teen Challenge started in Europe, Nicky Cruz was invited to preach at many evangelistic crusades, including this rally in Sweden.

THE FARM IN GERMANY

> **FIRST REHAB CENTER IN EUROPE** In 1971, Howard and Pat Foltz moved to Schachach, Germany, and established the first Teen Challenge residential recovery program for drug addicts in Europe. Modeled after the Teen Challenge Training Center, "The Farm," in Rehrersburg, Pennsylvania, it became the model for similar programs established across Europe.

The second phase of Teen Challenge's European ministry began in 1971, when the Foltzes moved to the Bavarian region of southeastern Germany. A German family had donated their farm, along with 12,000 chickens, intending that Teen Challenge could sell the meat and eggs to support the ministry. Howard and Pat decided instead to maintain the farm and establish a prototype residential center, similar to the Farm in Rehrersburg, Pennsylvania.

For the addicts who came into the program, the Bavarian farm was a lifesaving success. Its residents were mostly German, but it attracted workers and volunteers from across Europe, and missionaries often visited to see a Teen Challenge center in action, and to gather information for their own projects. At the same time, Howard travelled the continent, visiting churches and casting a long-term vision for the ministry. Two years later, more than fifty Teen Challenge centers had been established across Europe.[3]

The third phase of Howard and Pat's European mission came in 1973, when they moved to Wiesbaden, Germany to establish the Eurasia Teen Challenge Training Center. The Wiesbaden center provided additional training for Teen Challenge graduates and staff members preparing for careers in ministry. It was the first truly international Teen Challenge staff training institution, drawing students not only from virtually every nation in Europe, but from around the globe. The Training Center served a dual purpose for the fledgling Eurasia Teen Challenge organization—it raised up workers who could serve in a variety of capacities, and it gathered information on which Teen Challenge centers around the world needed leaders, and even which countries were ready for pioneers from abroad to start a new ministry.

> **NORWAY AND FRANCE** Teen Challenge ministries in France and Norway experienced early success in reaching out to drug addicts and discipling them in their new life with Jesus.

GERMANY WOMEN'S CENTER The first Teen Challenge women's residential program in Germany was started in 1973 and directed by Ursala Schultz.

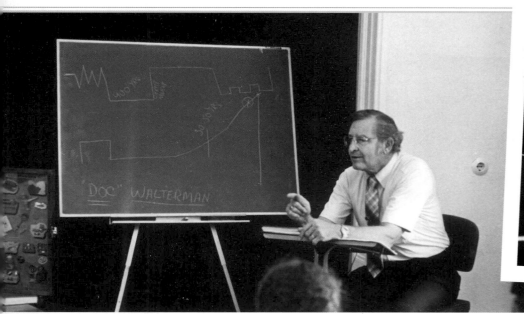

∧ **DEVORE WALTERMAN** Devore Walterman was one of the early pioneers of Teen Challenge, who helped to found and direct Teen Challenge ministries in Chicago and San Francisco in the early 1960s. He also dedicated many years of his life to training Teen Challenge leaders in Europe. In this photo, he is teaching at the Teen Challenge Training Center in Wiesbaden, Germany.

∧ **HOWARD FOLTZ TEACHING** Howard Foltz pioneered the Teen Challenge Training Center in Wiesbaden, Germany, a school dedicated to training leaders for Teen Challenge ministries across Europe. Its success soon attracted students from around the world.

Wiesbaden was a much larger city than the country village in Bavaria, filled with historical sites and monuments, but Teen Challenge made its presence felt nonetheless, through street witnessing efforts and media campaigns. "We were infamous," Pat recalled. When one of the Training Center's high-voltage videotaping sessions accidentally knocked out all electrical power in one quarter of the city, local authorities "knew exactly where to come." Teen Challenge's relationship with the community was largely positive, though, and several local churches lent their support.

The Eurasia Teen Challenge Training Center operated continuously until the mid-1980s, when staff training schools using the same model were established in other countries. Hundreds of future Teen Challenge leaders, pastors and Christian workers passed through the Wiesbaden center in the course of two decades, including Kevin Tyler, now the coordinator for Teen Challenge centers in the 14 former Soviet republics and Baltic states.

⟨ **CLASSROOM AT WIESBADEN** At the Teen Challenge Training Center in Wiesbaden, Germany, classroom instruction coupled with on-the-street experience in evangelism and coffeehouse ministry equipped leaders from around the world to work in Teen Challenge centers, or to raise up new ones if none existed in their home countries.

EURASIA SPREADS ITS WINGS

Eurasia Teen Challenge was so named because it included dozens of centers from Europe and a wide swath of western Asia—as far as the Middle East, India, and Pakistan. One of Eurasia Teen Challenge's core values from the start was to help Teen Challenge centers pioneer or mentor centers in other countries. The leading countries in this area, to date, have been Portugal and the United Kingdom, and many more have followed their lead.

When João Martins took the reins as national director in 1991, Portugal already operated five recovery centers, two re-entry houses, and 26 coffeehouses nationwide, and it had helped plant a Teen Challenge center in Macau, China. Under Pastor Martins's leadership, leaders from these centers also travelled abroad to pioneer Teen Challenge ministries in several African countries where Portugese is spoken, such as Angola, Guinea-Bissau, and Mozambique.

João Martins currently serves as the national director of Teen Challenge in Portugal. Teen Challenge Portugal operates a model program for reaching troubled young men and women, but João's vision extends far beyond the borders of his own country. He has been instrumental in helping to raise up Teen Challenge ministries in the Portugese-speaking nations of Africa. He also serves as the Vice-President of Global Teen Challenge. ❧

> **JOHN MACEY**, national director of Teen Challenge in the United Kingdom, has played a major role in helping to pioneer Teen Challenge ministries in India, South Africa, and Swaziland. The Teen Challenge ministries in Africa have faced not only rampant drug abuse but also the AIDS epidemic. As a result of AIDS, hundreds of thousands of children have been left orphans. Teen Challenge in Swaziland has developed residential recovery programs for drug addicts and orphanages for children whose parents have died of AIDS.

Teen Challenge in the United Kingdom under the leadership of John Macey was instrumental in starting centers in Bombay, India, South Africa and Swaziland. The first Teen Challenge center in Swaziland held its meetings in a mud hut—it has now grown into one of the largest drug rehab centers in Africa.

Thousands of miles away, Australians Doug and Anna Boyle founded the Teen Challenge center in Kazhakstan in 1994, a ministry that now includes five recovery centers, a crisis center, and a school, serving more than 500 residents, students, and locally based workers.

The work of planting new centers continues even as this book is being written—for example, Teen Challenge of Czech Republic is currently assisting a new program in Moldova.

The ever stronger bonds that Eurasia Teen Challenge centers forged across national and cultural lines helped foster the concept of an international Teen Challenge organization. Meanwhile, literally hundreds of Teen Challenge centers were starting independently in other parts of the world, but with little or no continental coordination. Starting in 1973, Teen Challenge held annual conferences in Europe geared toward fellowship and training, which attracted leaders from Africa, South

America, Australia and other locations well beyond Eurasia's membership area.

Early on, Howard Foltz recognized the need for an international body that could provide fellowship, support, and training for centers around the world, including those in the U.S. His early attempts to pull together such a coalition fell through. It would take a dramatic upheaval in world events to catapult Howard's dream into reality.

 Teen Challenge in the Netherlands helped with the young work in Poland in the 1980s, and a few years later, Poland assisted the new Teen Challenge starting in Belarus.

< **PRINCESS DIANA** visited Teen Challenge in Wales in 1993. She is pictured here with John Macey, national director of Teen Challenge in the UK.

^ **HOWARD FOLTZ** helped to train leaders in Calcutta and Delhi, who went on to establish a Teen Challenge center in India, a country with more than one billion people. Missionary Verlin Coleman in Delhi used the training provided by Howard to start several Teen Challenge "Tea Houses," which played a key role in pioneering 18 churches in the region.

< **STREET OUTREACHES** Evangelistic outreaches, both large and small, have helped Teen Challenge communicate its message of hope from the beginning. From tent crusades, to street rallies, to parks with clowns, a variety of locations and methods have been used to attract crowds and tell the stories of lives transformed by Jesus. This rally in the Dominican Republic was instrumental in helping to launch Teen Challenge in Santiago.

^ **KAZAKHSTAN TEEN CHALLENGE** In the 14 years since it started Teen Challenge Kazakhstan has grown to include 13 ministries.

Success Story in Central Asia

Doug and Anna Boyle, Australian missionaries to China, visited Kazakhstan in 1994 and saw a nation in tremendous need. Doug joined his friend Dr. Martin Bassett in leading a seminar on drug addiction, which was attended by nearly 250 Kazakhs. Forty volunteered to receive training in working with addicts. After two weeks of rigorous work, ten of them completed the training and became full-time Teen Challenge staff.

Teen Challenge Kazakhstan opened its doors in March 1995, and a year later officially registered with the government as an NGO. Over the past ten years, it has become one of the fastest growing Teen Challenge centers in the world. More than 500 students, staff members, and volunteers live and work at 13 centers nationwide, including residential programs for men, women, and adolescents; a vocational farm; a refuge and orphanage for women and children escaping physical abuse; and a primary and secondary school.

Since 1999, Teen Challenge has also run Koolagair ("Fast Horse"), the largest sports club in Kazakhstan. It started when Teen Challenge in Almaty purchased a vacant lot next to its Vocational Training Center, and neighbors rose up in protest—the lot had been a place for them to walk their dogs and dump trash. After hearing one neighbor scream curses at him from a fifth-story window, Doug decided that Teen Challenge had to become a blessing to its neighbors.

Doug bulldozed mounds of trash from the site, installed goalposts, and invited local kids to join a football club. Within a year, the club was attracting more than 500 kids to play soccer five afternoons a week. Today, Doug reports, "Many families who were against us are now saved. Our God is an awesome God!" ❧

PULLING BACK THE IRON CURTAIN

The need for Global Teen Challenge became even greater after the Berlin Wall came down, when Eastern Europe and the former Soviet republics opened up. Teen Challenge had actually found its way into several Communist countries before 1989, in part through underground distribution of *The Cross and the Switchblade*. "Wherever that book has had circulation," Don Wilkerson said, "Teen Challenge is uniquely embraced."[4] The book was wildly popular in East Germany, despite (or perhaps because of) its being declared contraband. Howard Foltz managed to visit East Berlin once before the Wall came down, travelling through Checkpoint Charlie to speak to a gathering of teens.

As the Iron Curtain began to fall, massive problems with drug addiction began to surface, and requests for help in starting recovery centers poured in to the leaders of Eurasia Teen Challenge. Tom Bremer, a music missionary from Madison, Wisconsin who had trained at the Wiesbaden center in 1983, and Jan Barendse received a huge number of these requests. Tom and Jan had assisted Atilla and Elizabeth Fabian who pioneered a Teen Challenge center in Hungary. In Poland, Tom assisted Zbigniew Urbaniak who pioneered the Teen Challenge which was sparked by Dave Wilkerson's crusade there in 1984. In 1986, as Communism stood on the brink of collapse, and as Tom fielded call after call from Christian leaders in Eastern Europe pleading for aid, Tom and Jan stood together on the mountainous border of Poland and Czechoslovakia and prayed for both countries. Later they would learn that within sight of their vantage point was the very building where Petr Ministr would found the first Teen Challenge center in the new Czech Republic.

FIRST EASTERN EUROPEAN CENTER IN HUNGARY Even before the Iron Curtain fell, word about Teen Challenge had spread across Eastern Europe. The first Eastern European Teen Challenge center was founded in Budapest, Hungary, in 1983. Pictured here are (left to right) Dr. Devore Walterman of Teen Challenge (USA), Al Perna, director of Eurasia Teen Challenge, and Attila Fabian, national director of Teen Challenge Hungary. Not pictured is his wife, Elizabeth Fabian, who served as the first director of the Hungarian women's center.

Tom turned his attention to Yugoslavia in 1989, where he established a Teen Challenge residential farm in the Croatian region and trained 32 young Christians in outreach ministry. When the Croatian and Bosnian Wars started in 1991, the work was put on hold while the country fought bitterly to redraw its borders. When Tom returned years later, "We had to start over, not with one country but with five. That was a hard time."[5] But with an increase in the number of countries came a corresponding growth in Teen Challenge centers—the farm in Croatia has since closed, but today there are Teen Challenge residential programs in Serbia, Macedonia, and Slovenia, and an active street outreach in Croatia. In 1998, Tom became the director of Eurasia Teen Challenge, and relocated its headquarters to Portugal, a country he viewed as a model for Teen Challenge leadership.

As the power of the Communist Party waned in the late 1980s, hundreds of churches in Russia, now free to operate more openly, started faith-based drug rehabilitation centers of their own. Most of them knew nothing of Teen Challenge, but the programs they established followed many of the same principles, like Bible-based training in practical living skills. The programs in Russia seemed a natural fit for Teen Challenge, but it would take nearly ten years for the organization to catch up with the movement God had started there.

⌄ **CHRISMA** Led by Tom Bremer (left, back row) and his wife, Terry, (left middle row), Chrisma was based in Wiesbaden, Germany and functioned as one of the Eurasia Teen Challenge outreach teams. They traveled extensively in Eastern Europe, conducting evangelistic concerts in the 1980s and early 1990s.

TOM BREMER Tom Bremer's first contact with Teen Challenge came in 1980, on a tour to Egypt with the Celebrant Singers ministry. Traveling on to India, he met Jan Barendse from Eurasia Teen Challenge. Over the next three years, Tom's ministry shifted to focus primarily on Eastern European countries, where he helped to raise up several Teen Challenge ministries. In 1998, he became the director of Europe Teen Challenge, a position he currently holds.

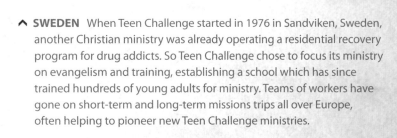

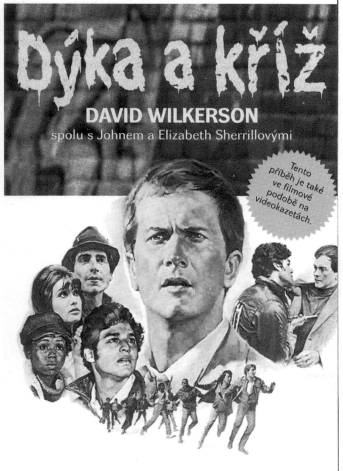

Dýka a kříž

DAVID WILKERSON

spolu s Johnem a Elizabeth Sherrillovými

Tento příběh je také ve filmové podobě na videokazetách.

„JSEM NARKOMANKA, KAZATELI. NENÍ PRO MĚ UŽ ŽÁDNÁ NADĚJE A TO ANI U BOHA!"

Její svět byla parta z ulice, sexpárty a tunely. Jejím předurčením byl zločinný život a brzká smrt. Marie však byla zachráněna spolu s tisíci takovými jako ona a to díky jednomu oddanému kazateli, který se rozhodl přinést poselství kříže do světa, ve kterém se řeší problémy dýkou.

Tento zázračný příběh, který se odehrál v Brooklynu v roce 1958 je stále aktuální a přináší naději lidem, kteří se dnes nacházejí v podobných situacích.

David Wilkerson se stal zakladatelem **TEEN CHALLENGE.** Dnes Teen Challenge působí ve více než 68 zemích světa a zachraňuje tisíce ztracených životů.

Potřebuješ-li pomoc, kontaktuj nás na této adrese:

TEEN CHALLENGE
Na Bendovce 24
181 00 PRAHA 8
www.teenchallenge.cz

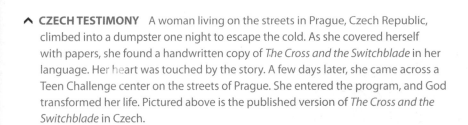

CZECH TESTIMONY A woman living on the streets in Prague, Czech Republic, climbed into a dumpster one night to escape the cold. As she covered herself with papers, she found a handwritten copy of *The Cross and the Switchblade* in her language. Her heart was touched by the story. A few days later, she came across a Teen Challenge center on the streets of Prague. She entered the program, and God transformed her life. Pictured above is the published version of *The Cross and the Switchblade* in Czech.

SWEDEN When Teen Challenge started in 1976 in Sandviken, Sweden, another Christian ministry was already operating a residential recovery program for drug addicts. So Teen Challenge chose to focus its ministry on evangelism and training, establishing a school which has since trained hundreds of young adults for ministry. Teams of workers have gone on short-term and long-term missions trips all over Europe, often helping to pioneer new Teen Challenge ministries.

Over the past 40 years in Europe many people have described that the two books which most influenced their life as a new Christian were the Bible and *The Cross and the Switchblade*.

— Tom Bremer, Europe Teen Challenge Director

A NEW INTERNATIONAL FELLOWSHIP

At the annual Eurasia Teen Challenge conference in 1995, directors from around the world gathered to create the Teen Challenge International Fellowship (later named Global Teen Challenge), an organization that extended beyond the Eurasia centers to include every Christian ministry that called itself "Teen Challenge." Its goal was to start new recovery centers, foster communication between those that already existed, and provide resources and opportunities for staff training, through curriculum, seminars, and regional conferences. At their first official meeting, the new board of directors elected Don Wilkerson to be the Fellowship's Executive Director. At the time, Don was a pastor at the Times Square Church in New York City. He immediately conferred a high level of stature on the new ministry, and his long experience as a director in Teen Challenge's early years gave him an unmatched breadth of wisdom that could turn the international vision into reality.

After accepting the challenge, Don's first order of business was to bring into the Fellowship existing Teen Challenge ministries—or centers, like those in Russia, that were doing similar work but didn't carry the Teen Challenge name—so that the resources long enjoyed by the Eurasia centers could become available to the rest of the world. From the start, he made clear that Global Teen Challenge would not become a controlling, bureaucratic organization that got in the way of effective ministry, but rather a tool to encourage work that God had already started.

Don Wilkerson travelled to Russia in 2003 and offered the churches Global Teen Challenge's services in training workers and sustaining their recovery programs. Most of the church programs decided to affiliate with Teen Challenge, and today the Teen Challenge International Coalition of Christian Faith-Based Rehabilitation Programs of Russia includes more than 230 programs.

Since Global Teen Challenge was established in 1995, new centers have opened in more than 25 new countries. Overall, the organization is not interested in running or controlling these centers, but rather in strengthening them. Typically, the Global administration will guide local leaders in establishing a Teen Challenge ministry utilizing local Christian workers. They also provide training for the new staff. In many countries, missions organizations, like the Assemblies of God, have helped in the establishing of new Teen Challenge ministries.

^ **RUSSIAN COALITION**   In June 2003, the Teen Challenge International Coalition of Christian Faith-Based Rehabilitation Programs of Russia was birthed when 126 Christ-centered rehab programs gathered in Moscow for a leadership training conference sponsored by Book of Hope. The late Bill Everett, Teen Challenge state director of Oklahoma, helped to pioneer this coalition of ministries. The coalition now includes 230 ministries across Russia, with more than 10,000 beds in their residential programs.

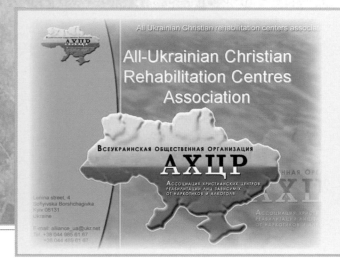

The All-Ukrainian Christian Rehabilitation Centres Association, which includes 82 programs in the Ukraine was founded in 2001. Teen Challenge collaborates with the programs in this association by providing curriculum and staff training. Jerry Nance, Global Teen Challenge President, recently participated in the association's national conference and provided training for directors and staff.

^ **MACEDONIA**   Tom Bremer (left), Europe Teen Challenge director, with Jonatan Vlaisavljevic (center) and his wife, Valentina (right), directors of Teen Challenge Macedonia. Jonatan and Valentina pioneered this ministry in 1995 which now includes a men's residential program. They have also conducted extensive drug prevention seminars in schools and use the Living Free support group model to reach many more through non-residential outreaches.

GOVERNMENT RELATIONS

While the majority of centers in the U.S. have strong connections with many local churches, international centers partner with a wide variety of denominations—or with none, if the local Christian community is small or non-existent. In Serbia, for example, Raskršce Teen Challenge planted its own non-denominational church, which is now one of the largest congregations in the country. On the other end of the spectrum, Teen Challenge in Kenya works closely with the powerful National Christian Churches of Kenya (NCCK). Its secretary-general has helped spread the word about Teen Challenge since the 1960s, when Dave Wilkerson gave him a copy of *The Cross and the Switchblade* film.

Teen Challenge's relationship with local governments also varies widely, from direct partnership to outright hostility. Teen Challenge has managed to enter many countries that are traditionally closed to outside religious groups, in part because of its focus on drug addiction, which even the most anti-Christian authorities will agree is a major problem worldwide. In those places, Don Wilkerson says, "It's a unique mission field, and we have no competition." Church-planting missionaries and social service NGOs (non-governmental organizations) can be found in virtually any corner of the globe, but in many countries, Teen Challenge is the only NGO that focuses on drug addiction. This fact can work to its advantage. In some countries, Teen Challenge has been allowed to operate even when other Christian ministries have been expelled, as governments recognize the importance of fighting addiction.

In the 1990s, after the fall of Communism, churches in Russia and Siberia were permitted to operate but not to own their own buildings. In a strange legal loophole, however, drug rehab centers were allowed to buy property, even if they were religiously affiliated. In this atmosphere, dozens of Teen Challenge centers were founded and essentially became church plants, which could purchase and develop worship spaces for local congregations.

< STAFF BEHIND THE SCENES

From the inception of Teen Challenge 50 years ago, volunteers and staff have played a vital role in providing support services to the ministry on the streets and in the residential programs. The secretaries, cooks, maintenance staff, and many others have provided the assistance that has made this ministry a success, though their names may never have become famous.

In former Communist countries, Teen Challenge's emphasis on freedom, victory over oppression, personal choice, and responsibility often fits the new political climate well. In Serbia, for example, Teen Challenge's promotional material reads as much like a tract against political tyranny as an advertisement for a Christian program:

> Raskršce Teen Challenge strongly believes in voluntary based decisions with regard to starting rehabilitation. . . . Students in the program soon discover that life at Raskršce Teen Challenge center is not based on compulsion, but on daily opportunities to make the right choice. The end result is a changed value system and a new life style. In an environment of understanding that every effort they make is entirely for their own benefit, students have an excellent opportunity to recognize and learn principles that build up character.[6]

In recent years Teen Challenge centers in European Union countries have faced a much different, and perhaps more difficult, challenge—rather than government restrictions, centers must contend with government programs that offer a different kind of "help" to drug addicts. In Portugal, Germany, Denmark, Switzerland, and the Netherlands, government programs provide addicts with housing, living subsidies, and even drugs, or synthetic alternatives. With the physical and criminal consequences of drug abuse thus largely removed, the incentive to enter a residential program—or to seek freedom from addiction by any means—is lowered. "In Western Europe," Tom Bremer says, "the laws are leaning heavily towards the medical model, methadone and heroin distribution, away from residential rehab, and they don't have space for the faith-based or recovery mentality anymore. And this is creating a great deal of difficulty."

In light of heavy restrictions and competition from the government, Teen Challenge in Switzerland has closed its residential programs altogether, and now focuses on outreach and evangelism, as Teen Challenge centers throughout Europe did in the 1960s.

One continual danger that Global Teen Challenge warns its members against is that their centers would become nothing more than Christian social service agencies. As Heinz Ulrich, director of Teen Challenge, Bavaria, Germany, puts it, "Our mission is not to do good social work. It's to do Christian discipleship."[7]

> **CLASSROOM** The key to life transformation for drug addicts around the world has been the Jesus Factor. Bible classes play a central role in providing a new foundation for drug-free living, but even more importantly, they introduce students to a personal relationship with Jesus. The *Group Studies for New Christians* and *Personal Studies for New Christians* curricula have been translated into many languages and provide the foundation for training new Christians around the world.

∧ TEEN CHALLENGE SERBIA The new Teen Challenge center in Serbia is home to that country's most effective drug recovery program. Sasa and Svetlana Ivanovic pioneered the program when they started taking drug addicts into their own home.

"Seeing broken lives restored back to families is one of the great joys of the Teen Challenge ministry to the glory of God."

— Malcolm Smith, Executive Director Western Australia and Global Teen Challenge Regional Representative for Asia Pacific

FUTURE CHALLENGES

∧ STUDENT WORK AND CRAFTS Teen Challenge centers in every part of the world face significant challenges as they strive to become financially self-sufficient. Many centers rely on student work projects, such as arts and crafts, to generate income. One of Global Teen Challenge's top priorities is helping these Teen Challenge centers identify and implement creative micro-enterprises to support their ministries.

eyond the issue of government relations, the most common problem facing Teen Challenge centers worldwide is a scarcity of funds. In the U.S. and other areas where healthy Christian communities exist, like South America, South Korea, and Australia, Christians provide the bulk of Teen Challenge's support. But in places without a wide base of Christian donors, Teen Challenge centers must find ways to become financially self-sufficient. One way to accomplish this is through income-producing work programs, like farms, jewelry and craft factories, bakeries, and construction projects. Another is through fee-based programs, in which an addict's family pays for the monthly program costs. Some centers have assisted others with initial capital investments, but one of Global Teen Challenge's central policies is that organizations or private donors in America will not permanently fund Teen Challenge centers around the world.

Each country in the Teen Challenge family, with its unique culture, religious atmosphere, and political system, has its own unique problems to overcome. The most pressing issue for Russia and former Communist bloc countries is the explosion of HIV and AIDS over the past ten years. Accurate numbers are impossible to verify, but rising infection rates have kept pace with rates of drug abuse closely enough to suggest a strong connection between addiction and HIV infection in these countries. The number of actual deaths is so far relatively low, but experts estimate that at least 1.7 million citizens of formerly Communist countries are HIV-positive[8], a figure that threatens a future even more devastating than the American AIDS crisis in the 1980s. Nearly 90% of all the infected live in Russia or the Ukraine, which gives special significance to Kevin Tyler's decision to locate his coordinating office there, as well as a Teen Challenge Leadership Training Center. The Teen Challenge residential recovery center in Kiev is under construction and nearly complete.

∧ Phanorinn Chhun (right), the director of Teen Challenge in Cambodia, with James Lowans, Director of New Hope Academy Teen Challenge in Factoryville, Pennsylvania. Four years ago, James came to Cambodia to help pioneer a Teen Challenge ministry. He has made nine trips since then, and currently serves as Chairman of the Board of Teen Challenge Cambodia. The close partnership between his Teen Challenge center in Pennsylvania and Phanorinn's in Cambodia has proven beneficial to both.

∧ Pictured in front of the main multipurpose building on the new Teen Challenge Cambodia property are (left to right): Kelly Robinette, Assemblies of God missionary; Phanorinn Chhun, Executive Director of Teen Challenge Cambodia; Rev. Ray Petts, Assemblies of God pastor from the United States, and James Lowans, Director of New Hope Academy Teen Challenge in Factoryville, Pennsylvania. When renovations are completed, the center will begin taking in new students in June 2008.

CAMBODIA

Well Qualified
Phanorinn Chhun

Growing up in Cambodia, Phanorinn Chhun felt a heavy burden whenever he saw families begging on the street, or young children sniffing glue from plastic bags. Phnom Penh, the capital city, is a distribution point for every type of drug, including methamphetamine, heroin, and cocaine, and addiction is rampant among young people, leading to high crime and HIV infection.

With the help of his Christian faith and a strong church community, Norinn managed to resist the temptations around him and earned a good education. But his heart continued to ache for the hurting people in his nation.

"Drug use has stabbed at the very core of Cambodian society," Norinn says. "Families are ripped apart, children are left without solid role models, workers are undependable, streets are filled with violence, the minds of our people are destroyed, and addicts have placed a burden on our society."

When Norinn's pastor told him that Global Teen Challenge was planning to start an addiction recovery center in Phnom Penh, he prayed about how he could help. The position of Executive Director had yet to be filled, but Norinn thought he wasn't qualified for the job. He didn't have any experience working with drug addicts—only his faith in Christ, a heart for the people of Cambodia, and a desire to see God work miracles among them. As it turned out, that was exactly what Teen Challenge was looking for.

The new Teen Challenge of Cambodia, led by Executive Director Phanorinn Chhun and located on an eight-acre property south of Phnom Penh, plans to take the first students into its residential program in 2008. ✴

> **AFRICA STREET OUTREACHES** Taking the gospel to the streets is one of the most effective ways Teen Challenge connects with those whose lives are trapped by addiction. Outdoor rallies, like this one in South Africa, also present a message of prevention to the young children who attend.

Sexual abuse is a huge problem in every country, and its link to drug abuse is well documented. Even the most traditional cultures, like those in China and the Middle East, have seen a rise in sexually transmitted diseases in recent years, and the rates are expected to increase. But Teen Challenge centers in some countries face particular challenges, like state-supported prostitution in Western Europe, South America, Australia, New Zealand, and Israel, and the child sex trade across southeast Asia. Teen Challenge has played an active role in fighting for an end to these practices worldwide and in offering support to their victims.

No country, of course, is free from drug addiction, and none has a monopoly on the suffering that comes with it. The names of the drugs may be different—in the slums of South American cities, millions of teens sniff industrial glue. In East Africa, adults chew khat, a drug that is practically unheard of in the U.S.—but in every country, a variety of drugs is available to both rich and poor. Heroin and cocaine use are widespread, and in every nation, without exception, the most commonly abused drug is alcohol. Don Wilkerson observes, "The subculture of the drug addict is very similar all over the world. And that's why Teen Challenge works all over the world." In Don's view, the only Teen Challenge centers that don't work well are those that depart from a residential, recovery model with strict discipline—in other words, those that view the center as a temporary shelter or flophouse, rather than a place where long-term recovery can take place.

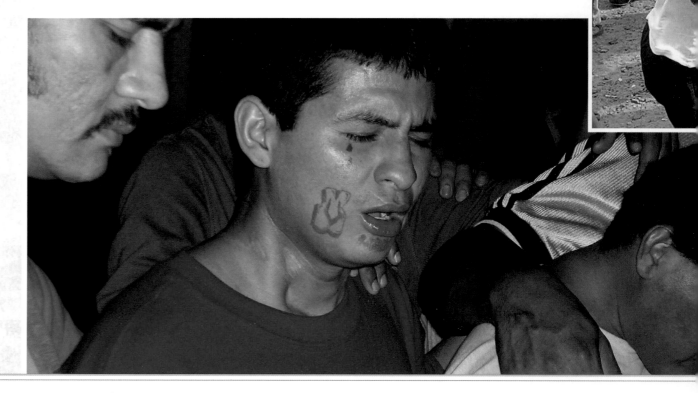

∧ **GANGS IN SOUTH AMERICA** Many Teen Challenge centers in the Caribbean and Latin America work with young people involved in gangs. Those who decide to leave their gangs can face serious consequences when they attempt to re-enter society and live as Christians. Victor was a former gang member who had just graduated from Teen Challenge and shared his testimony for the first time in church on a Sunday morning. As the Teen Challenge group left the church, members of a rival gang opened fire and killed Victor.

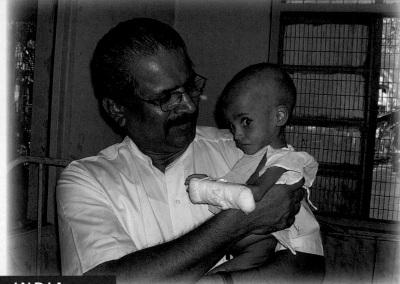

Courageous Leader
K.K. Devaraj

As a technician for the international Iranian Oil Company, K. K. Devaraj's only goal in life was to make money. But after a personal encounter with Christ, he gave up his job and devoted his life to full-time ministry, starting as a staff worker for Teen Challenge in Lebanon. In 1986, he moved back to India to earn degrees in both theology and sociology, with a focus on drug abuse.

When Devaraj saw firsthand the suffering that filled the streets of Bombay—starving children, drug addiction, people dying of AIDS and other diseases, and red-light districts that exploited women and children—he felt God calling him to open a Teen Challenge refuge center there.

Today, Devaraj oversees six safe houses for women rescued from forced prostitution, a night shelter for children whose parents work in the sex trade, an addiction recovery center, health clinics, a hospice for HIV-positive children, and orphanages for street kids.

"It takes courage," Devaraj says. "Silver and gold we do not have. And food and medicine is not enough. But what we have is the bread of life." ✒

Part of the glue that holds successful Teen Challenge centers together is the Teen Challenge curriculum. Some countries have adopted the Christian discipleship model of addiction recovery more readily than others, but it is Teen Challenge's written curriculum that shows them how, and which has fostered a common approach to discipleship training worldwide. Though developed for the U.S. initially, the curriculum has seen great success internationally, because its focus has always been on applying biblical principles to daily life. Dave Batty, who wrote most of the curriculum and has helped several countries implement it, put it this way:

> When you strip away the thin layers of language and culture, the hearts of people are very much the same. The struggles addicts deal with are basically identical worldwide. The Teen Challenge curriculum deals with those struggles directly, not through cultural means, but through the universal truth of Scripture.[9]

> **RAHUL** is one of many children that have been rescued by Teen Challenge on the streets of Mumbai (Bombay), India. Many are children of mothers involved in prostitution. Teen Challenge has started a weekly church service for these women and children, which has seen many accept Christ and find a way out of their destructive lifestyle.

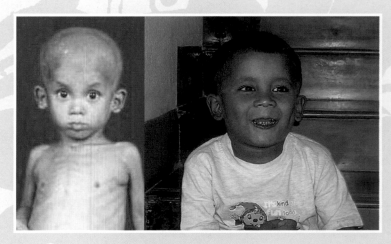

"We don't change a person's *religion*. We help change their *lives*. If a drug addict comes to us calling himself a Moslem, a Jew, a Christian, or anything else — we assume his "religion" *didn't work*, or he would not be an addict! We simply give them a belief and a faith they never had before.

— Don Wilkerson

The Cross is Still Mightier Than the Switchblade

In 2007 Jerry Nance was elected as the new President of Global Teen Challenge. Jerry's first order of business, he says, is to translate and adapt Teen Challenge's curriculum for even more cultures, and write new staff training materials on topics relevant to specific countries. He enlisted as Chief Operating Officer Dave Batty, who served for 20 years as the National Curriculum Coordinator for Teen Challenge USA and 10 years as Executive Director of Teen Challenge in Brooklyn, New York. Jerry also plans to tap the power of the Internet to spread the word about Teen Challenge to every nation, and to recruit new workers among college students, social workers, other professionals, and Teen Challenge graduates. When he looks to the future, Jerry says:

Drug addiction crosses every social and economic boundary and negatively affects virtually every country in the world. Over the past 50 years the ministry of Teen Challenge has established a proven track record in changing lives no matter the country, the culture, the drug of choice, or family history. As we address needs in the future, we must continue to depend on the power of the Holy Spirit, which will assure that the Jesus Factor continues. And our goal is Psalm 96:3, "to declare His glory among the nations and his marvelous deeds to all peoples."[10]

The challenge seems overwhelming. The United Nations estimates there are over 200 million people living in the grips of addiction. Global Teen Challenge has standing invitations from 37 more countries that want help in establishing Teen Challenge centers.

On the following pages you will read about miracles of transformation that have taken place across the globe. Their stories are just as dramatic as those first told in *The Cross and the Switchblade*. With God's help we anticipate that the future of Teen Challenge will be even greater than the past 50 years. ❧

NOTES ON CHAPTER 3

1. David Wilkerson, *Beyond the Cross and the Switchblade* (Old Tappan, NJ: Fleming H. Revell, 1974), p. 105-06.

2. All quotes from Howard and Pat Foltz come from Dave Batty's interview with them, conducted on June 4, 2007.

3. Wilkerson, *Beyond*, p. 106.

4. All quotes from Don Wilkerson come from Dave Batty's interview with him, conducted on June 29, 2007.

5. All quotes from Tom Bremer come from Dave Batty's interview with him, conducted on January 20, 2007.

6. *Raskršce: Teen Challenge Yugoslavia* (Novi Sad, Serbia: Raskršce Teen Challenge, 2007). Most of the information in this promotional booklet is also available online, at www.raskrsce.org.yu.

7. The quote from Heinz Ulrich comes from Dave Batty's interview with him, conducted on May 18, 2007.

8. Sam Jones, "The World Map of HIV/AIDS," *The Independent* (London), 1 December 2006, World AIDS Day, p. 6.

9. All quotes from Dave Batty come from Ethan Campbell's interview with him, conducted on September 4, 2007.

10. The quote from Jerry Nance comes from Dave Batty's interview with him, conducted on June 4, 2007.

"I cannot describe with words the pain
we have gone through because of his addictions;
neither can I describe the joy that I have for the freedom
my son found through Teen Challenge."

Mother of a Teen Challenge graduate

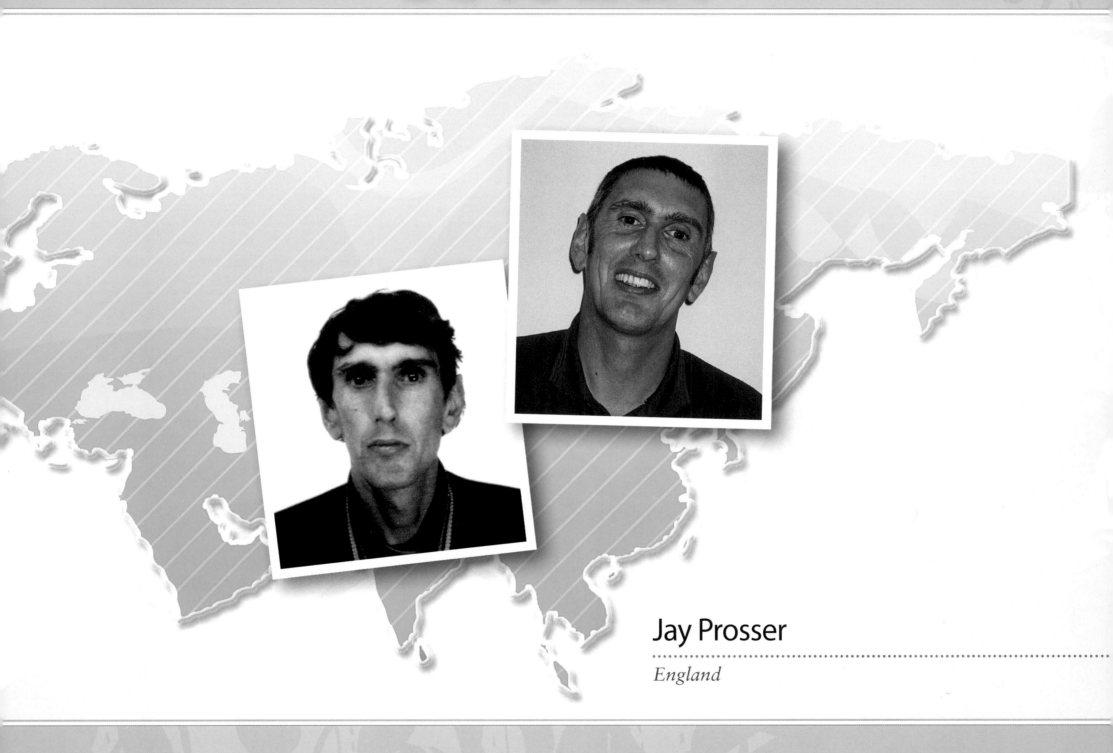

Jay Prosser

England

EURASIA

Portugal

Family on the Streets
João and Mary-Louise (Mimmi) Botica

When Mary-Louise (Mimmi) Botica came from Sweden to Portugal to work at Teen Challenge, she never thought it would become her life's work. She certainly didn't expect that the young man she met in a Lisbon slum would become her husband.

João Botica had been addicted to heroin for 15 years, and lived as a "human rag" on the city streets. He had gone to prison for trafficking drugs between Portugal and Switzerland, but prison didn't change his life. After his release, he was still a captive to his addiction. When Teen Challenge staff met João during an outreach to the Casal Ventoso ghetto, he felt hope for the first time. He accepted God's love in Jesus Christ, and started to believed it was possible to live free from drugs.

Day by day at the Teen Challenge center, God continued the work of restoration in João's life. Years later, he had grown into a man of strong Christian conviction, and he joined the Teen Challenge outreach team that had found him in Lisbon—the same team that Mimmi worked for. On January 10, 1998, they were married.

That summer, João and Mimmi took part in an outreach to the Quinta da Lage ghetto in the city of Amadora. They met many children on the street, but one in particular touched their hearts. Paulo was tiny for his seven years, from malnutrition, and covered with sores and lice. When João and Mimmi asked Paulo's mother if the boy could spend a few days with them, she said, "You can keep him."

During his first stay with them at Teen Challenge, Mimmi treated the cigarette burns and rat scratches on Paulo's face and body, and gave him medication for the parasites in his stomach. Paulo was amazed to find that in their home, he had a bed of his own, warm water in the shower, and a working toilet.

The days turned into years, and in September 1999, the Boticas gained legal custody of Paulo. In that time, he had learned to read and write and passed second grade. His appearance had completely changed, and people meeting him for the first time said he looked just like "Papá João."

With two success stories in their own family, the Boticas continue to work with suffering adults and children on the streets of Lisbon. Mimmi writes, "Sometimes it's difficult to deal with wounds from the past. A rejected, abandoned, and abused child has a lot of wounds—but the love of Jesus is superior. What we can't do, He can." ❧

Only a Few Words of Prayer
Eddie Gregory

Starting at age 16, Eddie Gregory tried a series of drugs to drown out the pain and emptiness of his life—first beer, then hashish, then heroin. The heroin numbed him completely, but in exchange, he had to give it his life. When Eddie's sister gave him a tract written by a Christian counselor, Eddie called the number listed on the back, and the man helped him get into Teen Challenge.

At first, Eddie had no use for the spiritual aspects of the program. If anyone recited Bible verses in his presence, he lost his temper. He found only one staff member, John, who was easy to talk with. On the third night of his stay, John asked if he could pray for him. Eddie agreed, but only to keep the peace.

Eddie recalls the moment in his own words: "John placed his hand on my head as he began to pray. Right there and then I felt something leave me. All the pressure of twenty years of psychological and emotional pain just suddenly lifted. It was incredible. Heroin, alcohol, cannabis—nothing the world had to offer me had worked. Yet here after only a few words of prayer, I felt free."

Eddie's road to freedom didn't come easily after that, but he knew that what Teen Challenge had to offer was real. He graduated from the program after his second try and settled in Dublin, where he works in the construction industry. ❧

The Only Way Out
Carlos Monteiro

As a young boy in Angola, Carlos Monteiro was sexually abused by a neighbor. The worst part of the experience was that his parents didn't believe him. The feelings of rejection and abandonment persisted as his parents divorced and his mother moved away.

Carlos left home at age 14 and began panhandling his way through Europe. By 18, he was addicted to morphine and intravenous amphetamines, and he stole cars for drug money. Nothing could stop his constant pursuit of drugs—not even prison, or an overdose and coma, or getting shot in the chest.

During one of his prison stays, Carlos met a man reading the Bible. The man told him the Bible was "the only way out of these walls." Carlos remembered his words, though they didn't make sense to him. Years later, he talked to a woman in a coffee shop who was also reading the Bible. She and her fiancé walked Carlos through the Scriptures, and showed him the freedom that Jesus offered.

Since his wife Júlia refused to let him come home, Carlos decided to give Jesus a try. He entered Teen Challenge just after Christmas, 1982, hobbled from sores on his legs and feet. His withdrawal from the drugs in his system was horrific, but when it was over, he felt God speaking and comforting him. His desire for drugs, even cigarettes, was gone, a feeling of freedom he could hardly recall.

In the program, Carlos sent numerous letters to his wife and family, hoping to be reconciled. They went unreturned until one day, he received a drawing from his 4-year-old daughter. That gesture opened a door of hope in his heart, and he began a new life with his family.

Carlos is now the pastor of a church and director of the Teen Challenge center in Loures, Portugal. 🖋

IRELAND

Gillian Booth

Rebel Trying to Fit In

Gillian Booth came from a loving family, but when her schoolmates bullied her for being a nerd, she grew desperate to fit in. She disrupted classes and rebelled against her teachers just to impress her friends. The problem was, her aggressive behavior soon drove them away.

After she dropped out of school, Gillian found a new crowd to fit into. These new "friends" lived on the streets, got high as often as they could, and had no moral standards. Often Gillian's parents picked her up from jail or the hospital, at a loss to understand what had happened to their formerly happy little girl.

At age 19, Gillian decided she'd had enough. She called the phone number on a leaflet she had picked up at a police station. "Everything on that leaflet," she says, "was what I was crying out for in my heart." A month later, she entered Teen Challenge.

In the program, Gillian often found herself crying uncontrollably, as she came face-to-face with the sober reality of what she'd done to her family. She learned to forgive herself and others through Christ, and stopped trying to survive life on her own.

Gillian graduated in 2005, and today she runs a successful youth club at her local church, reaching out to rebels like herself. She recently married her husband Sean and plans to attend college to study social work. 🖋

EURASIA

Wales, UK

The Evidence
Rhys Pritchard

Rhys Pritchard sold party drugs at clubs and raves, and the huge amounts of money he brought in made him feel important. But as he took more of the drugs himself, he ended up owing his suppliers more money than he could earn. He knew that soon they would come after him to collect their debts.

Rhys's paranoia grew so great, he visited a psychiatrist. The doctor prescribed Valium and temazepam sedatives, and soon Rhys was taking a whole week's prescription in a single day. When those pills ran out, he turned to heroin. Whenever fear or pain or a sense of failure threatened him, he shot up, and everything was all right—for a short time.

With thoughts of death creeping into his mind, Rhys cried out to God. Shortly after, a friend sent him a letter about the freedom she had found from drug addiction, and about Teen Challenge, which had helped her find it. In the letter, she included an application form.

At Teen Challenge South Wales, Rhys found a sense of purpose that went beyond earning money, and a healing from his paranoid fears that didn't involve drugs. Rhys now works on staff at Teen Challenge, where he participates with an outreach team called Evidence—a reference to the evidence of changed lives in its workers. ❧

England, UK

From Nutter to Vicar
Jay Prosser

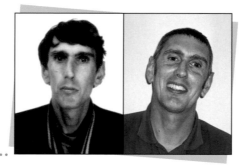

Growing up in a rough neighborhood in East London, Jay Prosser got by in life by acting the clown. But after losing his temper and winning a couple of fights, he realized that being a "nutter"—a crazy fighter—could win him even more respect. By his late teens, Jay belonged to several violent gangs, including the skinheads. He used every drug he could find, and mugged strangers for money.

Eventually, heroin addiction began to dominate his life, and Jay knew he needed to make a change. His friend Javier told him about Jesus, and invited him to church, but Jay resisted. So Javier gave him a copy of the pastor's autobiography, *Addicted*. Jay read about the man's life with astonishment—this London vicar had been a heroin addict, too, and

even more of a nutter than he was! Maybe this church was the place to find hope.

Javier enrolled in a beginner's Bible study course at the church, and made a commitment to Christ. His addiction still stuck with him, though, so Javier suggested Teen Challenge. The program proved difficult for Jay, especially when his girlfriend left him, but he came to see that God would never disappoint, even when the rest of the world did.

After graduating in 2000, Jay continued to work for Teen Challenge London, helping to staff the Crisis Centre and participating in outreaches. His favorite part of the job, he says, is walking down the streets where he used to use drugs, this time reaching out to people in the same desperate circumstances. ❧

WALES, UK

Restoring the Family
Paul and Cloe

Paul and Cloe had used drugs together since they were teenagers. Though the marijuana, LSD, Ecstasy, and speed often caused bitter fights, they always made up and found a way to stay together. That is, until Paul tried heroin.

After five years of watching Paul deteriorate into a lying, thieving junkie, Cloe turned to drastic measures. "I thought having a baby would give him an incentive to stop," she says, "but it didn't. So in the end, I thought if I can't beat him, I'll join him."

By the time their daughter Seren was 15 months old, Paul and Cloe had fed nearly everything they owned to their addiction. They stole from the offering plate at church and sold Seren's Christmas presents for drug money. "We realized we couldn't carry on," Cloe says. "We just had to sort ourselves out or Seren would never have a normal family life." With the help of Paul's mother, they entered Teen Challenge together.

Paul went to the Challenge House residential center for men, and Cloe and Seren to the Teen Challenge Hope House nearby. In their separate programs, they both committed their lives to Christ, learned good parenting skills, and though physically apart, grew closer as a family.

After graduation, Paul and Cloe got married and bought a house in Ammanford, South Wales. They both work full-time for Challenge House. ❧

Germany

The Prayer that "Didn't Work"
Wolfgang Mueller

Wolfgang Mueller never used hard drugs with his friends, but that didn't stop him from having a good time. At age 16, he belonged to a gang and an amateur rock band, and he often partied and got drunk with both. When a Teen Challenge worker invited him to the coffeehouse in Wiesbaden, Germany, he wasn't interested.

A few months later, Wolfgang and his friends went to a rock concert, only to find they couldn't afford the tickets. As they discussed what to do next, Wolfgang remembered that they were near the coffeehouse. He tried to persuade everyone to go, but only his best friend agreed.

On the way, Wolfgang said, "I'm going to ask those people questions they won't be able to answer. When we leave tonight, they will no longer believe what they think they believe now." At the coffeehouse, a Teen Challenge worker sat down across from them, and Wolfgang peppered him with pseudo-scientific questions about evolution and creation, along with deep philosophical questions like "What is the reason for living?"

To Wolfgang's surprise, the worker patiently answered all of his questions. He had never believed that people could actually know why they were created, or who their creator was. The idea that someone could have personal contact with God was a new revelation.

Wolfgang and his friend went back the next night, and again were impressed by the wisdom and patience of the Teen Challenge staff. But when a worker asked if they wanted to pray, they made a quick exit. On the bus ride home, Wolfgang decided to find out if prayer really worked. "We'll ask God to send sparks of light into a dark room," he told his friend. They experimented in the darkness that night, but were disappointed to find that nothing supernatural happened.

The next weekend, they returned to the coffeehouse to complain that prayer didn't work. The Teen Challenge workers listened, then explained God's plan of salvation, as offered in the Bible. Before the evening was over, Wolfgang and his friend had both accepted Christ into their lives.

Wolfgang worked part-time at the coffeehouse for five years, then full-time as a Teen Challenge staff worker, eventually becoming the director of Teen Challenge in Germany. He now lives in Idstein, Germany, where he serves as the Administrator for the County Department for Youth Welfare and Schools.

[Source: Don Wilkerson, *The Cross Is Still Mightier than the Switchblade* (Shippensburg, PA: Treasure House, 1996), p. 131-33.]

SPAIN

⌃ ARE YOU HUNGRY? The director's wife is cooking for everyone today.

⌄ SPAIN TEEN CHALLENGE
The men's dormitory at the Teen Challenge center in Spain.

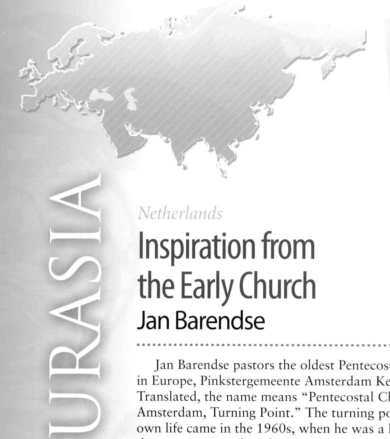

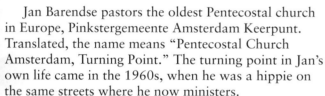

EURASIA

Netherlands

Inspiration from the Early Church
Jan Barendse

Jan Barendse pastors the oldest Pentecostal church in Europe, Pinkstergemeente Amsterdam Keerpunt. Translated, the name means "Pentecostal Church Amsterdam, Turning Point." The turning point in Jan's own life came in the 1960s, when he was a hippie on the same streets where he now ministers.

Jan received a Christian education early in life, but as a teen, he grew embittered with his parents and their religion. The reality he saw in the lives of church members didn't match the Christian ideals he read about in the Bible. So he turned to Marxism and other radical social theories.

After a few years working in a trade union, though, Jan realized the situation there was the same as in the church. Not even the most committed Marxists could fully live out their radical ideology. In response, Jan became cynical and depressed. He suffered from insomnia, and thought about suicide.

But all along, his early disappointment with the church kept haunting him. After reading Lloyd Douglas's novel *The Robe*, about first-century Christians, Jan returned to the Book of Acts and started asking questions: Why were Christians in the early church so enthusiastic? What was the source of their incredible strength?

One day while riding his motorcycle, Jan passed a big tent with a banner that said, "Bread for the Heart." His own heart felt empty, so he stopped and stood at the entrance. Teen Challenge outreach workers led a crowd in praise and worship. "I recognized them," Jan says. "They were the people described in the Book of Acts! They had strength, enthusiasm, and happiness."

Jan followed one of the workers to a small room in the back, and knelt down in prayer. He felt God's presence flow over him, and spontaneously he prayed for forgiveness. A sense of God's love so overpowered him that all his bitterness, hate, and loneliness disappeared.

After attending Bible school, Jan became the director of the first Teen Challenge residential program in Holland, then spent several years training other Teen Challenge staff throughout Europe. The church he now pastors was founded in 1907, and has hosted such well-known Pentecostal leaders as Smith Wigglesworth and Robert and Marie Brown. Their most recent Easter production, "Way of the Cross," attracted nearly 300 young people. 🌾

[Source: Don Wilkerson, *The Cross Is Still Mightier than the Switchblade* (Shippensburg, PA: Treasure House, 1996), p. 131-33.]

SCOTLAND, UK

Bus Ministry
Mark

From the age of 15, Mark sold drugs to terrorist militias in Northern Ireland. Before long, he was hopelessly addicted to crack and heroin himself.

Doctors told Mark he would never get off of heroin. But after hearing the gospel, he sensed Christ telling him, "No, you're free!" He locked himself in a room for eleven days and went through withdrawal cold turkey.

Mark knew he needed a fresh start, so he entered Teen Challenge in Scotland. Though many students complained about the program, Mark says he "loved every minute of it—because the Lord was there."

Mark now works as an assistant pastor at George Square Baptist Church in Glasgow, and serves as the chaplain of Wellington Academy in Greenock, 30 miles away. He also coordinates the Greenock Bus Team, one of several bus ministries throughout Scotland, which serves coffee and food to people on the street and refers addicts to Teen Challenge. 🌾

Saving What Was Lost
Rikke

Rikke had been sexually abused since age 12, and at age 18, she lived with a violent man who controlled her through beatings and heroin. She decided that if men only wanted sex from her, she might as well get paid. Broken in spirit, Rikke took to the streets as a prostitute.

After that, her life became an endless round of drug use, beatings, arrests, and psychotic episodes. No one could help her—not her family, who had given up; not her psychiatrist, who wanted to give her more drugs; not even the government, who couldn't find her a job, and threatened to take away her baby boy.

In a desperate gesture, Rikke knelt on the street and cried out to God. A group of Christians passing by invited her to their church. There, Rikke heard the words of Luke 19:10, "For the Son of Man came to seek and save what was lost," and recognized herself. The pastor asked if he could pray for her, and Rikke collapsed in his arms, spilling tears all over his expensive suit.

Rikke didn't think she could afford Betesda, the Teen Challenge of Denmark, but a donation allowed her to attend. After that point, everyone seemed willing to help her. Creditors began cancelling her bills, and the government allowed her son to return. Her violent ex-boyfriend came back and wrecked her apartment, but the social welfare office paid for the damages. When she confessed her past crimes to the police, they couldn't find her name in the computer, and told her everything was cleared up.

Ten years later, Rikke is now happily married, with three more children. She is working toward a degree in social work, and she hopes to return to Teen Challenge as a staff worker. ❧

Rikke heard the words of Luke 19:10, "For the Son of Man came to seek and save what was lost," and recognized herself.

ITALY

All or Nothing
Patrizia Scarpino

When Patrizia first shot heroin at age 17, she knew she'd found the answer to life's problems. When a group of young women tried to talk to her about Jesus, she didn't understand why she would need him. When others told her about a Christian recovery program, she said, "No thanks—when I want to quit, I will quit."

A year later, Patrizia was living on the street, having sold nearly everything she owned. In despair, she went to an interview at Teen Challenge, but the program seemed too restrictive—no smoking, no methadone, no medication for depression. Even worse, the program took up to two years, a seemingly infinite amount of time.

All the same, Patrizia was desperate enough to call back every week until a vacancy opened up. Like a prisoner facing his last meal, she shot up all the heroin she could find and got on the train.

In the program, Patrizia nearly fell asleep listening to everyone read the Bible and talk about God. But the other women in the program also prayed for her. Patrizia braced herself for terrible withdrawal symptoms, but they came and went without much pain.

Patrizia wanted to change her life, but she didn't want to become a saint, like these women seemed to be. She left the program after a month, intending never to use heroin again. A few days later, as she tried to shoot up in her church's bathroom, she realized that she would have to go all the way in her Christian life or not at all. She prayed that God would show Himself to her when she went back to Teen Challenge.

"So I returned," she says, "and from there began a new and marvelous adventure with God." Patrizia graduated from Teen Challenge, after spending the full two years there. At the center, she says, "I cried, I laughed, I got mad, I fought, but above all I fell in love with Jesus." ❧

EURASIA

Czech Republic

Answers to Life's Biggest Questions
Jirka Zavadzki

As a child, Jirka Zavadzki would watch the stars at night and imagine the immense size of the universe. He wondered about the purpose of life and what would happen after death, but he couldn't find answers. When he discovered drugs in high school, they calmed his restless questioning.

Jirka became a Christian, but then fell in love with a woman who dragged him back to his old lifestyle. This time, drugs took an even firmer grip on his life, as he started making and selling pervitin, a home-grown version of cocaine. This operation, financed through robberies, soon landed him in prison.

Jirka brought a pocket-sized Bible with him to jail, and while he read it, the Holy Spirit spoke. Scripture offered answers for the questions that had always tormented him, and challenged him to soften his heart and accept forgiveness in Christ. Jirka went through the Teen Challenge program after serving his prison sentence. Today, he and his wife work at the induction center in Tyra. ❦

CZECH REPUBLIC

Bringing Down the Walls
Markéta Midrlová

Markéta Midrlová didn't like going to Catholic Church with her family, but the services had a powerful influence on her. As a little girl, she felt God's presence all around, and once even thought she heard Him speak. But as a teenager, she built up walls inside to keep God and other people out. That way, she didn't have to feel bad about experimenting with sex, alcohol, and pills with her friends.

Those walls threatened to come down the day her best friend died in a car accident. But Markéta wouldn't let them—she simply took more and more drugs and tried to ignore her loneliness. Her parents noticed her constant cramps and hallucinations, and took her to a psychiatrist. He only prescribed more drugs, which Markéta abused. She moved out of her parents' home and bounced from one drug addict's apartment to another, occasionally living on the street.

One day, she met a woman who told her about Jesus and invited her to church. Markéta remembered that she didn't like church, but agreed to go anyway. During the service, a group of Christians gathered around to pray for her, and they told her about Teen Challenge.

At Teen Challenge, Markéta felt the presence of God again, but this time, she didn't try to keep Him out. She heard Him speak through Scripture and prayer, and saw him work through the love and acceptance of the staff. She graduated from the program in 2002 with a high school diploma and training in bookkeeping.

Markéta now works for Teen Challenge in Prague as a full-time bookkeeper. In 2003, she married a fellow Teen Challenge staff member, Pavel ❦

Serbia

Ministry of Hospitality
Saša and Svetlana Ivanović

Saša and Svetlana Ivanovic found freedom from heroin addiction in 1987, after reading *The Cross and the Switchblade*. Since then, they have devoted their lives to helping others trapped in the same addictions. Their ministry with drug addicts began on the first night of the NATO bombing in Serbia, when they took a new convert and former addict, Petrija, into their home.

As their ministry expanded, the Ivanovics decided to send addicts to a hospital for treatment, then invite them to their house for an extended stay. Word of their generosity spread fast. Soon so many people were seeking help, the Ivanovics knew it was time for a new strategy.

Saša and Svetlana visited more than 15 rehabilitation centers across Europe before opening Raskršce Teen Challenge in Novi Sad in 2000. In the first two years, more than 400 addicts received counseling through its men's and women's residential programs and day center. They also opened a coffeehouse, where addicts could get information and talk to counselors.

Raskršce Teen Challenge is registered with Serbia's Federal Ministry of Justice and works with several state institutions, such as the police department and municipal court in Novi Sad. After the NATO bombing, Teen Challenge volunteers also delivered humanitarian aid to a local psychiatric ward.

The demand for effective addiction treatment in Serbia continues to grow, just as it did when the Ivanovics first took hurting people into their home. The program plans to expand its facilities soon to a farm in the village of Cenej.

∧ **TEEN CHALLENGE POLAND**
Staff and students at the Teen Challenge center in Broczyna, Poland.

POLAND

No More Shadow
Piotr Damps

At age 26, Piotr Damps was, in his own words, "a shadow of a man." He had grown up in an abusive family, where he'd learned to rely only on himself, but that philosophy led only to addiction.

When Piotr first heard the gospel of Jesus Christ, it was the first time he'd heard that someone truly loved him. At once, his life had hope and purpose.

Piotr graduated from Teen Challenge in Broczyna in 2001, then spent a year of re-entry in southern Poland, where he worked with a children's ministry and drama evangelism.

Now Piotr is studying at the Theological Seminary in Warsaw. He and his wife Ania have a newborn baby. As he puts it, "The Lord makes dreams come true."

EURASIA

Romania

Into the Sewers
Catalin Baciu

From 1966 to 1989, under the rule of Communist dictator Nicolae Ceausescu, families in Romania were required to have many children, to boost the population. But rather than help the struggling economy, the policy simply filled the state-run orphanages with children abandoned by their parents. Many of these children, when they reached the age of 18, were simply turned out into the streets, with little job training, few social skills, and virtually no hope for the future.

Thousands of children and teens today continue to live homeless in major cities like Bucharest. Some spend their nights in the sewers, where it is warm in winter, but where living spaces are infested by rats, cockroaches, and lice. Most are addicted to industrial glue, which they pour into the bottom of plastic bags and inhale. The streets of Bucharest are literally filled with crowds of hopeless young people, continually breathing from plastic bags, ignored by every passerby.

After working with street children for eight years, missionary Catalin Baciu noticed a glaring gap in Romania's social services. There were orphanages for young children and government programs for adults, but nothing available for those in their teens and early twenties. This group, Catalin saw, had tremendous needs—they needed help to overcome their addictions, help in finding work, and help transitioning into society. Without support, young women turned to prostitution and young men to crime.

Catalin and his wife Oltita founded Teen Challenge Romania in 2004, and two years later opened its first residential center for boys. The center, located in a suburb of Bucharest, has a capacity of 18 students and a long waiting list. Other non-residential ministries include a coffeehouse crisis center, street outreaches, methadone clinic outreaches, and an outpatient counseling program for girls.

When he thinks about what prompted him to start a program to help street kids, Catalin says, "I put myself in their shoes, and I thought, man, we just have to do something for them." So Catalin walks through back alleys and into the sewer system, finding anyone who might need help and offering it. And his ministry doesn't stop when he goes home at night. Two of Catalin and Oltita's four children were rescued from the streets of Bucharest and adopted. 🌿

POLAND

A Bigger Love
Evelyn

When Evelyn met Adam, she fell head over heels in love. He was the answer—the one who would take away her suicidal thoughts, make life worthwhile, and conquer her addiction.

In reality, the only steady love for either Evelyn or Adam was heroin. They were married and had a baby daughter, Claudia, but they couldn't function without constantly getting high. Evelyn recalls, "The love of drugs was bigger than the love for our own child."

When evangelists from the Mission of New Hope in Bielawa told them about Jesus, they agreed that this was their last chance to get clean.

They left 2-year-old Claudia with relatives and entered separate Teen Challenge programs, in Janowicach and Broczyna. Their time was difficult but blessed, as God helped to correct their flawed ways of thinking.

Evelyn is now studying to become a therapist in dependency disorders at the Polish Society for the Prevention of Drug Addiction. She thanks God that Claudia, now 5, and her younger brother Tobias, 16 months, will grow up to remember their parents as sober and responsible. 🌿

MOLDOVA

^ **THE KITCHEN**
Look carefully—that flat surface with the chimney rising from it is actually the stove where all of Teen Challenge Moldova's meals are cooked.

^ **TEEN CHALLENGE WOMEN'S HOME**
Three women from the Teen Challenge with the staff (lower left) from Moldova.

ⱽ **MEN'S PROGRAM MOLDOVA** The Teen Challenge men from Moldova. Above their heads in the background on the right is a black tank, located at the top of their shower room. Hot water comes compliments of the sun in the summer. And in the winter?

CELEBRATING FIFTY YEARS OF MIRACLES
50
ANNIVERSARY CELEBRATION
TEEN CHALLENGE INTERNATIONAL

BELARUS

Sold Out
Oleg

Oleg tried drugs for the first time at age 16, when he let a group of friends gather at his place to shoot up an opium substitute. Over the next 12 years, he stole from his mother, went through several rehab programs, and stopped noticing everyone in his life. He sold everything in his apartment, including the refrigerator, to feed his addiction.

While Oleg spent two weeks in jail, an old classmate visited his mother and told her about Teen Challenge. She begged him to call, and Oleg entered the program in the Khoiniki district. He accepted Christ, and repented of the hurt he had caused his mother and friends. He also began to filter out the bad influences in his life, not only the hard drugs, but even alcohol and tobacco.

Oleg wants to attend Bible college in the future. He says, "I'm praying my plans would coincide with His plans."

EURASIA

Belarus
Breaking the Silence
Roma

While he was drinking and using drugs, Roma's conversation with his mother was limited to phrases like "Give me more money" and "Make me some food." His mother moved them from Russia to Belarus, hoping that a new location would separate her teenage son from drugs. But Roma soon found new dealers there to satisfy his addiction.

In the meantime, Roma's mother found Christ, started attending church, and pleaded with God to save her son. Roma thought she had gone crazy, but took her suggestion and gave Teen Challenge a try.

During a worship service on his very first day in the program, Roma heard a Christian song about a faithful mother, and his heart was instantly softened. He wanted to run home at that moment and beg her forgiveness.

Two months later, when she came for her first visit, Roma's mother hardly recognized him. She kept stroking his face and saying, "This is not my son." Now she no longer prays alone, and the two of them talk for hours, as if making up for long years of silence. "From the inky darkness of drug addiction," Roma says, "I returned home." ❦

LATVIA

BUILDING NEW CENTER
Workers from Teen Challenge in Iowa (right) came to Latvia to help build the new Teen Challenge center.

LITHUANIA

∧ BASKET WEAVING
Women in the Teen Challenge program at Lithuania weave baskets—it's therapeutic and it becomes a source of income for the ministry.

∨ TEEN CHALLENGE LITHUANIA
Students and staff at the Teen Challenge in Lithuania.

Buried Alive
Marina Makorin

Both of Marina Makorin's parents were doctors, and she earned good grades in high school and college. But after a friend encouraged her to try heroin, she was addicted to it at age 16. The drug became more and more the master of her life. She tutored young children in English, and would shoot up between sessions. In deep despair, at 22 years old, she called her mother and asked her to buy a casket. She wanted to be buried alive and end her misery.

Instead, her mom brought her to the Teen Challenge center in Moscow. Marina's first challenge there was detoxing from heroin, a process that made her very sick. After two nights of misery, she prayed, "God, if you can help me, please let me sleep." When she awoke hours later, she knew for the first time that God loved her.

Through the program's Bible study, classes, chapel services, and prayer, God transformed Marina's life. During that time, her mother and her boyfriend Roman also became Christians, and Roman went through the Teen Challenge program in Karabanovo, 60 miles from Moscow.

While students, both Marina and Roman received a call to full-time ministry. They married, and recently graduated from Bible school in the Ukraine. They are looking forward to a future of ministry, helping other young people find real life in Christ. ✐

EURASIA

Moscow, Russia
Left for Dead
Paul Boyko

Paul Boyko's drug addiction often took him to the brink of death. The last time he ever got high, a Moscow street gang found him and beat him into unconsciousness. Then they stuffed him into a plastic garbage bin and dumped it in a cemetery. An old woman passing by came across his body and called for help.

Paul knew that God had saved his life, and not for the first time. He vowed never to use drugs again, and after getting out the hospital, he came to Teen Challenge.

Paul now serves on staff at the Teen Challenge center in Karabanovo. Fellow staff and students alike praise his confidence and compassion, and the joy of Christ that is evident in his life. ❧

Siberia, Russia
Never Too Late to Start
Misha Kiruhin

Misha Kiruhin went to church for the first time at the age of 38. He had already spent 20 of those years bound to alcohol, heroin, and a life of crime. But his first service at the New Ilyinka Church in Novokuznetsk was the start of a new life. There he met Pastor Ilya Bantseev, who introduced him to Jesus Christ, then directed him to Teen Challenge.

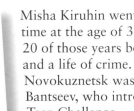

Today, Misha is the director of the Teen Challenge center in Kuzedeyevo, a small town just south of the city. It is the one of the oldest Teen Challenge centers in Russia, and miracles of deliverance continue every week. ❧

A Mother's Prayer
Eugene & Lena Kulagov

Eugene Kulagov started using prescription drugs like morphine and promedol in 8th grade, but as his need grew stronger, so did the drugs. He still managed to find success in boxing, in the Soviet Army, and at the Pedagogical University, where he majored in Physical Education, but his life was on a downward spiral.

During this time, Eugene's mother became a Christian and started to pray for her son. A friend invited him to church, and Eugene accepted Christ, turning away from 14 years of addiction.

Eugene and his wife Lena now direct the Teen Challenge New Life Center in Barnaul, Siberia. Graduates of this program have gone on to plant 11 new churches.

Eugene and Lena themselves attended training for national Teen Challenge leaders in Ishevsk, Russia, in March 2008. This new month-long training course is designed to raise up leaders to reach Russia's 4 million drug addicts. ❧

Kazakhstan

Strength in Small Numbers
Arman Kenzhebaev

Arman Kenzhebaev endured so much pain and shame during ten years of drug addiction, his relatives actually urged him to overdose and die. Arman called himself a Muslim, but he made no attempt to live out his religion's commands. He came to Teen Challenge in 1996, broken in spirit and seeing no prospect for his life.

In the program, still in its infancy, Arman was personally mentored by founder Doug Boyle, who taught him to search for God and seek His wisdom in every decision. After seeing the example of Doug and other workers who devoted their lives to helping others, Arman committed his life to Christ, and stayed at Teen Challenge as a staff member.

In 2002, Arman and four other workers started a Teen Challenge center in the Almaty province of Kazakhstan. Their building needed serious repair, and with only five staff members and one student, they desperately needed more hands for the job. "But God was strengthening us," Arman says, "teaching us how to manage wisely over the small amount of money we had."

Today, Arman serves as the regional director for Teen Challenge in the Almaty province, where five residential centers serve 120 men. In January 2005, he founded a church which today has 250 members. 🖌

Kazakhstan

Learning to Smile Again
Kamil Kadyrov

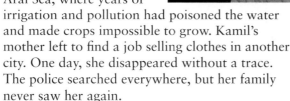

Kamil Kadyrov's family knew they had to leave their small town near the Aral Sea, where years of irrigation and pollution had poisoned the water and made crops impossible to grow. Kamil's mother left to find a job selling clothes in another city. One day, she disappeared without a trace. The police searched everywhere, but her family never saw her again.

Kamil's father soon remarried, but his new wife refused to take Kamil or his younger brother Yerbol into her house, and their grandmother could only take one of them. So at age 13, Kamil began his life on the streets, stealing to survive and drinking to blot out the pain of rejection. But even in his darkest moments, Kamil says, "God saw all my tears and heard the voice of my broken heart." At age 15, he came to the Teen Challenge juvenile boys' home, where he broke his addiction and learned to smile again. He also developed a heart for others. After living at Teen Challenge for the past five years, Kamil believes that God is calling him to help other boys who struggle with drug addiction. 🖌

KAZAKHSTAN

Just Enough Hope
Anya Krasnoborodkina

Anya Krasnoborodkina grew up in a happy family of five, until tragedy struck. Her father died, and the family sank quickly into poverty. Unable to provide enough money through work, Anya's mother found a new man. He was hardly a father, though, as he beat Anya's brothers and sexually abused her. He also drank heavily, and Anya's mother and brothers became alcoholics along with him.

Desperate to provide food for her family, Anya turned to prostitution, and became pregnant at age 17. She had enough hope left to keep her baby girl, Kristina. But when one of her brothers died of a drug overdose, she knew she had to get out.

Anya and her daughter have lived at the Teen Challenge Refuge Center in Kazakhstan for the past five years. Anya works at the center as an accountant, and Kristina is in the first grade. Anya's family is still not free from their addictions, but she continually prays for them and believes that God will work a miracle in their lives. 🖌

EURASIA

Pakistan
Success and Challenge
Mark Brink

Assemblies of God missionary Mark Hausfeld registered Teen Challenge in Pakistan as an official non-governmental agency (NGO) in 1997. The agreement with the Ministries of Anti-Narcotics and Health stated that Teen Challenge "will assist ... the Government of Pakistan and its response to the drug and alcohol abuse situation," and promised to do so "without interfering in political matters." The agreement made no reference to Christianity.

The promise to avoid politics, and a cautious attitude toward religion, is supremely important in Pakistan, whose culture and government are strictly Islamic. At the same time, the government recognizes the need for a solution to rampant addiction. More than seven million Pakistanis are addicted to drugs, and the numbers are growing, along with rates of HIV infection.

> More than seven million Pakistanis are addicted to drugs, and the numbers are growing, along with rates of HIV infection.

In the past ten years, Pakistan officials have been won over by Teen Challenge's undeniable success. Two residential centers in Islamabad house 20 men and 12 women. They offer vocational training, micro loans for small business development, and AIDS awareness presentations for schools, featuring interactive dramas in English and Urdu.

Two more men's centers have opened in Peshawar and Attock, a region known for drug smuggling. The Attock center sits on a six-acre lot between police headquarters and the Attock jail, and supports itself through raising peanuts, melons, wheat, and a herd of 50 goats.

For all of its success, Teen Challenge's Christian focus poses many daunting problems. For example, when two Muslim women were baptized at the Islamabad center, they didn't want to return home, for fear their lives might be in danger. In the "After Care" program, a Bible study for Teen Challenge graduates, men constantly pray for physical protection.

Pakistan Teen Challenge's current director, Mark Brink, writes, "We remain bold in our work but balance this with wisdom. We need your prayers." 🌿

PAKISTAN
Attock Center
3 Graduates

In 2004, *Pentecostal Evangel* reporter Ken Horn visited the new Teen Challenge center in Attock, Pakistan. The 9-month-old program, housed in an old army base, had 15 students, but with plans to expand to 40 or 50.

Turning off the Grand Trunk Road we enter Attock. A military sign reads, "Home of the gunners." We come to the Teen Challenge property and buildings. We are here for the graduation ceremonies of the Attock Men's Center.

The three graduates share their stories. Pervez was addicted to drugs for 14 years. The staff gave him so much love, he says, that he feels they are family. His biological family is also here.

Khalid was 15 years in addiction. He has been here a year and says, "Praise God, I am now well and healthy." The national pastor who recommended these first students stands and expresses his appreciation to the staff. The mother of a student weeps. "I am so happy my son was saved here," she says. A parade of gratitude follows.

A final testimony comes from the man who spent the most time in bondage to drugs—18 years. "Now I have been clean for 15 months," he beams.

"Thank you for giving me back my son," his mother adds emotionally.

Now Mark Brink gives a charge to the graduates. "You're going back into real life," he says. "You must be able to stand with God alone. Will you commit your life to serving Him?"

All three graduates answer, "Yes." 🌿

[Source: Ken Horn, "Pakistan Challenge," *Pentecostal Evangel* 1 Aug 2004, p. 21-22.]

India

Rescued From Slavery
"Janaki"

Janaki (not her real name) and her mother left their home in Nepal when Janaki was 7 years old, after her father admitted to having an affair. When they arrived in Mumbai, India, they met up with an old friend, who duped and robbed them. Taking advantage of their innocence and illiteracy, he sold both mother and daughter to a brothel owner in Kamatipura, where Janaki's mother was immediately put to work.

Janaki was sent to live in a hut with other children, under the supervision of a caretaker employed by the brothel. The hut was crowded and food was scarce, but even worse, Janaki was brutally raped in the night. She managed to escape, and was rescued from the streets by workers from the Children of Jubilee Home.

The mission of Jubilee Home, founded in 1996 by Bombay Teen Challenge, is "to prevent and protect every daughter of a commercial sex worker from entering prostitution in Kamatipura." Janaki is now safe and secure, receiving an education, and she hopes someday to be reunited with her mother. 🖎

NEPAL / INDIA

The Long Road to Freedom
Laxman Pant

Laxman Pant grew up in a Hindu family in Mahendranager, a western region of Nepal. For 14 years, he tried 7 rehab programs throughout Nepal and India, but finally concluded he would never get off of heroin. Then a friend told him about Jesus, and his life began to change.

Laxman came to Lucknow Teen Challenge in India through an outreach program in Nepal, and graduated in December 2007.

While at Teen Challenge, Laxman learned how to make handcrafted jewelry through a job training program called Jewels 4 God. In addition to training students in handcrafts and textiles, Teen Challenge also purchases buffaloes, to sell their milk for profit. 🖎

EURASIA

Nepal

Hopes for a New Center
Rajesh Poudel

Rajesh Poudel's drug use began with cough syrup, but soon progressed to marijuana and heroin. He was bound to his addictions for seven years, before coming to Lucknow Teen Challenge in India. Rajesh converted from Hinduism to Christianity, was baptized, and studied for three years at Lucknow Theological College.

Since July 2007, Rajesh has served as the coordinator of Teen Challenge in Nepal. There is currently no residential program in Nepal, but drug addiction is a growing problem there. With a team of volunteers, Rajesh has brought many Nepalese addicts to Lucknow for recovery. He hopes, with the Lord's favor, to open a new residential center within the next two years. ❧

> With a team of volunteers, Rajesh has brought many Nepalese addicts to Lucknow for recovery.

Singapore

A Mother's Last Hope
Ling Whee Yew (Calvin)

Calvin Ling knew many elaborate tricks to keep his parents from discovering his drug use. He demanded extra money for brand-name clothes, as well as his own phone line and cell phone, so his calls could be private. To avoid suspicion, he left his bedroom lights, stereo, and air conditioning running whenever he snuck out to get high. When his parents sent him to boarding school, to escape the bad influence of his friends, Calvin simply stopped going.

The last straw for his mother, Peh Ah Koon, was finding marijuana in his room. She knew that Calvin hung out with a bad crowd and often got into fights, but seeing drugs in her own house made her realize just how indulgent she had been. Broken-hearted, she called the police and turned in her son. Calvin was sentenced to four months in prison.

Calvin's parents appealed the sentence, and he was temporarily released to enter Teen Challenge. During their first few visits to the center, Calvin lashed out angrily at his parents, blaming them for ruining his future. But on their fifth trip, his attitude had completely changed. He apologized for the pain he had caused, and told them he had found peace through a relationship with Jesus.

As a gift of gratitude, Calvin gave his mother a Bible. By the time he graduated from the program in 1996, both his mother and younger sister Christine had accepted Christ, and his father Michael followed shortly after.

Singapore's justice system is notoriously harsh against drug offenders, but after seeing the change in Calvin's life, judge Yong Pung How lightened his sentence to two years of probation. "You were very lucky," he said. "You have a very good mother who has taken the trouble to try and sort out your life for you." ❧

Kyrgyzstan
Good Neighbors
Eldiar and Ayzada

Eldiar and his wife Ayzada lived just a few houses down from the new Teen Challenge center in Serafimovka, a small village about an hour east of Kyrgyzstan's capital, Bishkek. In the spring of 2006, Eldiar asked if he could meet with the directors, Murray and Karen Golder, and they invited him to dinner. The Teen Challenge students cooked up a big pot of plov, a traditional rice dish with carrots and meat, while Eldiar told his story.

Growing up, Eldiar had heard many stories from people in the village about what Christians were like. They killed animals, the villagers said, then drank the blood and poured it on themselves as they ran around at night. He figured the stories weren't true, but had to see for himself.

After a night of conversation and laughter, Eldiar and Ayzada decided that the Golders were actually pretty normal. As Eldiar put it, "You have ten fingers and ten toes just like us!"

Eldiar then told them about his own religious background. He had spent time in prison as a young man, and there converted to Islam, to keep from bringing shame on his family. For five years, he prayed five times daily and tried hard to turn his life around. His constant prayer was that Allah would show himself to him.

That night the Golders prayed with Eldiar, that God would show him the truth, and over the following weeks, Teen Challenge workers spoke with him regularly. By the third week, he had decided to become a follower of Jesus—no small decision in a culture that associates being Kyrgyz with being Muslim.

A few weeks later, the Teen Challenge staff invited Eldiar to a three-day conference in a nearby village. He agreed to go, hungry to learn more about his new faith. He returned with exciting news—one night, he had dreamed of a church with a bright light shining in the window, and from inside the light, Jesus had spoken to him. For Eldiar, it was confirmation that God had finally answered his lifelong prayer.

Eldiar and Ayzada made their new faith public in July 2006. Murray Golder baptized them in a small outdoor ceremony at the Teen Challenge center. ❧

Second Chances
Jamaalbek & Valentin

One of Teen Challenge Kyrgyzstan's biggest challenges is getting men to make a full one-year commitment to the program. Student dropout rates within the first few weeks are very high, which can frustrate the staff. But some of these dropouts return, and show more progress in their second try. Here are two of these two-time success stories.

Jamaalbek, a former history professor, lived on the rough streets of Bishkek as an alcoholic for 15 years. He stayed at Teen Challenge for only six days before going back to the streets, but the love and care he experienced led him back to Teen Challenge three months later.

When Jamaalbek reached the halfway point of the program, his family, in accordance with their culture, sent a middleman to check on his progress. The representative gave them a positive report, so Jamaalbek's mother, sister, and other family members came to visit, their first reunion in many years. In response to God's goodness in his life, Jamaalbek started writing poetry in Kyrgyz, which he set to music as hymns.

Valentin was a father of two who had divorced and struggled for many years with alcohol. He stayed at Teen Challenge for nine months, but dropped out with only a short time left to complete the program. Immediately, he went back to his hard-drinking lifestyle.

Valentin's mother was a strong believer in Jesus, and when she fell ill and seemed close to death, she asked Teen Challenge to find her son and bring him home. Teen Challenge staff hunted him down and literally plucked him off the street, with a message that God loved him and his family needed him.

Valentin saw his mother through her illness, then decided to give Teen Challenge another try. This time, he turned all of his problems over to God, and found that doing so made a difficult program easier to bear. After graduation, he served as Teen Challenge Kyrgyzstan's very first intern. ❧

 A mother's illness and a mother's love brought Valentin to Christ

EURASIA

Uzbekistan
Near Death Experience
Sergey N.

Sergey started drinking at age 16, and soon became a terror to his family. He stole from the house, constantly fought with his parents, and embarrassed them in front of relatives. During one fight, he pushed his father down the stairs and broke his leg.

Finally, Sergey's mother Svetlana went over the edge. When Sergey came home drunk, she poured a can of gasoline on him and pulled out a match. Sergey's screams brought the neighbors, who pulled Svetlana away. Her only hope then was that he would die of liver failure, and put an end to the nightmare.

Sergey entered Teen Challenge in 2005 on the advice of a friend, and his entire life transformed. After completing the program, he went through training to become a counselor and teacher.

Best of all, he and his mother learned to forgive each other. Svetlana now sees her neighbors' intervention on that fateful night as heaven-sent. She says, "I cannot describe with words the pain we have gone through because of his addictions; neither can I describe the joy that I have for the freedom my son found through Teen Challenge." ❧

UZBEKISTAN

A Mother's Changed Heart
Sergey T.

Sergey's father died at the dinner table, while drinking a bottle of vodka, and his mother Valentina took two full-time jobs to support her five children. With no adults to steer him on the right path, Sergey started drinking at age 7, and kept going for the next 35 years.

"Sergey's life was a mess," Valentina recalls. "He went to the military and came home closed, then he went to prison and came home even more closed."

Valentina, Sergey, and the other siblings all became Christians in 1997 and started attending church together. But Sergey's drinking didn't stop. When he came home late at night, his mother would yell at him and call him a useless drunk. Finally, Sergey said, "Mom, when you start to love me and look at me with different eyes, I will change."

Valentina's attitude toward her son changed as she grew in her Christian faith, but Sergey's addiction only got worse. He lived on the streets, and every week Valentina asked the church to pray for her son. Their prayers were finally answered in 2005, when a Teen Challenge graduate met Sergey on the street and showed him where to go for an interview.

Sergey now works as Teen Challenge's education coordinator, and he plans to start attending college in 2008. "God has restored our entire family," Valentina says, "and our pain has been turned to joy." ❧

Macau, China

Two Fathers
Xu Kangzhi (Ah Chek)

Shortly after Xu Kangzhi ("Ah Chek" to his friends) was born, his father's animal husbandry business began to fail. He blamed the bad luck on his newborn son. As Ah Chek grew older, his father beat him mercilessly, and humiliated him at every opportunity.

At age 12, Ah Chek reached his breaking point. When his father burned his mouth with a cigarette, Ah Chek hit him with a chair. He ran out as his father shouted, "Don't come back!"

To survive on the streets of Macau, Ah Chek joined a gang called the Black Society. He fought, robbed, and committed arson for them, and took drugs to numb the fear of getting caught.

The drug use led to addiction, and soon Ah Chek was bouncing in and out of prisons and rehab centers, both in Macau and mainland China. In one rehab program, one that wasn't working, a missionary told him about Teen Challenge.

At Teen Challenge, Ah Chek learned from staff members who cared for him in a way no one ever had. They disciplined him for wrong actions, but with love, and he saw that they genuinely wanted to ease his pain. They told him to cry to Jesus for help, and he did.

As Ah Chek grew to know the Lord better, he felt the Holy Spirit prompt him to ask: "How can I ask my Heavenly Father for forgiveness if I don't forgive my father on earth?" For the first time since childhood, he returned home, and in that visit reconciled with his father. Ah Chek and his wife Elisa have since gone back often to spend time with the family. Ah Check now serves as the director of the Teen Challenge program in Macau, China. ✌

KOREA

△ TEEN CHALLENGE KOREA
Jonathan Aird and his wife, Sungjoo, are pioneering a new Teen Challenge in Seoul, Korea.

The Spirit of the Lord is on me,

because he has anointed me
to preach good news to the poor.

He has sent me to proclaim freedom for the prisoners and recovery of sight for the blind,

to release the oppressed,
to proclaim the year of the Lord's favor.

LUKE 4:18-19 NIV

AFRICA

Sipho

Swaziland

AFRICA

Kenya

Long Year Off
Dan Owuor

In Kenya, students graduating from secondary school usually take a year off before going to college. Dan Owuor spent that year, 2000, going on excursions with friends, chewing miraa (also known as khat, an addictive stimulant), drinking whiskey, and doing hard drugs. His one year off turned into several.

In 2003, Dan got into a drunken fight with his girlfriend's mother, and her sons tied his hands to keep him from getting violent. After that, Dan resolved never to use alcohol again, but two weeks later, he was drunk again. After another binge, he woke up in the hospital surrounded by family. His brother Fred told him he had been hit by a car and nearly killed, and that the family had been praying all night.

In the hospital, Dan gave his life to Christ, grateful that God had saved him. He realized quickly, though, that just being a Christian wouldn't be enough to turn him from his lifestyle. After his father's death, Dan wanted to help his family financially, but all his money was wasted on liquor and women.

He asked his mom to find a rehab facility, and she sent him to the only one she could afford. Teen Challenge Kenya, which sustains itself financially through donations and student work projects, offers its services free of charge.

In the program, Dan discovered not only loving counsel and care from the staff, but also the free gift of God's grace. Dan was the first student in this brand-new program, which officially opened its doors on February 5, 2008. ❧

∧ Current home of Teen Challenge Kenya, which officially opened for ministry on February 5, 2008.

∧ This ½ acre plot will be the future home of Teen Challenge Kenya. Pictured here are (left to right), Ben Luyali, TC staff, Lucas Orimba, TC staff, Joseph Karanja, TC staff, Dan Owuor, first student at TC Kenya, and John Martin, Executive Director.

KENYA

Dead-End Job
Daniel Kamau

Growing up in a single-parent family with ten children, Daniel Kamau often skipped meals when his mother couldn't afford them. Still, he managed to make it through primary school with high marks, and was invited to secondary school. To pay the school fees, Daniel found a sponsor at his church, and Mrs. Kamau took up a side business, buying vegetables at a Nairobi market and reselling them in their village.

Daniel graduated from secondary school, but his grades weren't high enough for college. After a year of unemployment, in desperation, he took a job in Nairobi with a brewer of illegal beer, called changaa. Drinking beer was part of the job, but soon he was smoking, too, and frequently getting drunk. Between shifts, he often slept on the road or in drainage ditches.

After 15 years of this life, a friend told Daniel about a new Teen Challenge program he thought could help. As one of the first students in the program, Daniel recommitted his life to Christ.

The prospects of gainful employment in Kenya are bleak for the majority of young people without college degrees. But Daniel and others at the Teen Challenge center are trusting God for their futures, and for their nation. ❧

Ethiopia
Up from the Streets
Wondwossen Tegabu

As a young man living in a rural area, Wondwossen Tegabu ran away with his girlfriend to Ethiopia's capital city, Addis Ababa. They didn't have enough money to survive for long, so Wondwossen ran away from her, too, and lived on the street. He smoked hashish, sniffed benzene, and stole wallets and briefcases in the train station for money.

Once, while drunk, he climbed on top of a moving train and fell. The train severed his right leg. He was reduced to begging by day and stealing at night.

Wondwossen came to an Addis Hiwot (New Life) Teen Challenge after seeing a friend become a Christian and conquer his addiction. There, at a chapel service, he saw dozens of street boys singing and praying at full volume. In March of 1998, after nine years of suffering on the street, he gave his life to Jesus. Today he works at the New Life center, where he trains students in tailoring. 🌿

ETHIOPIA

Hope for Girls on the Street
Tigist Demeke

Tigist Demeke ran away from her uncle's abusive home after she was raped by a cousin. But her life on the streets of Dilla, Ethiopia, wasn't much better. She begged for food, used whatever drugs she could find, and slept with men without regard for pregnancy, AIDS, or other STDs.

At the invitation of a group of Teen Challenge workers, Tigist entered the New Life Teen Challenge Development Program. For the past ten years, this program has sought to improve the lives of street people in Ethiopia, especially girls from ages 12 to 28, by educating them in the areas of reproductive health, HIV-AIDS, and employment.

Tigist describes the education she received at New Life Teen Challenge: "I used to think that I was hopeless, so I engaged in alcohol and drug abuse and unprotected sex. Now I am relieved from addiction and risky sexual behavior because I have got counseling, HIV-AIDS knowledge, and the skills to protect myself and help others who are on the street. I used to earn money through ways that put my life in danger, but now I work as a peer educator."

Now 21 years old, Tigist says she plans to protect herself by waiting for a husband who is willing to go through counseling and medical testing with her. As a peer educator, she facilitates group discussions among those who come for counseling, stages dramas for the outreach ministry, and refers those she meets on the street to Teen Challenge. 🌿

AFRICA

Swaziland
A Young Evangelist
Manqoba Diamini

Manqoba Diamini spoke in public for the first time at age 13, when he announced to thousands of people at Swaziland's 2002 National Day of Prayer that he was HIV positive. He told the crowd in Prince of Wales Stadium that only God, working through changed lives, was the answer to the AIDS crisis in Africa.

Earlier that year, a Teen Challenge staff worker named Carol Cooper had met Manqoba at a police station. He had been abandoned by his parents, and was sick and tiny for his age. Carol took him to the Teen Challenge Lighthouse Care Centre, to live with seven other children who were either orphans or addicted to drugs.

For six years, doctors have told Manqoba that his time on earth is short. His response has been to minister to others, touring with Teen Challenge as a spokesman for AIDS awareness. ❦

Swaziland
A Life of Death
Bongani Mgodloli

In Swaziland, death from AIDS is a way of life for many families. Bongani Mgodloli's family was no exception. As a young boy, he watched his mother Nelisiwe slowly waste away, then his father Sibusiso. Bongani and his two brothers moved in with their aunt and uncle, who lived in a mud hut with three children of their own and were unemployed.

With no food in the house, the Mgodloli brothers searched a nearby forest. When they came across a bee hive, Bongani climbed up to it, anxious to scoop out the honey inside. The bees swarmed, and within minutes their two-year-old cousin had been stung to death. In anger, Bongani's aunt and uncle beat him, denied him food, and tried to drive him away.

Eventually, a social welfare officer intervened. The youngest brother was sent to an orphanage and Bongani to Teen Challenge.

Bongani came to Teen Challenge violent and full of rage. His aunt and uncle died of AIDS shortly after, and Bongani believed they had cursed him, since he had not asked their forgiveness. He developed a fear of bees and other insects, and a fear of relationships—since everyone he loved had died. Only the undying love of God, working through his people, could give him hope.

Bongani accepted Christ at Teen Challenge, and came to see that his deep anger stemmed from a past full of rejection and loss. He also saw that God did not hold him responsible for all the death that surrounded him, but planned to give him new life. Bongani attends school now, and aspires to become a youth pastor, to bring the same hope to other young men in Swaziland. ❦

Jose Mario and his wife (left) with three of the girls in the Teen Challenge program in Cacuaca, Angola with Domingos Cristovao (right), the national director of Teen Challenge Angola.

Jose Mario

Hard to Kill

Jose Mario had tried to quit using drugs so many times, he finally gave up and decided to kill himself. He drank poison, but it didn't work. Then he threw himself in front of a speeding car, but he survived the attempt.

The turning point for Jose came while he was in prison for drug-related crimes. Pastor Domingos Cristovao, the director of Teen Challenge Angola, came to visit and told him about the freedom he could find in Christ. After his jail sentence, Jose entered the Teen Challenge program in Benguela, and experienced that freedom for himself.

After graduation, Jose continued to work for the ministry and eventually became the program director at Benguela. He and his wife are now the directors of a Teen Challenge center for children in Cacuaca, Angola. ✍

The first Teen Challenge in Swaziland started in a mud hut. Since then, it has grown into one of the largest Teen Challenge ministries in Africa.

169

Guinea-Bissau

"We Will Bury Our Son . . . and You Will Go"
Domingos Te

The day before the beginning of a four-week Global Teen Challenge leadership training conference in Lisbon, Portugal, coordinator Duane Henders received a strange phone call. A pastor named Domingos Te introduced himself, and said he was waiting at the Lisbon airport. "I am here for the training," he said.

"But you didn't sign up for the training," Duane said. "You didn't send in your registration money."

"No," Domingos said, "but I am here for the training." Domingos explained that he was from Guinea-Bissau, a former Portugese colony in West Africa. He had read about the conference in a Teen Challenge brochure.

On the drive back from the airport, Domingos shared the rest of his story. He had pastored a church of 200 members in Guinea-Bissau, until reading a newspaper story about drug addicts who had poured gasoline on a man and burned him to death. Domingos and his wife felt God calling them to do something. They resigned from their small-town church and moved to a drug-infested neighborhood in Bissau, the capital city.

For the past six months, Domingos said, "I've just been trying to make friends with drug addicts." Six of them were coming regularly to a Bible study, but the Tes realized they needed training on how to lead them out of addiction. When they heard about the four-week training in Lisbon, they knew one of them had to go.

But finances were extremely tight. "My church said we are crazy," Domingos told Duane. "They won't support us, and my denomination won't help." The Tes put all of their resources into a single plane ticket to Portugal.

Shortly before Domingos was scheduled to leave, his 18-month-old son got sick. The local hospital didn't have the necessary medication—their only option was to buy it at full price from a pharmacy. The Tes searched the city, but the only medicine they could find was far too expensive. The day before Domingos was scheduled to leave, his son died.

He told his wife, "I can't go to Portugal for training." She corrected him: "You must go, because God has called us to this work with drug addicts, and we don't know what we're doing. So we will bury our son, and you get on the plane and go for training."

After hearing the story, Duane immediately offered to cover all of Domingos' expenses with a scholarship. Teen Challenge Portugal offered to help get his ministry off the ground.

Upon his return, Domingos pestered the mayor of Quinhamel until she gave him two acres of land to build the nation's only addiction recovery program. The Tes and a group of volunteers built the building one brick at a time, making the adobe bricks as they went.

Today, Teen Challenge of Guinea-Bissau has over 50 students and is planting a church in Bissau in one of the worst areas of the capital, because other churches are not reaching out to these people. Duane Henders calls the ministry "a phenomenal work that has been carved out of nothing." ❧

Shot to the Heart

Ricardo Heilbron

The .357 magnum bullet tore through Ricardo Heilbron's chest and lodged just seven millimeters from his heart. All alone in a puddle of his own blood, he thought life was over.

But God had other plans. Ricardo woke up in the hospital, where he met a pretty nurse who continually invited him to church. When he had recovered enough, Ricardo went with her, and that very night prayed to accept Jesus. He saw clearly everything that had been stolen from him in life, and he knew it was time for change.

But Ricardo had a dilemma. He was a drug dealer for the 28's, the largest and most violent gang in Cape Town, South Africa. Over the past eight years, after a grueling initiation, he had been expelled from school, stabbed in the back, and sent to Pollsmoor prison. The only way out now was for the gang to kill him or his family.

Ricardo cried out, "Lord, I want to change and serve you but I can't do it here." The next morning, a loud voice in his head woke him up: "Leave now and I will make a way!" Ricardo didn't understand, but he obeyed. Though still wounded by the bullet lodged near his heart, he climbed over a wall and fled. As he ran down the road, a car pulled up beside him. The man inside said, "Get in. I know a place where you can get help."

At Teen Challenge, Ricardo found healing for his addictions and freedom from the bondage of violence and sin. He now works on staff and helps rescue others trapped in gangs. 🔖

A Timely Tent Meeting

Anthea Groenewaldt

Anthea Groenewaldt grew up watching her mother smoke Mandrax, a depressant combined with marijuana, in the shack where they lived behind her step-grandfather's house. She watched as her stepfather verbally and physically attacked her mother, and starting at age 11, she was sexually abused herself.

Her mother warned her against using drugs, but Anthea followed her example rather than her words. She smoked marijuana at age 14, then moved on to Mandrax, speed, and heroin. She dated a 21-year-old man who said he worshipped Satan—and Anthea told him she wanted to try that, too.

With her boyfriend, Anthea's life plunged into a weird, nightmarish world of animal sacrifices, blood-drinking rituals, and sexual orgies. She broke into homes for money to support her drug habits. She slept in graveyards, praying for demons to enter her, and covered her body with tattoos and piercings.

Meanwhile, Anthea's mother had given her life to Christ and stopped using drugs. At a tent meeting near her home, the director of Teen Challenge invited the crowd: "If you have a child addicted to drugs, bring them to the front. If they are not here, you come anyway."

At that very moment, Anthea was returning home, and she saw her mother in the tent, running to the front. Anthea stepped inside the tent, and a woman sitting nearby told her to go up, too. Anthea cursed at her, then suddenly blacked out.

When she awoke on the ground, Anthea was surrounded by six pastors, all praying loudly. She tried to get up and run away, but passed out again. It felt as if a physical struggle were tearing her body apart.

Eventually, Anthea got away from the tent meeting and went home to smoke more Mandrax. But something strange happened then—for some reason, she felt guilty. Anthea hadn't felt any guilt for the past two years, as she robbed others and led Satanic rituals. But now, smoking a joint was too much. She went to Teen Challenge the next day.

In the program, Anthea met Jesus personally. He gave her a freedom that Satanism, and the demons she had prayed to, never could. The rage and hunger for power that consumed her were replaced by peace and the power of God to heal and restore. Anthea continues to work at Teen Challenge, which leads outreaches to men and women trapped by addiction and cults. 🔖

"My addiction left me in a coma when I was 19.

Jesus has set me free from the bondage of drug addiction and

delivered me from a life of crime, violence, and hatred.

He has restored my family to me. He has healed and purified

my mind and body. He has taught me how to love again.

For this I thank the Lord Jesus Christ – and Teen Challenge."

Jacob Hill

Australia

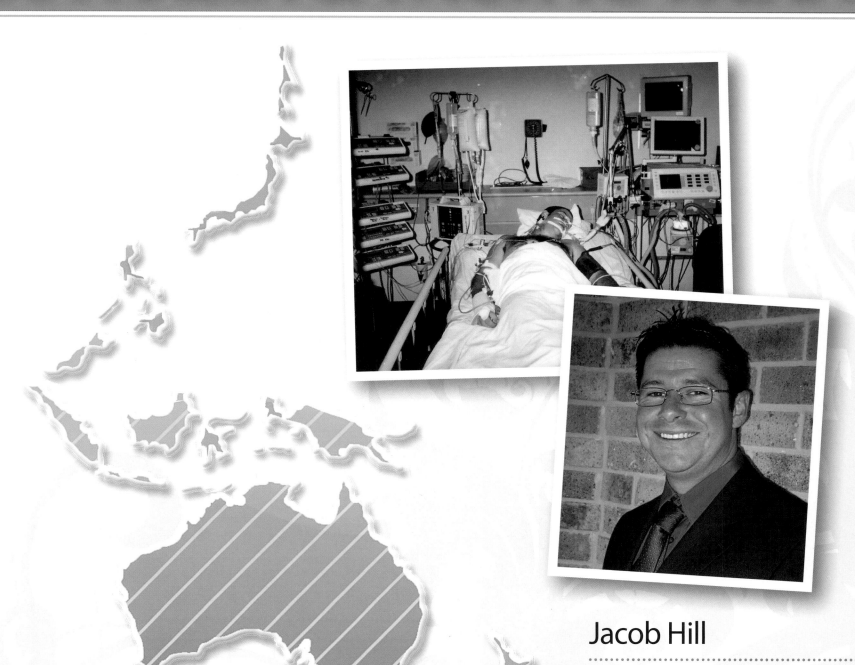

Jacob Hill

Australia

AUSTRALIA & PACIFIC ISLANDS

Japan

Healing in a Foreign Land
Kazuhiko Furukawa

Kazuhiko Furukawa didn't speak much English, but the staff and students at Teen Challenge in Perth, Australia welcomed him with open arms. For ten years, Kazza had been struggling with an addiction to anti-depressants and sleeping pills, the result of a car accident in Japan that left him partially crippled and numb on one side. He came to Australia in 2004, but after his plans to live on a ranch fell through, a local Japanese church referred him to Teen Challenge.

What astonished Kazza most about Teen Challenge students was their stories of mental and physical healing. Over time, he saw a miracle in his own life, as a new relationship with Christ healed his depression, and the physical after-effects of his accident improved.

Today, Kazza considers Teen Challenge of Western Australia his "second home," and its Executive Director, Malcolm Smith, has preached at Kazza's home church, Yamato Calvary Chapel in Tokyo. After graduation, Kazza and his family moved back to Japan to help establish a new Teen Challenge youth center. ❧

Philippines

Missionary Kid
A.J. Del Rosario

A.J. Del Rosario's parents were Christian missionaries, who often moved the family back and forth from Texas to the Philippines. At age 14, A.J. decided that everything they did was fake, that nothing mattered, and that he might as well indulge his pleasures. First he tried marijuana, then crystal meth, and soon was kicked out of school.

A.J. parents responded by sending him to an 8-month training program for future missionaries. For A.J., it was a chance to use drugs without their interference. He went to Hong Kong and China on a missions trip, and found drugs there, too.

But A.J. couldn't keep his addiction hidden for long. His father found him after a four-day crystal meth binge, and sent him to a mental institution. As he detoxed, A.J. had intense dreams about hell, and for the first time cried out to Jesus. After a few more unsuccessful attempts to handle the problem on their own, A.J. and his family decided to try Teen Challenge.

A.J. had never done as much hard work as he did in the Teen Challenge program, but in the midst of physical struggle, he promised his life to God. When he wanted to give up, he remembered the faith of his childhood, and everything God had already done for him. When asked what the future might hold for his life, he says, "I'll let God decide on that." ❧

NEW ZEALAND

Work in Progress
Ben

Ben grew up in a Christian home, where his father worked as a teacher and his mother was a stay-at-home mom. But when his family moved to the countryside, Ben stopped working hard in school and found a new, rebellious crowd to hang out with.

Just before his 16th birthday, Ben was arrested for stealing a car, carrying a knife, and breaking and entering. Over the next three years, he would earn 11 more criminal convictions, as life spun out of control. He dropped out of school, held a string of jobs, and was fired from most of them. Along the way, he tried every drug he could find.

In court for one of his crimes, a judge offered to give Ben a suspended sentence if he attended rehabilitation. A friend's father found Teen Challenge online.

> "God is changing me from the inside out," he says, "and I am looking forward to what the future may hold."

Ben is now nearing the end of the Teen Challenge program, where he has rediscovered his relationship with God. He knows he still has a long road ahead, but he is grateful that his parents never stopped supporting him. "God is changing me from the inside out," he says, "and I am looking forward to what the future may hold." ❧

New Zealand

Time Out
Terry

....

Terry grew up in Porirua, New Zealand, the third oldest in a family of ten children. He got involved with a gang, started drinking and doing drugs, and at age 18 served his first of many jail terms.

By age 25, Terry was desperate for help. His sister's friends invited him to church, and there he started to turn his life around. His past wouldn't go away so easily, though, and Terry had to serve yet another prison sentence.

A pastor from his new church visited him in jail and told him about Teen Challenge. Six months later, Terry is now halfway through the program. He calls this time of life his "time out," and he plans to work in building construction after graduation. ❧

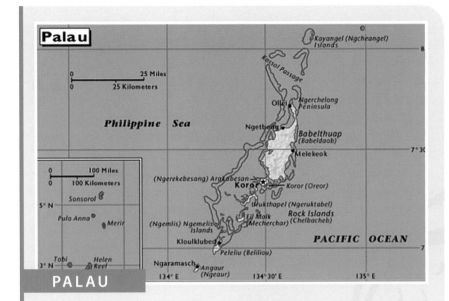

PALAU

The Smallest and Youngest

With only 177 square miles and 21,000 people, Palau is the fourth smallest nation in the world. It is also one of the youngest—in 2007, Palauans celebrated their 13th Independence Day.

But this South Pacific island's drug problem, unfortunately, is not small at all. Palau ranks among the highest in per-capita alcohol consumption of all the islands in Micronesia, and suicide rates among its young people are unusually high. The most popular drug is the traditional betel nut, an addictive stimulant that can cause mouth cancer, similar to chewing tobacco.

The Palau government offers drug rehabilitation through its Behavioral Health program, but many of its patients have made repeat visits, as they continue to struggle with addiction. As Dale Eytzen, head of the Teen Challenge Palau Steering Committee puts it, "We need Teen Challenge in Palau, and we need it yesterday!" With the help of local churches, Teen Challenge of Palau plans to open a residential addiction recovery program in 2008. ❧

 Palau ranks among the highest in per-capita alcohol consumption of all the islands in Micronesia, and suicide rates among its young people are unusually high.

AUSTRALIA & PACIFIC ISLANDS

Australia

Don't Look in the Mirror
Jenny

Despite earning straight A's in high school, excelling in sports, and working part-time as a model, Jenny suffered from extremely low self-esteem. To win her friends' approval, she started smoking, binge drinking, and using drugs, and she made excuses when her boyfriend John beat her up.

One night while coming home from a pub, John broke her nose with a vicious punch. At the hospital later that night, nurses removed the mirrors from Jenny's room, so she wouldn't see herself while in her drug-induced psychosis.

Desperate to help their daughter, Jenny's parents took her to a "drug summit" at their church. One of the speakers, a Teen Challenge graduate named Jade McSherry Lewis (whose story is also included in this book), inspired Jenny to want something better from her life. A few weeks later, as Jenny faced charges for drug-related crimes, the judge sentenced her to a rehab program. She chose Teen Challenge.

Jenny says that the main thing Teen Challenge instilled in her was a healthy attitude toward herself—she deserved God's condemnation, but received instead his love and favor. With that understanding, she regained her sanity, her health, her family relationships, and her plans for the future.

Jenny completed the Teen Challenge program in 2002 and will soon graduate from college. She works as a youth leader in her church and visits high schools to share her story. "In the end," she tells students, "the people I took drugs to please were the ones who hurt me the most. Now I have faith in God, who has given me a new life with the courage, strength, and wisdom to live it." ❧

AUSTRALIA

Witness on Rollerblades
Casey

After Casey's mother died, her father in Chile didn't want to take her in, so Casey was placed in the care of Family and Children's Services. At age 14, feeling that she'd lost her only home, Casey gave herself up to marijuana and speed.

One afternoon in Joondalup, a lakeside suburb of Perth, Casey sat crying and feeling hopeless. A girl named Chantel glided up on rollerblades and asked what was wrong. Chantel said that she had once been a heroin addict, but had found freedom in Jesus Christ. Casey didn't usually listen to Christians, since they made her feel bad, but this girl seemed so happy and willing to help.

When Casey came to Teen Challenge, a photo on the wall caught her eye—it was Chantel, with a note that she had graduated from the program. Throughout the program, as she accepted Christ and made difficult changes in her life, Casey constantly remembered that happy girl on rollerblades, a reminder of where she wanted to go with her own life.

Near the end of the program, in 2002, Casey participated in a 700-kilometer bike marathon from Esperance to Perth, to spread the word about Teen Challenge. She said, "I hope that I can be an encouragement, in the same way that Chantel was an example of God's power and an encouragement to me." ❧

Australia

Olympic Dreams

Jade McSherry Lewis

Jade McSherry's ultimate dream was to run in the Olympics. And she was well on her way—as captain of her high school track team, she won medals at international competitions in Singapore and Malaysia.

But at age 16, Jade took time off from training to focus on academics, and she hung out with a new set of friends. Many of them did drugs, had casual sex, and constantly went to raves. Jade went with them, and tried Ecstasy and LSD. It was okay, she thought, since she was just experimenting. Then she tried speed, and everything slid downhill.

After that, all that mattered was shooting up. When speed lost its thrill, Jade turned to heroin. When she got sick, she simply used more, and shoplifted for money. Her grades slipped, she lost weight, and the thought of returning to the track team became impossible. Her new boyfriend was abusive, and when her parents put a stop to the relationship, their lives were threatened.

Jade first heard about Teen Challenge from that same boyfriend, who showed up one day claiming that Jesus had changed his life. He hadn't finished the program, and he didn't stay clean, but Jade

could see that something powerful had taken hold of him.

Jade wanted to stop using drugs, but she didn't want to be brainwashed by a group of crazy Christians. She resolved to go through the Teen Challenge program without letting anyone convert her.

The hardest part of the program, besides detoxing from heroin, was facing the shame and guilt of her wasted life—her sports, her schooling, her Olympic dreams. Her new friends Monique and Channy suggested that she turn to Jesus for help. "Jesus can help me!" Jade cried in frustration. "Not unless he's got a secret stash for me to share!"

But rejecting their advice didn't make the pain go away. Reluctantly, she knelt with Channy and prayed, "God, if you are real, then I invite you to come into my heart and help me live my life."

God took up her invitation, and Jade grew in her newfound faith, especially through the mentoring of staff and other students. Near the end of the program, she and Channy prayed about ways to speak to more young people about drugs. In April 2000, they organized a 700-kilometer bike marathon across Australia, with Teen Challenge staff giving presentations at schools along the way.

Jade spent three years on staff at Teen Challenge, and now works full-time as a motivational speaker. She and her husband Tristan Lewis have reached thousands of high school students with their message of warning and hope. 🌿

[Source: Jade Lewis, *Golden Haze: Jade's Story* (Carlisle, Western Australia: Print Hotline, 2004).]

A Missionary at Home

Vivien Wilson

As a nurse working with the Queensland Aboriginal Health Program, Vivien Wilson always had a strong desire to help others. After recommitting herself to the Christian faith of her childhood, Vivien decided to take her passion and skills around the world. She spent several years working for World Vision, bringing medical care to war and disaster zones like Ethiopia, Mozambique, Rwanda, and Liberia.

In 2001, while preparing for a trip to the Sudan, Vivien read a newspaper article about the town of Papunya in Australia's Northern Territory. The article focused on a young boy, one of many, who was addicted to sniffing gasoline. Vivien felt God tugging on her heart to stay home.

For the next two years, Vivien worked as a nurse in the Northern Territory town of Alice Springs. Then in 2003, tragedy struck—a young man she had worked with, Jayden Price, was murdered. Jayden's mother organized a memorial concert in Alice Springs, and invited Teen Challenge leaders from across the country to speak, determined that Jayden's death would not be in vain. From that concert, and meetings between Vivien and Teen Challenge leaders, Teen Challenge Centralia was born.

From her years of experience in the Northern Territory, Vivien crafted presentations and curriculum materials that would appeal specifically to Aboriginal culture. Where past anti-drug efforts focused on brain damage and other physical problems caused by sniffing, Vivien emphasized the spiritual nature of addiction and the power of prayer. She also made Teen Challenge's presentations more visual, to capture the attention of young people who didn't have high literacy levels.

So far, her approach has worked. The community has rallied around her cause, as parents come forward with stories of how prayer saved their children, and Vivien reports that the children themselves are as eager to learn as ever. Teen Challenge Centralia currently offers outpatient services and education, and Vivien plans to open a residential facility soon. 🌿

"Teen Challenge offers hope to every young person
who has lost their way through drugs or alcohol abuse. Its success lies in the
spiritual transformation which takes place in those being rehabilitated
and it is my prayer that there will always be sufficient public support
to help this ministry rescue the perishing."

Howard Cooke

Governor General of Jamaica

Jose Martinez

Dominican Republic

AMERICAS

Winnipeg, Canada

Single Dad
Sean Goulet

Sean Goulet decided to get help after his girlfriend left him to raise their 3-month-old son Anthony alone. Sean was in no position to care for a baby. He was 19 years old, an alcoholic and pothead whose prescription drug use was starting to take over his life. He had attempted suicide and spent time in hospitals and jails.

Desperate, Sean stumbled into a church and went to the front at the altar call. "I need Jesus," he told the pastor as he cried.

For a few years after Sean accepted Christ, life looked up. He made friends at church and found a good Christian school for his son to attend. At age 9, Anthony accepted Christ for himself.

The one area of his life Sean hadn't cleaned up was his heavy drinking. Whenever his spiritual life felt dead, he turned to the bottle. Eventually he grew disillusioned with his whole faith, and decided he needed something more. Soon he was hopelessly addicted to cocaine.

 "I need Jesus," he told the pastor as he cried.

Sean kept up appearances at church, or at least thought he did. But one day over coffee, his pastor gave him a shocking ultimatum. If Sean didn't stop using drugs, he said, Anthony was destined to become just like him, or worse. Sean got angry, but then the pastor said something that triggered a change in his heart—he told him to go to Teen Challenge.

Two weeks later, with Anthony safely at the home of another Christian family, Sean packed his belongings and moved into the Teen Challenge center in downtown Winnipeg.

In the program, Sean found himself often annoyed with the immature students and hard-nosed staff, but came to see it was the result of his own self-righteous attitude. He also reconciled with his father, whom he had blamed for so many of his own problems.

A year after graduating from Teen Challenge, Sean married Jenny, another Teen Challenge graduate and single parent. Along with Anthony and Jenny's son Eric, the Goulets are now a complete family. Sean is in his second year of Bible college, and currently pioneering a boys' club and drop-in center in Winnipeg. ❦

BRITISH COLUMBIA, CANADA

Advice from a Mountie
Christine Hunt

As a child, Christine Hunt grew up in British Columbia feeling lost and confused. Though she attended church on Sundays she never had a personal relationship with Jesus. As a teenager, she turned to drugs and abusive relationships for acceptance. By age 22, she was living homeless on the streets of Main and Hastings in Vancouver, Canada. Her family in Ontario took her back in when it appeared she had stopped using drugs, but in reality, she had simply switched her addiction to alcohol and prescription medication.

She relapsed again into IV drugs and was back on the streets in British Columbia, when a Royal Canadian Mounted Police officer told Christine that the only way to find freedom was through Jesus Christ. In response, she went back to church, gave her life to the Lord, and entered the Teen Challenge women's center in Abbotsford.

At Teen Challenge, Christine found the acceptance and love she had been craving since her teens. She also found freedom from the bondage of addiction. After graduation, she became an intern through the Leaders in Training program. Christine now works as the Intake and Outreach Coordinator for the women's center, and recently travelled to Uganda as a short-term missionary. ❦

Change of Heart
Tim Woudstra

Just before going into the Teen Challenge program, Tim Woudstra signed his wife's divorce papers. She'd had enough of his addiction to crack cocaine, along with his lies, thefts, neglect of their children, and constant unemployment.

As Tim moved through the program, he gave his life to Christ and shifted his priorities. At the same time, his wife's heart began to change as well. When Tim graduated on April 28, 2006, he was reunited with his whole family. Tim now works as a loan officer with a credit union in Athabasca, Alberta. ✷

50
CELEBRATING FIFTY YEARS OF MIRACLES
ANNIVERSARY CELEBRATION
TEEN CHALLENGE INTERNATIONAL

Ontario, Canada

The Gospel in Pictures
Troy McLeod

As a native First Nation Canadian, Troy McLeod spent his early childhood on a reservation in Newaashiiniigmiing, which means "land surrounded by water" in the Ojibwa language. But when his parents separated and moved away, Troy began to rebel, smoking marijuana and getting involved with petty crime.

In junior high, Troy was picked up by the police for theft and given two weeks at a detention center run by Mennonite Christians. There, Troy read the Bible for the first time—a Picture Bible for children. Before he left, a staff member gave him a Picture Bible of his own, and Troy read it cover to cover.

But his lifestyle didn't change right away. In high school, Troy sold LSD, mushrooms, and marijuana to his classmates, and soaked up the popularity. When his own drug use got out of control, he dropped out.

Troy finally made a decision for Christ during another prison stay, when a group of volunteers from the ministry Prison Fellowship prayed with him. But the continued chaos of his life after prison showed that he still needed Christian discipleship. Troy decided to try Teen Challenge after hearing men give testimonies about the program at a church service.

At Teen Challenge, Troy found the balance his life had been missing from an early age, through the program's rigid schedule of chores, classroom instruction, worship, and prayer. Along the way, he also picked up a strong work ethic. In 1999, shortly after graduating from the program, Troy jumped into a river to save a man from drowning, and earned a national Medal of Bravery from Governor General Adrienne Clarkson.

Troy attended Full Gospel Bible College in Saskatchewan, where he was elected Student Body President, then earned a degree in Microbiology from the University of Saskatchewan. He plans to attend medical school in the fall of 2008. ✷

AMERICAS

Mexico

A Different Kind of Help
Domingo Pineda

Until he was 30 years old, Domingo Pineda tore his life apart with crack cocaine, solvents, alcohol, and other drugs. A string of good jobs allowed him to satisfy his addictions while keeping up a respectable front.

The turning point came in a moment of crisis in 2004, when he asked his mother and brothers for help. They agreed, and Domingo waited to receive their money. Instead, they brought him to Teen Challenge. Domingo was upset at first, but quickly realized that what they had given him was far more valuable—a chance to be free from drugs, and a relationship with his Savior.

Domingo now works as a counselor at the same Teen Challenge center where he found help. "I cannot count all the miracles that I have in my life," he says. ❦

Mexico

A Grain of Sand
Arturo Israel Medina García

Arturo Israel Medina García tried Alcoholics Anonymous and several other programs, but nothing could free him from addiction until he came to Teen Challenge. There, he met God who forgave him for his past, and treated him with a kindness he didn't deserve. For the first time, Arturo thought of himself not a drug addict, doomed to live with his addiction forever, but as a new creation.

Arturo continues to serve as a staff member at Teen Challenge. When he reflects on his work in the ministry, he says, "Now instead of being a danger to society, I am a help, and I contribute in the fight against addiction. It is something that is consuming my country, but I am putting my little grain of sand into this cause." ❦

> "Now instead of being a danger to society, I am a help, and I contribute in the fight against addiction."

^ Anthony Richards (left) with Don Wilkerson and Karissa McCarter, then director of Teen Challenge Jamaica.

JAMAICA

Two New Families
Anthony Richards

Anthony Richards, director of the Teen Challenge Men's Home in Jamaica, saw a student named Eric Currie sitting by himself, looking sad. When Anthony asked what was wrong, Eric explained that he had no family in Jamaica, his mother was dead, and he was all alone. Anthony was at a loss for words, but said, "Eric, just trust the Lord. He will provide."

Eric did, and so did God. He gained a new family of Christian brothers and sisters at Teen Challenge, and made a commitment to work there for two years after he graduated. Better yet, when his commitment was up in May 2006, Eric married the love of his life, Maureen. When Pastor Errol Bolt said, "You may kiss the bride," Teen Challenge students in the congregation shouted, "Eric, you graduate now!"

Eric and Maureen have gone into business together and started a family of their own, with two children. Eric continues to mentor recent Teen Challenge graduates. ❦

The Bahamas
Man of the House
Eric Fox

Eric Fox was the youngest of seven children and the only boy, raised by a single mom. From the age of 10, everyone looked to him to lead the family. But the only male role models he could find were criminals. Eric wanted to be successful like the rich drug dealers he knew, so he started selling and smoking marijuana.

By age 15, he had dropped out of school. Soon after that, he discovered free-based cocaine. He went through an endless revolving door of secular rehabs, only to return with the same habits. Finally, in 1988, one of his sisters took him to Teen Challenge.

He gave his life to Christ, and transferred to the Teen Challenge Training Center in Rehrersburg, Pennsylvania, where he travelled with the choir. In 1996, Eric moved to the Cayman Islands to worked at a drug treatment program called Canaan Land Home, and now serves as the Program Director for Teen Challenge Bahamas. He and his wife Caren have four sons. ✺

▼ Eric shares Christ with a drug addict on the streets.

Up from the Garbage Dump
Alberto Bámaca

Alberto Bámaca followed his parents' example: by age 12, he had become a hopeless alcoholic. In his late teens, drinking longer satisfied him, so he turned to harder drugs and crime. After a dozen prison stays, his girlfriend left him, and took their three children. Alberto lived in a garbage dump, and kept himself alive by stealing and eating whatever food he could find.

Alberto entered Desafío Juvenil (Teen Challenge) of Guatemala in 1986, as one of its first students. The first thing director Richard Conti did was burn his clothes and shoes, which were filled with lice and fleas. It took several days for Alberto to scrub the black filth from his body. But he wasn't just getting clean on the outside—he accepted Christ, and God began to cleanse his inside as well.

After graduation, Alberto visited his children regularly, and told his girlfriend everything God had done for him. As a result, she came to accept Christ in her own life. They married in 1994, and have since had another son. Alberto now serves as the director of Desafío Juvenil. ✺

AMERICAS

Uruguay

Place of No Return
Estefani Gomez

Estefani Gomez grew up watching her father use drugs, get violent, and abuse her mother. She hated it, but when her parents separated, Estefani began to act the same way. Her mother went to church and tried to tell her about God, but instead Estefani shouted, "I hate you!" If her own father didn't love her, she thought, how could God?

So she got high and slept on the streets, until her mother came to find her. To spite her, Estefani attended a Spiritist church and dabbled in Satanism. She slept in cemeteries and painted her bedroom black with bright pairs of eyeballs, a reminder of the demons that were watching over her. All the while, drugs ate her alive, body and soul.

In 2006, after a nearly fatal overdose, Estefani came to the new Teen Challenge center in Uruguay, "Hogar Esperanza." Everything about the program felt new and strange. People hugged her, and talked with her, and worried about how she was doing. She had never felt such love. Strangest of all, she could feel the love of God, too.

But Estefani was still terrified inside. For months, horrible nightmares kept her awake. Sometimes she would even run to the supervisor's room and jump into her bed for comfort. But during an Easter service in 2007, all of her fears dropped away at once, replaced by a simple desire to serve the Lord.

The Spiritist Church had told Estefani that Christian programs were dangerous places, from which people never returned. In a sense, they were right. Estefani never returned to her old life. After a few painful visits, she even reconciled with her mother.

When she completed the program, Estefani became one of the first two graduates of the Teen Challenge women's center in Uruguay. She now attends Bible school. 🌿

🔺 (top photo) Estefani Gomez in center with red jacket.

(bottom photo) Estefani on left.

Barbados

Just One Hit
Edward

Before he started using hard drugs, Edward would hear stories about addicts and tell himself, "I'd never be like those people!" Sure, he drank alcohol and smoked marijuana, but he had those habits under control. When a friend told him about crack cocaine, he wondered, what harm could just one hit do?

After that first hit, Edward was instantly addicted. He also became addicted to sex, a desire brought on by the cocaine. Soon he had lost the trust of his family and any respect for himself. He journeyed across Barbados, looking for a rehab that could set him free. After several attempts, some of the centers refused to take him back.

Edward came to Teen Challenge in desperation, uncertain whether a Christian program would be any better. But in the program, he accepted Christ's sacrifice for him, and allowed God to lead his life.

After graduating from Teen Challenge, Edward stayed clean for three years, the longest he had ever gone since that first hit of crack cocaine. During a stressful time in his life, he relapsed, but he is now back at Teen Challenge, scheduled to graduate in 2008. 🌿

< Ricardo Zelaya prays with men at a
Teen Challenge evangelistic rally

War Zone

Ricardo Zelaya

Ricardo Zelaya's parents sent him to the U.S. at age 15, as civil war engulfed El Salvador. They didn't know their son would place himself in a situation just as dangerous in America. Ricardo skipped his high school classes to smoke marijuana, and stole from the people he lived with. Eventually, he moved on to cocaine, and when he returned to El Salvador, started stealing from his parents.

When Ricardo discovered crack, his downfall was swift. Soon he was living on the streets, begging for spare change, in and out of Narcotics Anonymous programs. One program he tried was a Christian ministry, but he was expelled after two months for using drugs. On his way out, a staff worker told him about Teen Challenge.

Ricardo found freedom there, and a relationship with God he'd never had. He graduated from the program in 1998 and now serves as the Executive Director of Teen Challenge El Salvador. 🌿

AMERICAS

Barbados

Two Tragedies
Lisle

As a talented singer and songwriter, Lisle performed rap music in bars and nightclubs across the island of Barbados. Life couldn't get any better, until his best friend and music partner was brutally murdered.

Lisle had used alcohol and marijuana for many years, but this tragedy plunged him into a deadly addiction to crack cocaine. He found himself in jail again and again, usually for robbery to support his habit. Meanwhile, his music career withered away.

Lisle came to Teen Challenge as a last resort, after hearing about the program in jail from a visiting minister. He asked God to clean up his life and help him discover a true calling.

Near the end of his program, Lisle's mother developed terminal cancer. Rather than letting this new tragedy push him back into drugs, Lisle thanked God for turning his life around in time to be a blessing to her. He was able to spend much time with her before she died, healing the heart he had broken through years of rebellion.

After graduation, Lisle picked up his music career where he left off, this time as a ministry, with rap music that praises God. ❧

Trinidad & Tobago

Hope on the Steps
Anthony Virgil

Anthony Virgil was a 40-year-old, HIV-positive crack addict living on the streets of Trinidad when he heard about Teen Challenge. For two nights, he slept on the front steps of the center, refusing to leave until someone gave him help.

At that point, Anthony's family had given up on him, having spent all they could on programs that didn't work. Even the Trinidad government, for whom Anthony worked as an electrical contractor, had tried to help by paying for rehab.

When Anthony entered Teen Challenge, he gave his life to Christ, and found freedom from 18 years of addiction. As one of the older men in the program, he served as a role model for younger students. As a former government worker, he had the chance to present his story at a state-sponsored drug awareness rally.

Anthony's older brother, the assistant chief of police in the city of Barataria, held a press conference after his brother's graduation and presented a $5,000 donation to Teen Challenge from the Trinidad Police Credit Union. ❧

For two nights, he slept on the steps of the center,

refusing to leave until someone gave him help.

A Voice in His Head
Winston Collymore

Winston Collymore was a police officer in Trinidad, responsible for arresting drug pushers. But after trying crack cocaine himself in 1995, those same pushers became his friends.

Winston abused his office in every way he could to get more drugs. He took bribes from organized criminals, stole cocaine the police had confiscated, and robbed rival dealers. He went through drug rehab programs, but only to keep from losing his job. Finally, he stopped going to work anyway, overwhelmed by physical fatigue.

His new profession became house break-ins, petty hustles, and running from his former colleagues. He even stole from his family, who moved away and kept him locked out.

Then, in January 2005, a strange phenomenon began to occur. Whenever Winston started to smoke crack, he heard a voice in his head that said, "Teen Challenge." After a few months, wondering if he had gone insane, he asked a friend what the words might mean. "There is a rehab called Teen Challenge," the friend said.

Winston entered the program on April 11, 2005, and his life started to change immediately. He developed a relationship with God, and after a few months, the very thought of cocaine and his old life made him sick. While in the program, he also found healing for a medical condition that caused blood clots, and in response, Winston recommitted his life to Christ.

Winston now operates his own landscaping business in Trinidad. He has also reconciled with his family. One of his uncles gave him a piece of land as a "welcome back to society" gift, which Winston uses for gardening. ❧

Honduras
"I've Got to Change!"
Reynaldo

In high school, Reynaldo joined a gang called Gang-18, in order to be cool and to keep getting good drugs. For his initiation, he had to commit a robbery. Reynaldo was scared at first, but after the first few tries, he came to enjoy stealing. Eventually, it gave him as much of a high as the drugs. Gang-18 became known as the one of the most violent gangs in Honduras.

As their reputation grew, so did their competition, and Reynaldo was forced into more and more violence. One night, on the way to fight a rival gang, Reynaldo and his friends were attacked, and several were killed. Reynaldo barely escaped with his life. A persistent thought started to enter his mind: "I've got to change."

Unfortunately, he didn't keep that thought to himself. He shared his fears with other gang members, including his own brother, and they turned on him violently. As Reynaldo ran for safety, six AK47 bullets shattered his legs. A doctor told him that he would never walk again.

In the hospital, Reynaldo heard about Teen Challenge, a program that offered a way out of his whole lifestyle. For protection, an ambulance secretly drove him to the Teen Challenge farm.

Reynaldo was scared, because he was still weak and couldn't defend himself from rival gang members in the program. But instead of a fight, he was greeted with something he'd never thought possible from gangsters—hugs and smiling faces.

For the next few weeks, these ex-gang members helped him dress in the mornings, carried him to classes, brought him food, and even washed his clothes and dishes. If God had the power to change them so completely, Reynaldo thought, surely God could change him, too.

He asked Jesus to become the center of his life, and became a servant to God rather than a slave to drugs. Since then, Reynaldo's legs have completely healed, and now he walks, runs, and even plays football. ✺

A Tragic Temptation
Jonathan Urena

Jonathan Urena's descent into drug abuse came early and swift. He smoked his first cigarette at age 11, and by age 14 was smoking crack cocaine. As an adult, he tried seven different rehab programs, but none could break the hold addiction had on his life.

At Teen Challenge, Jonathan found a God who didn't condemn him for his past, but helped him to look forward with a purpose. For the first time, he felt blessed just to be alive, and he loved to tell everyone about his new life in Christ.

After Jonathan had spent three months in the program, his brother killed himself, a tragedy that broke his heart and led his thoughts into dark places. Jonathan was tempted to leave the program, but knew that if he was serious about change, he would have to persevere even in this most difficult trial.

He stayed, and graduated in January 2008. Jonathan now serves as a Teen Challenge intern, with plans to enter ministry or the field of education. ✺

AMERICAS

Ecuador

No Easy Way Back
Eduardo Páez

Eduardo Páez became a juvenile delinquent after his parents divorced, drinking and smoking marijuana. At 24 years of age, married with three kids, Eduardo discovered cocaine, and became a delinquent in his own home. He would leave for days at a time, and he robbed from the family to get money for drugs.

Eduardo's wife brought a pastor to the house, who told Eduardo where he could find help. In April 2001, he came to Teen Challenge. Eduardo found it difficult to accept that he had been wrong about so many things, and that he needed to seek forgiveness in Christ. But once he did, an entirely new life began.

Even after graduating from Teen Challenge, Eduardo didn't regain the trust of his wife and kids right away, and reconciliation was not easy. But now, he says, "I can say after six years, that he has restored my family. I believe that God will fulfill his promises, and He will give back all the devil tried to take away." ❧

Ecuador

The Only One We Can Trust
Luis Condo

Though all his friends warned him to stop drinking, Luis Condo sacrificed everything in his life to alcohol. He lost his job with Coca-Cola, and his wife left. He found another girlfriend, but eventually she left with everything that was in his house. With nowhere left to go, Luis moved in with his mother, and started drinking himself into oblivion.

Luis's family convinced him to get help at Teen Challenge. After three days in the program, he wanted to leave, but something wouldn't let him. "Now I know that person that kept me was God," Luis says, "my King and personal Savior, the only one we can trust."

Luis graduated from Teen Challenge in 2007 and currently works on staff. ❧

 "Now I know the person that kept me was God …"

DOMINICAN REPUBLIC

New Language, New Life
Jose Martinez

Jose Martinez went to prison in the Dominican Republic with a heroin addiction so unshakeable, he was ready to try anything, even prayer. He began to attend Christian services, and though they didn't solve his problems, a seed of truth stuck with him.

Jose came to a Teen Challenge center in Florida in 1999, not knowing any English. Three months later, with the help of God's grace and his new American friends, he could speak fluently. He also felt God's love dissolving the roots of his addiction, bitterness, and distrust.

Jose went on to graduate from the Teen Challenge International Ministry Institute in Jacksonville. Today he is a pastor and the director of Teen Challenge in Santiago, Dominican Republic. The men's residential center has a capacity of 25 students, and a women's center will open soon, under the leadership of Jose's wife Nelly. ❧

Brazil

Christian Cradle
Adriana and Tadeu Vargas

Adriana Vargas and her boyfriend Tadeu first started using drugs at college parties. After two years, they dropped out and began a life of bouncing from job to job, losing friends, and living only for the next high. They moved in together and promptly sold everything they owned—furniture, appliances, even clothes—to pay for their addiction.

Adriana's parents lived far away and continued to send money, thinking that she simply had a hard time finding work. Five years later, when she decided to seek help from Teen Challenge, she finally had to tell her parents the truth.

Adriana and Tadeu, now married, entered Teen Challenge at the same time and stayed for two years. Adriana calls the program a "Christian cradle," where she found new life in Christ and a new sense of purpose. She and Tadeu were baptized together, and began to plan a future in ministry together as well.

Tadeu now works as a manager at a large furniture store, one that fired him years earlier for drug use. Both Adriana and Tadeu lead Sunday School Bible lessons for kids and work with young people in their church. Since graduating from Teen Challenge, Adriana has also seen several of her family members come to faith in Christ, including her 83-year-old father. 🌿

BRAZIL

Hope Lives Here
Sidney Gonçalves de Araújo

At age 13, Sidney Gonçalves de Araújo joined a group of friends gathered around a can of shoe-repair glue and sniffed it. The glue gave him the best feeling he'd ever had, one that made him forget about his chaotic home life. It wasn't long before he was hooked.

At 15, Sidney joined his uncle in shopping for marijuana in a shantytown in the city of Itatiba. Soon he was smoking pot and drinking heavily, and involved in the local black market.

After his grandmother died, Sidney slipped into a deep depression and thought about suicide. Then a friend told him about Desafio Jovem, the Teen Challenge center in Itatiba. Through an outpatient counseling program, Sidney met others who were going through the same struggles he was, and worked one-on-one with a counselor every week. With the help of his new friends, and a renewed relationship with God, Sidney began to plot a new course in life.

"Today," Sidney says, "I have a life I thought never to be possible for me." He finished his studies and now has a full-time job that allows him to support his mother and brother. 🌿

AMERICAS

Brazil

A Center for Lunatics
Rafael Camargo dos Santos

Rafael Camargo dos Santos was so in love with crack cocaine, he stopped eating. When his family noticed how thin and weak he had become, they tried to help—even though Rafael had stolen from them and done everything he could to drive them away.

Rafael thought that rehab centers were only for lunatics, but he gave in to his family's demands to enter one. His first try at a secular center ended in failure, but then his mother's pastor, a recovered addict himself, told him about Teen Challenge.

At Teen Challenge, Rafael found the love of God, shining through the people who were willing to help him. "I am so grateful," he says, "that this is where God dealt with me, shaped me, and changed my life completely." Four years after graduation, Rafael continues to volunteer at Teen Challenge, helping other young people experience the same life change. 🌱

PARAGUAY

"The Factory of New Life"
Luciano Rubio

After Luciano Rubio's parents divorced, he decided to run away and see the world. At age 14, he snuck aboard a merchant marine ship, and began a new life of travel, hard work, drinking, and drug use. Over the next 11 years, he visited more than 40 countries and learned five languages, but he grew ever more antisocial.

At the end of his merchant marine career, Luciano was a hardcore cocaine addict who had lost all sense of reality. He spent three years in prison for drug trafficking, then six months in a psychiatric ward. The only way out was the program he now calls "the factory of new life."

At Teen Challenge, Luciano found a new family, one that gave him the love he had been missing for 20 years. He learned about Jesus through a Bible one of the pastors gave him, and through watching the example of that pastor's life.

As a result of his bad decisions as a young man, Luciano currently has many health problems, and he is waiting for a liver transplant. Though doctors have often told him his time is short, God has kept him alive and active in the Teen Challenge ministry for the past 16 years, and he now serves as the Director of Teen Challenge Paraguay. Luciano and his wife have three sons and a daughter. 🌱

A Prisoner's Dream
Antonio Gonzalez Romero

Antonio Gonzalez Romero moved to New York City from Colombia at age 17. He studied industrial mechanics at Polytechnic University in Brooklyn, then moved to Long Island with his daughters in the 1970s. He divorced his first wife, but life was good as long as he made plenty of money.

But love of money turned out to be Antonio's downfall. With connections in New York, Cuba, and Colombia, he worked with the Mafia to traffick drugs into the country. He was arrested in 1985 and sent to prison in Miami, on a 120-year sentence.

In jail, with no hope of ever getting out, Antonio found hope in Christ. From his cell, he promised to serve God regardless of the circumstances—without knowing that his circumstances were about to radically change. When his case was appealed, a judge determined there wasn't enough evidence, and Antonio was set free.

Antonio decided to get a fresh start in life by joining a friend in Chile who was starting a furniture factory. But when he arrived, his friend gave him a much different proposal— with Antonio's contacts, he said, they could "fill Chile with cocaine" and become millionaires. Antonio stayed faithful to the commitment he'd made in jail, and after a long argument, the two men parted ways.

Antonio's troubles were far from over, though. He stayed at the furniture factory, building it into a respectable business, until an old business partner from Colombia accused him of drug running. Eager for a major drug bust, Chilean officials convicted Antonio on the slightest evidence, and he spent the next three years in a Santiago penitentiary.

Far from destroying his faith, however, Antonio's undeserved time in jail only increased his love for Chile and its people, and he prayed that God would reveal a way to serve them. As soon as his sentence ended, in September 1992, Antonio set about starting a ministry for drug addicts.

The Assemblies of God denomination donated a piece of land for the project, and with the help of pastors Rodney Hart and Luciano Rubio from Global Teen Challenge, the Rehabilitation House of the Potter opened in 1997. The ministry that started with just two students and an ex-convict with a vision now has two centers with a capacity of 50 men, along with outpatient services for women. ✺

Please, please, please help me to get into Teen Challenge A.S.A.P I can't stand this hell any longer …

— A drug addict's email pleading for help

CELEBRATING FIFTY YEARS OF MIRACLES

50

ANNIVERSARY CELEBRATION

TEEN CHALLENGE INTERNATIONAL

"As I studied the early years of this ministry,

it became clear that the success of Teen Challenge does not lie in the grand strategies of Dave Wilkerson or any other Teen Challenge leader. It is truly a sovereign work of God—He chose to raise up this ministry, using ordinary people to do extraordinary ministry."

Dave Batty

When I first began working as a volunteer at Teen Challenge in Philadelphia, I was a 19-year-old college freshman who had never seen the destructiveness of sin as I did that summer of 1968. That summer, I also saw the power of God, breaking the chains of addiction and seeing people enter into a personal relationship with Jesus. I was hooked, not on drugs, but on ministry to those who were deeply damaged and desperate for change.

In the past 40 years of ministry with Teen Challenge, my wife Patty and I have witnessed incredible miracles of transformation—from our early years in Philadelphia (1967, 1968) and Brooklyn (1971-1975), to the 20 years as National Curriculum Coordinator, developing the curriculum for Teen Challenge, and then back to Brooklyn for 10 years as the Executive Director.

I deeply appreciate the opportunity to work with Ethan Campbell on this project. His writing skills brought a level of excellence to this book. I also want to express special thanks to my wife Patty and her support through this project.

As I studied the early years of this ministry, it became clear that the success of Teen Challenge does not lie in the grand strategies of Dave Wilkerson or any other Teen Challenge leader. It is truly a sovereign work of God—He chose to raise up this ministry, using ordinary people to do extraordinary ministry.

One common thread that runs through all the Teen Challenge ministries around the world is obedience. God called a person and the Teen Challenge ministry was birthed in a city, or a nation. Those who pioneered these ministries responded with simple steps of obedience and miracles followed—and still are occurring today! Those who worked and those who supported the ministry financially may never get public recognition, but God keeps good records.

One of the biggest problems with writing this book is that the story of Teen Challenge and the miracles of changed lives is much too big a story to be told in one book. With over 1,000 Teen Challenge ministries, there was room to include one or two testimonies representing a ministry, or a nation, yet tens of thousands of miracles that have occurred in over 80 countries around the world.

Incredible stories were not included because of space limitations. Thousands of family members have come to Christ through their loved ones who came to Teen Challenge. But beyond that are the hundreds of thousands, probably millions of people who have been influenced by Teen Challenge alumni. Pastor A.R. Bernard, whose testimony is on page 15, is just one of those. Only in heaven will we know the full impact of this ministry.

"The Jesus Factor" continues to be the key to transformations today. God is raising up a new generation of Teen Challenge leaders—"fresh legs" as Jerry Nance says, who will carry on this ministry.

Every hurting person that comes to Teen Challenge today is still high risk for failure, because of their past. But in the hands of God, every one of them has great potential. I awake every day with a sense of anticipation—God, what miracle are you going to do today?

Expecting new miracles,

Dave Batty, *Chief Operating Officer*
GLOBAL TEEN CHALLENGE
Email: DBatty@gmail.com

"I've discovered that God likes to tell stories —

or rather, that He likes to tell the same story, over and over again.

It is the story of the Resurrection. God likes that story so much,

He wrote it into history, and He retells it every day."

Ethan Campbell

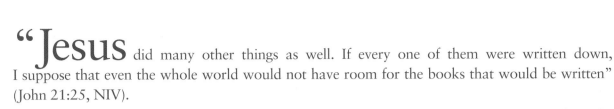

"**Jesus** did many other things as well. If every one of them were written down, I suppose that even the whole world would not have room for the books that would be written" (John 21:25, NIV).

Any writer who attempts to tell the story of Teen Challenge can relate to this last verse from the Gospel of John. As long as the book might be, untold numbers of miracles must be left out.

Dave Batty and I began our research in late 2006, when we sent letters and e-mails to hundreds of Teen Challenge centers around the world. We asked each center to provide a brief description of its history and current ministry, along with testimonies of changed lives. Over the next year, thousands of letters, histories, testimonies, and pictures overflowed our filing cabinets.

Through this project, I've discovered that God likes to tell stories—or rather, that He likes to tell the same story, over and over again. Every Teen Challenge testimony follows a similar pattern. A young man or woman makes bad choices—the wrong friends, the wrong response to a personal crisis, the false hope that a substance will bring salvation along with its high. Swiftly the sinner is brought to a point of desperation, where often the only choice left is a reckless cry to God or death.

Then comes what a lyric poet would call "the turn." At once, entirely apart from human wisdom or strength or moral goodness, God plucks the helpless person from this self-made pit, onto firm footing, then restores everything that has been lost and more.

In other words, it is the story of the Resurrection. God likes that story so much, He wrote it into history, and He retells it every day.

Anyone who has worked even briefly as a Teen Challenge staff member could compile a personal storybook of changed lives. I witnessed dozens during just one year as a choir director at the Brooklyn center. Some of them, like Canzada Edmonds and Vivian Hernandez, have found their way into this book.

With more space, I could also tell the story of Harry Davis, who graduated from Teen Challenge at age 63. Or George Callen, who spent two decades living homeless. Or Paul and Elizabeth Smith, who came to Christ at the same time without knowing it, in jail and at Teen Challenge. Another Teen Challenge graduate, Dave Henry, gave us valuable tech support.

My greatest thanks, of course, goes to Dave Batty, whose interviews, phone calls, persistent attempts to reach Teen Challenge centers in remote places, and eBay shopping supplied much of the information in these pages. This book is the fruit of his vision, and he shepherded it from start to finish.

Thanks also to my wife, Alice Yu, who tolerated my many late nights hunched over a computer, hammering out yet another story. And to my colleagues and students at The King's College, who endured a distracted English professor in the months before our deadline.

I can't begin to thank David Wilkerson adequately, for his faith and courage. At Teen Challenge Brooklyn's 40th anniversary banquet, he told me, "Stay on your face before the Lord." I haven't always followed that advice, but I've certainly never forgotten it.

Ethan Campbell

BROOKLYN, NEW YORK

Special Thanks

to all who helped make this book a success.

Thisbook would not be possible without the contributions of many people. We appreciate the generous help we received from all. Most of the photographs on these pages are amateur shots, not done by professionals, yet they capture well the story of Teen Challenge.

Thank you to all of the current and former Teen Challenge students who gave us their testimonies, either in writing or through personal interviews. Whether your story was featured in this volume or not, the Lord knows it—and one day, we will hear them all.

We are deeply grateful for the incredible design work by Don Jones. He transformed our text and photos into a work of beauty.

A special thanks to all the early pioneers of Teen Challenge who shared their stories with us, especially Frank Reynolds, Mike Zello, Howard Foltz, and more. Almost all peppered their interviews with, "Now, this is off the record ..." There are many stories — some humorous, others tragic—that are not included here. While these men entertained us with their lively stories, they also proved that "eyewitness accounts," especially those nearly 50 years old, cannot always be trusted. Whenever we pointed out that someone's story differed from what someone else told us, a common response was, "Well, that's their version of history." Clearly, our text is not inerrant.

We want to express special appreciation to Kay Ware Zello, who had the foresight 47 years ago to realize God was doing something that future generations should remember, and kept a detailed scrapbook of her first summer at 416 Clinton Avenue in 1961. She provided us with a treasure of authentic pieces of history.

Over the past two years, several people have been a tremendous help to us. At Teen Challenge Brooklyn, Dave Henry, Khalilah Tyre, and Brooke Easton worked many hours to gather and organize testimonies, pictures, and historical articles. Special thanks to Mike Hodges and Patty Baker at Teen Challenge USA, and to Jerry Nance and Bernie Gillott at Global Teen Challenge.

We also appreciate Dave and Don Wilkerson taking time to share their stories with us. Their numerous books and articles also provided rich insights into the history of this ministry.

A special thanks to all those around the world who translated testimonies into English. Some of their stories brought us to tears.

We are grateful to *Life* magazine for their special part in Teen Challenge history, publishing the story of the Michael Farmer trial in their February 24, 1958 issue. In the years following, *Life* magazine ran other stories on Teen Challenge, and several of their photos are included in this book.

Thanks also to Bob Combs, for his historical photo book *God's Turf* (Fleming H. Revell, 1969). Several of his excellent photos are also included.

We also want to express appreciation to Google and Amazon.com, who made it possible to gather historical information, old records, and books which in years earlier would have been almost impossible to locate. Detailed websites from Teen Challenge centers around the world proved to be valuable resources as well.

But most of all, we want to thank Jesus Christ. He alone has made all of the miracles recorded in this book possible.

Dave Batty and Ethan Campbell

"Most of all, we want to thank Jesus Christ.

He alone has made all of the miracles recorded

in this book possible."

CONTACT INFORMATION

If you would like more information about Teen Challenge,
or if you or a loved one needs help overcoming a substance abuse problem,
please contact the appropriate address listed below.

USA Information

For a complete list of Teen Challenge centers in the USA
visit the website of Teen Challenge USA

Teen Challenge USA
PO Box 1015
Springfield, MO 65801
Phone: 417-862-6969

www.TeenChallengeUSA.com

Global Information

For a complete list of Teen Challenge centers in countries
around the world, visit the website of Global Teen Challenge

Global Teen Challenge
PO Box 511
Columbus, GA 31901
Phone: 706-576-6555

www.GlobalTC.org

Teen Challenge Brooklyn
444 Clinton Ave.
Brooklyn, NY 11238
Phone: 718-789-1414   Toll-free: 877-813-1414

www.TeenChallengeBrooklyn.com

TEEN CHALLENGE
INTERNATIONAL
The Faith-Based Solution for the Drug Epidemic

Now to him who is able to do immeasurably more

than all we ask or imagine, according to his power that is at work

within us, to him be glory… for ever and ever! Amen.

EPHESIANS 3:20-21 NIV®